TO HELL AND BACK

TO HELL AND BACK

Mel Rolfe

GRUB STREET · LONDON

Published by Grub Street,
The Basement,
10 Chivalry Road,
London SW11 1HT

First published by Grub Street in hardback 1998
This edition first published 1999

British Library Cataloguing in Publication Data
Rolfe, Mel
To hell and back: true life experiences of Bomber Command at war
1. Great Britain. Royal Air Force. Bomber Command. 2. World
War, 1939-1945 – Personal narratives, British 3. World War,
1939-1945 – Aerial operations, British
I. Title
940.5′44′941

ISBN 1 902304 36 5

Typeset by Pearl Graphics, Hemel Hempstead

Printed and bound in Great Britain by
Biddles Ltd, Guildford and King's Lynn

Cover painting by Mike Steele-Morgan. It depicts a Halifax rear gunner in action
and is entitled '110 at 7 o'clock.'

DEDICATION

This book is dedicated to everyone who served in Bomber Command during the
war. To the brave young aircrews who survived and to those who did not. To the
loyal ground crews who worked tirelessly night and day to keep the bombers
flying, and to every man and woman who served at Bomber Command airfields,
all with the common goal: victory over the enemy.

ACKNOWLEDGEMENTS

I must thank all the former Bomber Command aircrew who patiently told me their
stories, together with the following who, in some way, contributed to this book:
Bob Adams DFC, John Burford, Pete Dean, Freddy Fish DFM, Jack Fletcher
DFC, Bill Littlemore, John Macfie, Professor Reginald Jones, Ron Stewart, and
The Grantham Journal for allowing me unlimited access to its printing facilities.

To their names I would like to add that of my dear wife Jessie, whose love and
undiminishing support has again helped me to give birth to a took. Uncomplaining,
she read and helped tidy up my manuscripts and boosted my spirits when they
threatened to sag. I must also mention my stepdaughter, Heather Salway, who has
proved herself indefatigable at promoting my books and finding vital accessories
for my tape recorder.

CONTENTS

INTRODUCTION

Bomber Command aircrews were sent to hell every night to bomb enemy targets during the Second World War. Many – over 55,500 – did not come back. This book is about courage, adventure, life and death. Above all, it is about courage, for we would not have won the war without the brave young men of Bomber Command, all volunteers, some barely out of school, who flew into enemy territory, defying enemy flak, night fighters, and the probing searchlights. They flew into hell, the lucky ones came back to tell their stories. *To Hell and Back* contains some of those stories about ordinary men who were required to do an extraordinary job: to bomb Germany into submission. Many were too young to vote, but they were old enough to fight and die for their country and our freedom.

CHAPTER ONE

INTO THE DRINK

Five men sat in a tiny yellow rubber dinghy looking anxiously into the grey sky. The sea was running heavy, with water constantly pouring over them. Barefoot, their flying uniforms hung about them as uncomfortably as cold sodden blankets. There was a dull rumble in the sky to the west and rain threatened. A few hours ago they were the exhausted crew of a twin-engine Whitley bomber, returning to England after a terrifying trip to Berlin.

Now, adrift in the North Sea, they were unexpectedly happy. The dwindling rumble in the sky was not thunder but the sound of the two snarling engines of an American-built Lockheed Hudson Royal Air Force maritime reconnaissance aircraft as it gained altitude and turned slowly towards England.

Shivering and hungry, their spirits were high. The Hudson had found them, a tiny vulnerable speck in a heaving predatory sea. Before leaving, it had flashed a message that help was on its way. They should be picked up that afternoon. The men, grinning at each other, shared their emergency rations and talked about how delicious the first beer would taste that night.

It was the morning of 24 September 1940. The war was into its second year. Britain, retreating from the grinding hordes of Nazi Germany had, three months earlier, salvaged some pride by successfully evacuating over 337,000 Allied troops from Dunkirk. The weary pilots of Fighter Command were bravely embroiled in the Battle of Britain against the massed ranks of Luftwaffe bombers. London reeled against the Blitz, but the previous night Bomber Command had launched a unique offensive on Berlin, concentrating 129 bombers, most of its raiding force, against one German city. Another 80 bombers attacked Boulogne, Calais, Flushing and the now-occupied Channel Islands, without losing an aircraft. The total aircraft sent into battle that night exceeded 200 for the first time. Less than two years later, the then Bomber Command chief Sir Arthur 'Bomber' Harris would despatch the first 1,000 bomber raid.

The bombers attacked eighteen separate targets in the German capital: seven railway yards, six power stations, three gasworks and two factories making aircraft engines and components. Three bombers were lost.

One of the Whitley bombers sent to Berlin was based with 77 Squadron at Linton-on-Ouse, in the heart of rural Yorkshire. It was piloted by Pilot Officer Andrew Dunn, a tall good humoured Ulsterman, who possessed a daredevil streak which sometimes drove him to indiscretions, leading to an occasional balling out by his squadron commander, Wing Commander 'Bull' Jarman. Dunn had at least once buzzed the airfield with a lumbering Whitley, causing windows to rattle in Jarman's office and turning the faces of high-ranking officers scarlet. He was, however, a brave man and an exceptional pilot, already holding a Distinguished Flying Cross.

Many crews who served in the Armstrong Whitworth Whitley Mark V heavy night bomber called it the Flying Coffin, some derisively, others with affection, for they knew how much punishment could be soaked up by this faithful plodding workhorse.

The Mark V Whitleys were powered by two 1,145hp Rolls-Royce Merlin X engines. Few who served in them accept the bomber reached the claimed maximum speed of 230mph unless it was corkscrewing out of danger or had a powerful wind behind it; or that it could climb to an alleged service ceiling of 18,000ft. What cannot be disputed is that the Whitley, together with the Vickers Wellington and Handley-Page Hampden, led Bomber Command's early offensive against Germany. The robust Whitley had an all metal stressed skin fuselage with immense box spars in the wings. It carried four .303in Browning machine guns in the Fraser Nash rear turret with another machine gun in the nose.

The Whitley had a five-man crew, pilot, second pilot, observer and two wireless operator/air gunners. In the bomb bay were two 500-pounders and five at 250lb, together with incendiaries.

Sergeant George Riley was in the rear turret when Dunn's Whitley, P5046KN O-Orange, took off for Berlin at 10pm. It would be Riley's ninth bombing operation. The other wireless operator/air gunner, Sergeant Dudley Allan, was that night taking his turn at the wireless operator's switchboard.

Twenty-year-old Riley, born at Old Trafford, had played trials for Manchester United's junior team. He wanted to be a pilot but was persuaded into a less glamorous job with the promise that he could train as a pilot later in the war. The call never came.

Riley was a practical joker, having a lively imagination which, combined with good humour and a positive outlook, extricated him from numerous extraordinary situations.

Dunn and his crew had been briefed to attack an aircraft factory at Spandau, on the outskirts of Berlin.

Navigation was an exceptional art in the early days of war. Much depended on dead reckoning.

'There were few navigational aids in those days,' says George Riley. 'We had the loop aerial which involved taking two bearings. This gave the observer some idea of the wind and the direction in which he was flying. But it was a bit more awkward to get a fix. The observers would be briefed by the met officer about the winds. They were not always right and at that time we probably lost as many aircraft from bad navigation, getting lost and crashing into hills as we did from flak and night fighters. The second pilot, who doubled up as bomb aimer, reported landmarks, especially bends in rivers, small towns and villages. If they coincided with the observer's route we were going in the right direction. But we had the track to follow. We usually found the target and dropped our bombs. We tried to avoid areas where fortified resistance was concentrated. Later, observers would be known as navigators.'

That night the met officer had predicted cloud over the target, but good visibility up to six miles. The wind was west-south-west, veering to north-west later and less than 10mph. Berlin, known to aircrews as The Big City, was heavily and fiercely defended. To reach it they passed between, but well away from, the cities of Bremen and Hanover at 10,000ft.

The rear turret was cold and noisy. Freezing air rushed in through the aperture through which the guns pointed. The cold, together with the ceaseless noise of the two engines, made this the most inhospitable position in the Whitley. Riley had to shout to make himself heard over the intercom; years later he would suffer from Menière's disease, which caused dizziness and nausea, probably caused by flying in non-pressurised aircraft.

Riley peered into the darkness for signs of enemy night fighters during the long haul over Germany. He saw flak and a few thin wavering searchlights, nothing to worry about. Flak grew more intense as they drew nearer to Berlin at 8,000ft until the sky appeared filled with the bright arcs of tracer shells which seemed as if they must pulverise everything en route to the capital. Powerful searchlights swept the sky, probing for victims. Another bomber ahead of them was caught in the glare of a searchlight then flak began slamming into Dunn's Whitley. Searchlights moved swiftly to enfold it in a chilling embrace. Dunn immediately sent the bomber into a corkscrewing stomach-churning plunge to escape the dazzling light as more flak began to thump into O-Orange.

'The searchlights were so bright we didn't see the tracer coming up,' recalls Riley. 'We imagined all the flak was aimed at us. It was an unhealthy position to be in. I felt very vulnerable in the rear turret, being flung around like a pea, hanging on tightly to my guns. I was amazed how Dunn threw the bomber about, as if it were a Tiger Moth. When we got low enough I fired down the beams of the searchlights and knocked out two or three. We had flown from 8,000ft more or less on to the deck.'

Riley saw the empty streets and gaunt buildings of Spandau illuminated palely in the light of the searchlights while the guns below pumped up a continuous stream of shells at them, shrapnel rattling against the bomber. The lumbering Whitley was not equipped to duck and dive. It was no midair ballet dancer, more a stolid road worker in hobnail boots. The German gunners soon found their range, delivering a shell which tore a 15in wide hole in the fuselage. A fuel tank was holed, too, but the Whitley escaped briefly from the searchlights and Dunn sent someone back to inspect the damage. Apart from the leaking fuel tank nothing critical had been hit. They moved towards the target, a storm of flak continually bursting around them and searchlights stabbing like bloodstained daggers.

With the bomb doors open the crew held their breath as Dunn set the aircraft on a straight and level course. This had to be maintained for at least two minutes if they were to hit the target. Riley watched the Whitley's bomb load strike the factory they had been sent hundreds of miles to destroy. Part of the great mass of buildings burst into flames.

They turned for home and were chased by flak but escaped Berlin without sustaining further damage. They did, however, have a serious problem which Dunn explained to his crew over the intercom. The bomber had gulped down extra fuel while corkscrewing and further petrol had leaked from the tank which had been hit. Riley had to concentrate on Dunn's words as they crackled through his ear phones.

The pilot's voice was weary. 'We haven't got enough fuel to get back to England. We should make it to within sixty miles of Flamborough Head before ditching, or we can bale out now over Germany, or later over Holland. What do we do chaps, bale out and take our chances, or keep going and ditch?'

Nobody fancied being held prisoner for the rest of the war so they voted for ditching in the North Sea, not an enviable prospect, but they all had unshakeable faith in Air Sea Rescue.

Dunn was happy for the Whitley to be swallowed up by the safety of the dark after the witches' cauldron of Berlin. He flew as low as possible in an effort to save fuel, but they were caught again by searchlights near Bremen. Further corkscrewing helped evade the flak but the straining engines had swallowed more precious petrol.

They droned on, crossing Germany, passing over Holland and soon spotted the shimmer of the North Sea. Some became jittery, believing the Whitley would nosedive to the sea bed, carrying them with it as soon as they touched the water.

Riley was positive. 'I knew we'd make it,' he says.

He cut the dinghy loose from its position near the escape door, picked up the Very pistol and stuffed its cartridges under his shirt to keep dry.

Landing on water is not easy, nor is it soft, even with the most skilled pilot at the controls. Dunn and his second pilot remained in the cockpit while the others braced themselves in the fuselage against the main spar. The Whitley had only a few pints of petrol left as it skimmed the waves, engines bellowing.

The bomber struck the sea with the explosive impact of a runaway train ploughing into buffers. There was a moment of awed silence after Dunn switched off the engines. The crash had upset Riley's watch which stopped at 5.50am.

The door, hinged at the top, opened outwards, useful for aircrew baling out in the sky, but awkward in the tossing water. They chopped away the hinges with an axe and the door fell into the sea. The inflated dinghy was launched and soon four men were in it. Riley was last out. He dived into the water, grabbed the ropes which were fastened round the dinghy and yelled: 'For God's sake pull me in!'

'I felt my boots dragging me down and had to kick them off,' he recalls. 'They were leather, lined with lamb's wool, good flying boots. I clung to the dinghy. I was scared, I suppose. Dunn cried: "Hold on a minute!" while they sorted themselves out. They dragged me in and we sat round the edge of the dinghy holding on to the ropes with our feet in the middle. Dunn had lost his boots too and he told the others to throw theirs over the side after someone kicked his bare toes. The dinghy was small, like those you would find on the beach fifty years later.'

Dudley Allan suddenly shouted he must go back to the sinking bomber for his parachute. Then he was in the sea but the others dragged him back into the dinghy. He slumped over their legs and went to sleep. His companions were worn out. The Berlin operation had been draining. Getting out of the bomber and into the dinghy without drowning had used up their remaining energy. Now they had a deranged wireless operator on their hands. Perhaps he had thought that ditching was not such a good idea, imagining himself still flying over land with time to bale out.

Dunn, Riley, second pilot Sergeant Derek Gibbons and observer Sergeant Bernard Savill, who held the Distinguished Flying Medal, watched the Whitley slip slowly beneath the water in less than a minute.

The dinghy was pathetically small, too small to expect five men to fit into it and survive the battering from a rough sea and the numbing cold. It was no bigger than a tractor tyre and apart from keeping an eye on the semi-conscious wireless operator, they had to hold tightly to the rope to avoid falling into the water. After two hours Allan started hallucinating and his abject misery affected them all. The North Sea looked big enough from the air. Sitting on it in a tiny bobbing dinghy the sea was immense, endless in all directions. Although Allan had sent SOS signals with their position to England their optimism had been severely dented. It would surely take a miracle for anyone to spot them.

They concentrated on staying afloat and alive. Riley does not know how the dinghy remained afloat for they were sitting in water up to their waists and it was pointless trying to bale out because sea was continually splashing on top of them.

When the aircraft arrived it almost took them by surprise. It was a Lockheed Hudson. They had heard the drone of its engines drawing nearer and half expected it to pass without pausing. But it had seen the dinghy. It was 10.50am. Just to make sure they had been spotted Riley got a Very cartridge from inside his shirt and dropped it into the pistol. The cartridge was wet but it soared into the air. The Hudson waggled its wings and they waved joyfully from the waterlogged dinghy. Later, an Aldis lamp flashed from the aircraft.

Dunn, who had become increasingly morose, snapped to Riley: 'Read what it says, you're the wireless operator.'

Dunn moaned again when Riley was unable to change position to follow the flashing lamp as the Hudson circled, afraid of falling into the sea and being swept away. The message was: 'Good luck, help on its way.'

The Hudson, which pinpointed the ditched aircrew as 100 miles east of Hartlepool, circled them until 12.35pm when it was relieved by another aircraft. A third took over at 1pm. A high speed launch was sent to pick them up but as the weather closed in, hiding the little dinghy, the rescuers returned to England.

The frozen airmen tried to get warm by sipping some of the emergency spirit ration, but that and the helter-skelter motion of the dinghy over waves lashed by wind and heavy rain made them wretched with sea sickness.

The searchers did not give up. A Hudson and a launch went that afternoon to where the dinghy had last been seen but were unable to find it and the boat became lost in the murk. Another Lockheed found them later, a miracle of observation, and dropped a container of food and drink. The men paddled desperately to reach it, but the seas were too high and, overcome by frustration and deep gloom, they watched their food parcel disappear.

The Lockheed's observer, who had logged their position, noted the dinghy was drifting at around three knots, although the wind kept shifting, making its discovery extremely difficult. One of the airmen became light-headed, relaxed his grip on the rope and fell into the sea. They dragged him back, but he rolled out again. They rescued him a second and third time, but when he went overboard once more they were too weak to reach him. Stunned, they watched their friend vanish.

There was now more room in the dinghy but the four who remained were in silent shock, although Dudley Allan remained semi-conscious. They sipped a little emergency water and nibbled dry biscuits. Riley tried, unsuccessfully, to smoke the sodden cigarettes. He ate a morsel from a tin of what seemed like concentrated Bovril, but couldn't keep it down.

That night, huddled together, fearfully pounded and drenched by sea and rain, they were locked in a monstrous nightmare that seemed to show no mercy. They all prayed, the others openly, Riley quietly to himself. Only he retained a nutshell of hope that the Hudsons would return and they would be saved as he watched a strange silvery phosphorescence slithering over the waves. He became needlessly alarmed, believing it might be a flotilla of electric eels, intent on puncturing the dinghy.

Four Hudsons left their base just after six next morning and two destroyers joined the search. One Hudson saw the missing launch heading home, but nothing was seen of the dinghy until after 11am. It was circled for two hours and the waving men below believed they might, after all, see home again. Another Hudson took over and the destroyers, sixteen miles away, were alerted. The second Hudson came as low as it dared, dropping flares and emergency rations but these too floated tantalisingly away. The aircraft lost the dinghy in a squall but continued to search. By 2.30pm the sea was hidden as a fierce storm struck. The four men clung grimly to the dinghy ropes, their hands like raw swollen lumps of meat.

Riley recalls: 'To let go was to give up hope for we'd have been thrown into the sea. The Very cartridges didn't work and we tried to use a marine distress rocket when we saw the aircraft but it was soaking wet, went "pop" and fell over the side. Dunn said we'd use it as a paddle but we just went in circles. We were controlled by the tides. We had no idea where we were going, although we thought we did, but there was no point we could fix on. We seemed to drift all over the North Sea. We hallucinated. We thought we could see land and buildings, but we were ninety miles off the coast, drifting further away. We saw what appeared to be beach groynes and the pilot made us paddle furiously towards them but they were all in our minds. Dunn had become a bit of a tyrant, Captain Bly in charge of a dinghy. He wasn't like this normally. When we needed to go to the toilet we did it in our trousers. It was embarrassing and humiliating, but we got used to it. There was no room to remove any clothing and if we'd tried doing it over the side we'd have been washed away. I somehow tied my hands underneath the dinghy ropes to keep myself aboard.'

The next night, as their strength faded, one drifted into an hallucination, perhaps convinced he was walking on the airfield back at Linton-on-Ouse. He stepped into the sea, into unreality, and disappeared. Now there were three.

The RAF and the Royal Navy had not given up the struggle to find them. Aircrews were a valuable commodity, expensive to train at a time so many were being killed. At first light five Hudsons were instructed to search over 5,000 square miles off Flamborough Head. They frequently fought off inquisitive German aircraft and one sent packing two Heinkel 115 torpedo-bombers which it found investigating the British destroyers *Ashanti* and *Bedouin*. The ships were part of what had become a massive search and rescue task force for the dinghy. A Bristol Blenheim bomber and another rescue launch were called in, but the boat, hammered by the raging sea, had to limp leaking back to port.

Low on fuel, the Hudsons turned for England and four Ansons sent to replace them failed to find the little dinghy.

The first light streaks of dawn touched the bobbing dinghy next morning, their fourth afloat, as five Hudsons and four Ansons were sent on what now seemed an impossible task. Visibility was poor over a turbulent sea. The elusive dinghy was spotted by a Hudson which marked the spot, but the airmen had disappeared yet again when two more aircraft passed over where the Hudson had seen it. Three more Ansons guided the two destroyers to the bearing they had been given, but the dinghy had become invisible.

Then, at 2pm they were found by a Hudson which flew in low, dropping a float and a watertight bag of comforts, and remained circling. Riley was exhausted. He had already saved one man who had fallen into the sea that morning. He could barely move, but knew this would be their last chance. Frozen muscles creaked as he bullied his weakening arms to haul the dinghy through the heaving sea to the bag. Riley drew it aboard. He opened the bag, at first ignoring two flasks, one containing water, the other spirits, and reached for a precious packet of cigarettes. His joy was short-lived, the cigarettes were soaked, impossible to light. His two companions were in bad shape. The cold had eaten into them, devouring their spirits and the will to live.

Riley recalls: 'We had seen so many aircraft, some no more than dots in the sky, we had hoped so much for a boat. I tried to pour the spirits into their throats, but it went over the side of their mouths. They might have been unconscious, but I had an idea they were both dead from exposure. I had a drink myself and sat there thinking that was it. I'd got beyond feeling cold. I must have dozed off.'

A second Hudson joined the first and together they circled the pathetic scene below, determined not to let them out of their sight. It was after 4pm when the horrified crews of the Hudsons saw one of the airmen slip slowly off the dinghy and disappear.

The Hudsons stayed with them until 5.30pm, dropping flares and guiding the two destroyers until there was no chance the dinghy would evade them again.

'The next thing I remember,' says Riley, 'is the noise of an engine, "bom! bom! bom!" as I came to on a bed aboard the destroyer HMS *Bedouin*. I don't remember being picked up. It had been getting dark. Another hour, perhaps, and I would have been dead as well. I looked up, a naval officer smiled and said: "You'll be all right. Is there anything I can do for you?" I asked for a cigarette before passing out. When I came to I was in a hospital bed at Rosyth. My hands and feet were badly swollen. My flesh was scored by the parachute harness which I'd been wearing. A doctor asked about my background and what I liked to eat. I told him I had a rice pudding every day as a child and he said it was probably them that had saved me.'

It was more likely that Riley was pulled through by the simple stubborn optimism which flourished in a man whose spirits were kept high by an unquenchable sense of humour. Dudley Allan, the other man rescued from the dinghy, died later. The sparely built Riley had lost two of his eight stone when rescued, but he was alive.

Allan is buried in a cemetery at Farnham, Surrey. The names of Dunn, Gibbons and Savill are recorded at Runnymede on the memorial for servicemen who have no known grave.

Later, after long spells in hospitals, Riley was to fly again, first as a wireless operator with 106 Squadron, which was equipped with Lancasters at Syerston, Nottinghamshire.

Riley again: 'I needed to get over that terrible experience in my own way. I had to fly again.'

Towards the end of 1943 he was allowed compassionate leave to be with his dying father in Manchester. His father died and Riley had a phone call to tell him that his crew had not returned after a bombing trip to Hanover. They were all killed.

The loss of his father and second crew made it even more difficult for Riley to erase the horror of being adrift on the North Sea.

'I phoned Leonard Cheshire whom I'd met on Whitleys. He was commanding 617 Squadron at Coningsby and asking for volunteers. He said: "Pack your bags and join us." That's what I did.'

Riley's new skipper was Flight Lieutenant Paddy Gingles, DFC, DFM. The two men became great pals. Gingles, a low-flying specialist, also had a mischievous sense of humour and they shared many pranks throughout the rest of the war.

Riley relates with relish his part in smuggling squadron cook Sergeant Arthur Rowsell aboard their Lancaster at Woodhall Spa for a sortie to a German rocket site at Wizernes, France, with a 12,000lb Tallboy bomb, cheerfully risking Cheshire's wrath. Riley and Gingles hijacked a parade of air cadets to get into Maine Road and watch an England wartime international from the touchline, without tickets. And once, trying to board a packed train to Manchester from Blackpool after a football match, they were invited by the engine driver into his cab. Riley stoked, Gingles drove, and they arrived in Manchester, laughing, covered in soot, seeking a pint at the nearest pub.

Riley, who flew on forty-nine operations, was never decorated. Although medals were not given for every act of loyalty and courage, perhaps a special award should have been struck and presented to men like Riley. He was one of the few fliers in Bomber Command who survived the entire war, which killed over 55,500 of them. An apprentice french polisher, aged eighteen, he had joined the RAF on 3 September 1939, the day Britain had declared war on Germany. Still there when Germany surrendered on 5 May 1945, he says, quite simply: 'I wanted to be part of it.' That he most certainly was.

CHAPTER TWO

ONE STEP FROM ETERNITY

Bill Belton had never been up in an aeroplane at night before he stepped into a Wellington for his first bombing operation over Germany. Nor had he received any of the training that prepared young aircrew for their life and death struggles in the air. He came innocently from a desk straight to the front gunner's seat in a bomber and was expected to get on with it.

It may have been an error by a hard-pressed Air Ministry clerk which caused Sergeant Belton to be posted directly to 156 Squadron at Alconbury, near Huntingdon, instead of an operational training unit. He had passed out at Newmarket as a fully fledged wireless operator/air gunner and was looking forward to some serious cross-country flying training. Nothing came more serious than that first trip on 25 July 1942, which took him over Germany to bomb the huge river port of Duisberg in the ferociously defended, heavily industrialised Ruhr, known by sardonic aircrews as Happy Valley. However, this was a novel, but not initially a frightening, nor even daunting experience for him.

'I was what was known as a spare bod, someone who did not fly with a permanent crew. Someone was short of a gunner and I took the position,' says Belton, equably. 'Although I'd never flown in my life at night before I was not particularly frightened on that first op. I got more nervous as my number of operations built up and they got worse and worse. Terrible do's, all of them. Later I saw other bombers shot down and blown up. Some of my pals were in them.'

In other sorties they were attacked by German night fighters and flak. Death was always there waiting to happen. It was one thing dying quickly, without pain or knowledge. Chaps talked about the merit of that. But no one wanted to die. Dying was for the other fellows whose luck had run out. Everyone wanted a life with a future which stretched farther ahead than the next operation, with no more killing and no more being shot at.

Some men were less able to cope with stress than others. There were those who could cheerfully dissipate the private doubts, agonies and fears that lodged in their minds by a good night out in the mess, the local pub or dance hall. Others were less able to deal with the mounting burden of stress which, for them, instead of being diluted by a few pints of beer, built up into an almost tangible and insurmountable barrier. The fact that Belton was a spare bod throughout his career in Bomber Command did nothing to bolster his security which would have been strengthened by having the companionship of a permanent crew.

'We took a 4,000lb bomb to Duisberg,' says Belton. 'I can remember the engines were roaring at a tremendous rate and we just about managed to get off the runway. We got over the target without incident. I didn't see a lot, there was not much flak. The bomb doors were open and we were flying straight and level over the target. With the words "Bomb gone!" I had the worst fright of my life for as the bomb was released the aircraft, now much lighter, leaped into the air. I hadn't been told that would happen. I hadn't been told anything. At that moment I thought we'd been hit by a shell.'

Sergeant Bill Belton served six pilots during his thirteen operations. When his latest skipper approached Belton a few days after the Duisberg trip, he was cleaning his guns in the rear turret before that night's sortie. The pilot, frowning, said: 'You don't look very well this morning, Bill.'

The gunner replied: 'I'm all right, a bit stuffed up and a sore throat that's all.'

The pilot insisted: 'Go and see the MO.'

Belton reported sick and the medical officer excused him flying for forty-eight hours. That night his skipper, with a new rear gunner, was lost over Germany. The entire crew were killed. The incident clearly demonstrated what a lottery living and dying was in the bomber war and how important it was to have friends and confidantes with whom anxieties could be shared.

Belton, a Norfolk farmer's son, was in a reserved occupation and had not needed to join any of the services.

'I thought my King and country wanted me and felt most passionately that this was the right thing to do, for the Germans were no friends of mine,' says Belton. 'The evacuation of people from towns in France and the shooting of women and children had left a deep impression in my mind. I had also heard of them shooting down parachutists. I had hatred for the Germans and I've never liked them since.'

On 14 September 1942, a day after his twenty-first birthday, Belton flew with another new skipper, Sergeant Andy Proudfoot, to bomb Wilhelmshaven. The night before he had been to Bremen and on 16 September when he was to fly in the rear turret again with Proudfoot, this time to Essen, Belton was tired. They were all tired, but with a war on, they had to push themselves beyond the limits of what a couple of years ago they would have thought totally impossible.

The Pathfinders of 156 Squadron were now based at Warboys. The Pathfinder force was set up in August 1942 to locate and illuminate targets in an effort to improve bombing accuracy. Five squadrons, 7, 35, 83, 109 and 156, based in Cambridgeshire and Huntingdonshire, became the nucleus of 8 Group. Eventually, a Master Bomber was appointed to control major raids.

In those days, 156 Squadron flew Wellington Mk IIIs. Later they would be equipped with the four-engine Lancaster. When Vickers' assistant chief designer, Barnes Wallis, built the Wellington he incorporated into it an ingenious geodetic lattice work of steel which gave the bomber tremendous ruggedness and ability to absorb considerable punishment and still complete its job. The metalwork was covered by a fabric skin. The Wellington had six .303 machine guns in front and rear turrets. The aircraft's portly comfortable appearance earned it the nickname of 'Wimpey', the tubby friend of Popeye. The first Wimpey flew in December 1937.

'I can remember very distinctly the afternoon before the raid on Essen,' says Belton. 'I was billeted in a Nissen hut at the village of Oldhurst near Warboys. It was miserable weather and I was feeling quite tired after the recent raids. I got up at 2pm, the same time as my friend, front gunner Alex Duke. We had been stationed together a few miles from my home at Marham, then at Alconbury and now I was flying with him. We were making our beds and, looking up, our eyes met and somehow I had a feeling something unpleasant was about to happen that night. I thought this would be my last trip.'

Aircrews had premonitions and were often waylaid by dark thoughts and unsettling moods. And for Belton, a superstitious man, this was to be his thirteenth operation. He always wore the same shirt and tie which he had been wearing when he last made it safely back to base.

'Then,' recalls Belton, 'I looked out of the window and thought how wonderful life was. The hedges and trees were green around us and the birds were singing but tonight we were going to bomb Germany. I thought I wouldn't come back, but I was determined it wouldn't happen if I could possibly help it.

'Cycling down to the mess, then about half a mile to the operations room, we saw we were down to take off at about 11.30pm. The rest of the day went like a flash as we had to check all our equipment and see our guns were correct. As we were briefed around 8pm, the perspiration of fear began to trickle down my back.'

An hour before takeoff the crew bus picked up the five men to take them to Wellington X3822 F-Freddy which was standing quietly at dispersal. Towering over them at 6ft 5in was the skipper, former school teacher Andy Proudfoot who, in his mid-thirties, was the daddy of them all. The rest of the crew climbed leisurely into the bomber. There was the navigator, little Sergeant Bert Couchman, quiet, unassuming and cheerful. Pilot Officer Ron Tinkler was wireless operator, the only officer aboard. The pilot was in charge and Tinkler took his orders amicably from the NCO pilot, but on the ground, Proudfoot was expected to salute the wireless operator, who was a pleasant broad thick-set man with dark hair. Rear gunner Belton was a stocky figure of 5ft 8in, who loved sport, playing football at sixteen for

King's Lynn in the Eastern Counties League, and hockey for the town. Front gunner Sergeant Alex Duke, a Geordie, had hated working at Boldon Colliery near South Shields and came to London as a bricklayer. His main interest, like many aircrew, was drinking beer. Belton remembers often carrying his pal back to the billet from a drinking session.

'One night we were drinking in the village of Oldhurst. Beer was ladled out from a gallon jug. I went home by myself, after Alex. I heard a sound from a dyke and found him at the bottom of it with his bike. He hadn't been able to climb out and had a tin of treacle in one hand and a slab cake in the other for his supper. I hauled him out. It was opposite the church. The door was open so we went inside and prayed that we would survive the war.'

Belton had trouble before taking off for Essen. He got into the bomber and put his parachute on the hook behind the rear turret which was too small for a gunner wearing bulky layers of clothes to combat the cold – and a parachute.

'I checked everything in the turret and to my horror, my sight which I had to aim from did not light up. It was known as a ring and bead sight. When you turned a little knob the light should have come on. Mine did not so I asked the wireless operator to call up the gunnery officer. He was there within minutes. It was a hot, tiresome business getting in and out of the cramped turret with all my heavy gear and perspiration was soon running down my face and legs. The officer said he had fixed it for me. I clambered back into the turret, yet again the light failed. What was I to do? Once more I asked for help. The officer who came to my assistance was very nice but again, when we were about to take off the sight had failed. We had to go and I told the pilot it was okay.'

They took off at 8.02pm, the Wellington's two 1,370hp Bristol Hercules radial air-cooled engines hauling them into the cool autumnal sky.

Belton recalls: 'The weather had improved and I shall never forget the sight of the sun going down with the western sky cloaked in a lovely salmon colour. That soon disappeared and we were in near darkness, although I could see other aircraft below flying towards our target.'

F-Freddy was part of the illuminator force whose job was to light up the vast Krupp armament works in Essen for the main force which was following. The aircraft carried target indicators and marker flares, no bombs.

Aircraft from the training groups were among the 369 heading for the German city. Thirty-nine bombers would be lost, including twenty-one Wellingtons, nine Lancasters, five Stirlings, three Halifaxes and one Whitley. Among these heavy losses would be F-Freddy.

Proudfoot reached the target area without incident at 18,000ft. It was 9.55pm. The guns did not open up immediately and he stooged above the city for five minutes looking for the target. At 10,000 to 12,000ft there was 8/10ths cloud with some ground haze. The moon was up. On the starboard quarter, two coning searchlights swept the sky and flak streamed up. Ground detail was not visible and it was decided at first not to drop the marker flares as the target could not be definitely identified. The bomb doors were opened at 10.00pm as Couchman, the navigator, waited patiently at his bomb panel. Tinkler, the wireless operator, stood near Proudfoot in the astrodome peering at the ground and the two gunners waited with their guns for possible attack by night fighters.

Seconds later Belton reported a Focke-Wulf FW190 150 yards dead astern, slightly above. A cannon shell hammered into the bomber. Alex Duke, the Wellington's front gunner, takes up the story:

'After we'd been hit Bill told the pilot to fly straight and level. It was a hell of a gamble. The normal instructions were to corkscrew, but it paid off.'

The German fighter broke away, but surged in to make another attack from the port quarter.

Belton again: 'I had the problem with the sight, but as bullets were pumped into us I immediately fired into their path and kept on firing, long bursts from my Browning .303 machine guns. To my delight I saw the fighter go down in flames on our port side.'

The FW190 was last seen with flames pouring from its fuselage and both wings, diving out of control into cloud at about 8,000ft.

Duke recalls: 'All I saw was German tracer flying past the front of the aircraft. I was a bit scared. It all happened so quickly and, at first, you don't know what the hell's going on.'

As F-Freddy made a steep banking turn to port, the interior of the Wellington cockpit was illuminated by the flames from the German fighter and Andy Proudfoot, the skipper, believed the bomber was on fire. He then discovered his starboard aileron was damaged as he experienced great difficulty in coming out of the turn.

The wireless operator was struck in both feet by shrapnel, but staggered back to the astrodome after pushing the photo flare down the 'chute. He flopped down in considerable pain on the rest bed and Proudfoot decided to leave him there until they had returned to base. The intercom unit was probably hit during the attack for communication between the crew became difficult.

Belton, having sustained slight wounds above his left eye and to his left forearm, had little time to savour the triumph of his kill.

'Everything happened in seconds,' he says. 'Then I heard a distorted noise on the intercom and the skipper was saying we must bale out because he thought we were on fire. By that time we were going straight down and had no chance to escape because we were held immobile by G-force. I prayed: "Please God, save me." I thought I'd had a good life and waited for the blank when I should be no more. Then I heard more crackling from the intercom and the voice of Bert Couchman, the navigator, exclaiming: "Pull her out, Andy. Come on, you can do it".'

Duke recalls: 'At that point I thought I was going to die. I had no thoughts, just fear. I would have baled out, but the bulkhead door behind my turret was locked from the outside. Andy pulled us out of the dive and the navigator unlocked my door.'

A course was then set at 296 degrees for Kampen, but the skipper had great difficulty maintaining height as the fabric had been stripped from along the top of the fuselage from the astrodome to the tail. Part of the trailing edge of the starboard wing and part of the aileron had been shot off.

Belton remained in his turret keeping a vigil for marauding fighters after reporting that the turret was u/s because the hydraulics had gone. The Wellington limped for home, gradually losing height. At 10.45pm, near Emmerich at 6,000ft Belton reported a German fighter approaching from dead astern. The fighter opened fire with one short burst, missing the Wellington as the skipper side-slipped into the tops of clouds at 5,000ft, but he was unable to take evasive action because of the damaged aileron. Shortly afterwards the oil pressure on the port engine began to fall and they slipped to 700ft over the Zuider Zee, where they nearly fell foul of another German aircraft.

'We met a fighter almost head on,' recalls Duke. 'It had its light on, but I didn't fire at him. They usually worked in pairs and if there was another one about we didn't want to draw attention to ourselves. I let him go thinking discretion was the better part of valour. The port engine had been banging, we were running out of fuel and had been losing altitude. The skipper warned we might have to ditch in the North Sea.'

The rasping noise from the port engine sounded even more unhealthy as Proudfoot opened up the starboard engine to stagger up to 1,200ft. As they crossed the Dutch coast, south of Ijmuiden, F-Freddy was coned by searchlights and fortunately escaped the light flak that was fired at them. About forty miles from the English coast the crew saw what they believed was a British bomber shot down into the sea.

It was about this time that Belton, virtually cut off by the u/s intercom, decided to leave his turret, find out how the rest of the crew were getting on and see how badly the bomber had been damaged. He was in pain from his wounds, but could move without difficulty. He undid the locking device behind him, grasped two handles above, and eased himself into the fuselage. Suddenly, a simple manoeuvre turned into a life and death struggle as Belton found himself plunging out of the aircraft. Part of the fuselage behind the turret had been shot away. He was half-way out of a great ragged hole in the floor. His left boot went sailing into space as the gunner screamed in wild terror, thrashing about helplessly in the dark. His cries for help were lost in the brain-numbing roar of the engines, especially from the painful clattering of the one on the port side. No one was aware of the drama going on behind them. Belton clung desperately to the exposed geodetic metalwork, as the freezing wind gleefully snatched at him and gnawed into his bones. He was not wearing a parachute, for there was no room in the turret for such luxuries. His 'chute was now almost certainly on the ground near Essen, waiting to be turned into silk dresses for shabby German fräuleins. At one point it seemed his strength would ebb away and he would fall. Then, with one muscle-wrenching superhuman effort, he dragged up one leg and, gasping, rested his knee on the fuselage floor. Painfully slowly, inch by tormented inch, he clawed himself out of the hole, the torn metal ripping through his tunic. At last, badly shocked, he lay on the floor panting, amazed that he was still alive, the wind squealing through the hole in a manic rage for having lost him.

He gathered his senses then staggered gingerly forward through the fuselage, carefully testing with his feet before each step. The fuselage was peppered with holes and wind streamed in where the fabric was ripped away. He found the wireless operator, his feet badly injured, lying on the rest bed. The navigator was hunched over his charts, the pilot alternatively peering ahead and looking down at the sea. Their concentration was total.

The port engine cut about thirty miles from the English coast. Andy Proudfoot tested all controls and found the undercarriage was u/s. The hydraulics had failed. The emergency system and hand pump were also not working. This posed a serious problem for the five men aboard.

Belton explains: 'Without an undercarriage we would have to land on our belly. The only way out of a Wellington was through a door in the floor between the wheels by a ladder which was held in the plane. Most of our target indicators and flares had not been dropped so when we landed there was a real chance of being blown up. The only other way out was through the astrodome. We would only have seconds after hitting the deck.'

The comparatively simple job of undoing the catch to release the astrodome turned into a nightmare. The closer they got to England the more frantic became Belton's struggles.

'There was only one point to undo,' Belton recalls. 'It was a sort of bolt to pull up then push back. I stood on tiptoes, pulling and pulling until the sweat poured off me, but it would not come. I thought if I didn't release it we'd be cooked alive. Time was ticking away. I told myself not to panic.'

F-Freddy dragged itself over the English coast at less than 300ft as Belton continued to do battle with the astrodome. A rich mixture of fuel had been used throughout their return from the target and the nacelle tanks were dumped over the RAF base at Marham, Norfolk.

'Andy asked if I'd like to bale out over Norfolk,' Duke recalls. 'I asked him what was our altitude and he didn't know, so I declined his offer. I would have been happy to bale out if there had been enough height, but I think we were too low, we had lost height continually since we were hit over Essen.'

The others went to their crash positions, lying down, hands behind their necks beside the main spar. The lights of the airfield at Warboys were visible as F-Freddy made its wobbling approach at 100ft, tilting from side to side. Andy Proudfoot called up the control tower to say he was making an emergency landing. When control asked him to circle the airfield to allow other bombers to land, Proudfoot said brusquely: 'We are coming in now' and ordered a red Very light to be fired.

The Wellington was lined up with the runway when Belton's curses and brute strength combined to release part of the astrodome which fell into the cockpit, leaving only a small 18in by 2ft gap through which the crew could escape. There was time only for him to think: 'How on earth are we going to get out of that little hole with our bulky flying suits?' before the bomber hit the runway with a grinding screaming crash and burst into flames. The injured wireless operator was half carried to the front of the aircraft.

'We had a lot of trouble getting Ron out,' Belton recalls. 'One of us was outside pulling while the others pushed him up. It was a tight squeeze for us in our flying suits, particularly for Ron and flames were licking all round us. We escaped climbing through the flames. I was singed, but not really burned. All the time there was a risk of the bomber exploding.'

No one knew how long they had before the curtain of fire became so fierce it would be impossible to get out. The pilot left through the escape hatch above his head, which the others could not reach. He saw several figures running from the aircraft which was then well ablaze and thought everyone was clear. Proudfoot ran to the edge of the runway and saw only two members of the crew. Looking round, he saw someone being half dragged along. He ran back and found Alex Duke, the front gunner, helping Ron Tinkler, the wireless operator, limp slowly away from the aircraft from which ammunition and marker flares were exploding. The skipper took Tinkler's other arm and between them they got the injured man to the edge of the runway where they waited for the station ambulance. Couchman, the navigator, was last out of the aircraft, his clothes in flames which Duke helped him beat out. Couchman sustained third degree burns to his hands and legs helping Tinkler and the others.

Tinkler and Couchman were both taken to Ely Hospital as the Wellington burned out on the runway, causing problems for incoming aircraft. Someone then noticed that rear gunner Bill Belton had disappeared. His crewmates knew he had left the burning aircraft safely and an initial search was made in the area around the runway. When he wasn't found the Home Guard was called in to organise a search. Belton was discovered some time later cowering behind a tombstone in Warboys village churchyard. It was clear the traumas of previous operations and that night had temporarily scrambled his mind.

Belton says: 'I didn't know what had happened until three or four years later when I was hypnotised to support my claim for a pension. When I knew everyone was out I ran like hell away from the burning aircraft, crawled through the barbed wire around the perimeter track and kept going. I was in a bad state when they found me, rambling, delirious with shock. I believed I had just parachuted into Germany and was terrified of my captors. I was taken off to Ely Hospital.'

The Krupp works in Essen was hit by fifteen high explosive bombs and by a crashing bomber, loaded with incendiaries. Bombing was scattered and many other towns were hit, although Bomber Command believed this was the most successful attack on Essen, causing thirty-three large and eighty medium fires.

Belton was awarded the Distinguished Flying Medal for the part he played in helping the others escape. Bert Couchman's courage was rewarded with the British Empire Medal.

The skipper, Andy Proudfoot, was not decorated. Instead, he was chewed up by his commanding officer for landing the stricken Wellington on the busy runway and not on the grass. Proudfoot flew again until shot down on a sortie to Duisberg in which three of his crew were killed and he became a prisoner of war. Front gunner Alex Duke flew a total thirty-eight operations, doing two more trips with Proudfoot before having a sinus operation, fortunately missing the ill-fated Duisberg trip.

Bill Belton did not fly again. His self-confidence was so shattered by the Essen operation he became uneasy crossing a road. After some months in different hospitals, he went on courses, first to train as a gunnery instructor, then as an airfield control officer. He was invalided out of the RAF on 5 September 1944 as physically unfit for further service and returned to work on the farm with his father.

CHAPTER THREE

FIGHTERS' MOON

Pilot John Lawrie and his crew got out of the truck and stared in dismay at the Lancaster waiting for them at dispersal. 'Christ!' muttered someone bleakly, 'it's not ours.' Repairs to their usual aircraft, U-Uncle, the ground crew said, had not been finished in time. They had been given LM-180 G-George, an almost new Lancaster III. They regarded it with a mixture of suspicion and loathing. They knew every leak and rattle in U-Uncle, a Lancaster II, with four air-cooled radial Bristol Hercules engines. This Lanc had less powerful in-line Packhard-built Rolls-Royce Merlins. Its call sign G-George had been taken from a 'dead' aircraft lost over Caen on 30 July. A subdued crew climbed into the aircraft and went to their usual positions, counting up the bad omens.

It was 12 August 1944 at 514 Squadron, based at Waterbeach, near Cambridge. The crew had learned after breakfast they would be on ops that night and needed to check their bomber from nose to tail. Apart from Lawrie, who had done one more, this would be their thirteenth operation. Unlucky for some. They went through the ritual of running through their checks.

Flight Sergeant Bob Chester-Master, of the Royal Australian Air Force, the rear gunner, was nineteen. He recalls: 'As I climbed through the fuselage to the rear turret, I checked the parachute storage area and straps to ensure all was well. It was necessary for crews to thoroughly check their working area to ensure no gremlins had infiltrated the systems. Climbing into the turret was easy in just my uniform. It would be more difficult later, wearing all my flying gear. Ground power to the plane was on, so testing started. I rotated the turret, depressed the four .303 Browning machine-guns, cocking and firing several times to make sure everything was in good working order. Repairs couldn't be carried out during flight as the intense cold would make your hands freeze to the metal and it was impossible to work wearing heavy leather gauntlets.'

The engines were fired one by one, escalating to high revs, then settling. The bombs and ammunition for the guns would be put in later by the armourers. The afternoon was occupied with section briefing. Chester-

Master and fellow Australian Flight Sergeant Sam Burford, the mid-upper gunner, made their way to the gunnery section.

Although they were not told the target until all crews were together later at squadron briefing, they learned the number of airfields in the area and the possible number of fighters waiting to greet them. The main briefing would be at 8.30pm, when they were given details of expected weather conditions, cloud, height and density, where the heaviest anti-aircraft fire could be expected, and most likely areas for fighter activity. By now it was time for supper. Beside the plates of those on ops was a Benzedrine 'wakey-wakey' capsule. Old hands slipped them into a pocket until shortly before takeoff. New bods gulped them down straightaway. If the sortie was called off, they would pass a sleepless night playing cards, while the veterans caught up on some kip. After supper they collected flying gear, parachutes and mae wests. Crews could also sign for a pistol in the event of baling out over enemy territory. Chester-Master strapped his on with no anticipation of using it.

Chester-Master again: 'In my case, flying gear consisted of uniform, already on, electrically heated inner flying suit, slippers and gloves, outer flying suit, gauntlets and boots, all necessary as the rear turret was not heated and temperatures at 20,000ft were minus twenty to thirty degrees centigrade, darned cold. Without this gear I could not survive.'

That night's target was the Opel works at the west German town of Rüsselsheim, near Mainz where, it was believed, wings for V1 flying bombs were being made. What really made crews sit up was being told they would fly to and from the target on the same track. This was a dangerous manoeuvre, stirring up a hornets' nest on the way out, and knowing the natives would still be buzzing on their return.

In the rear turret Chester-Master carried out his pre-takeoff checks and reported 'all OK' to the skipper. His mind wandered. Would this trip be a piece of cake or not? Would they have trouble? Would they get back?

Pilot John Lawrie sat down in his left-hand seat in the cockpit and began running through pre-flight checks with engineer Tom Young. Bomb aimer Martin Carter settled in the nose. Reg Orth dropped his charts on the navigator's table where he would be isolated from the glare of searchlights and the flash of flak by the curtain between himself and the flight deck. Nearby, the H2S radar set would play no part in tonight's raid. Lancaster IIs lacked H2S and Orth was not familiar enough to use that or the Fishpond, a tail warning radar for detecting night fighters. Astern of Orth, wireless operator George Durland arranged his pencils and pads and plugged in the jack for the headset. He turned on the TR 1154/55 transmitter-receiver and started his intercom check.

The pilot, Flight Sergeant Lawrie, a New Zealander of farming stock from Otakeho, in Taranaki Province, was twenty-two. Navigator Flight Sergeant Orth, was a square-jawed, fair haired, slightly taciturn Australian from Penrith, New South Wales. Sergeant Durland, the wireless operator, a former apprentice in the leather trade, came from Walsall. The flight engineer, Sergeant Young, of Falkirk, Scotland, was joint owner of a 1935 Ford Seven with Orth and Chester-Master. The rear gunner spent several happy leaves with Young and his family. Sergeant Carter was a slow laconic loping Londoner, who loved his pipe, hated baths, but was a bang-on bomb aimer.

Mid-upper gunner Burford, nineteen, had worked in a pharmacy before joining up. Brisbane-born Chester-Master was a shipping clerk before the war. He completed 60 hours' dual and solo on Tiger Moths until it was decided there were too many trainee pilots. Besides, he was told, his legs were not long enough. Chester-Master, at a shade under a sturdy 5ft 5in, thought this excuse, if true, should have been conveyed to him months ago, before wasting money on pilot training. He was not too short, however, to sit in a gun turret.

The crews of 191 Lancasters, 96 Halifaxes and ten Mosquitoes had been briefed for the Rüsselsheim raid. Thirteen Lancasters and seven Halifaxes would not return. Other targets attacked that night included Brunswick, Falaise and three flying bomb sites, while 143 training aircraft mounted diversionary sweeps over the English Channel. Altogether, 1,167 sorties were carried out that night.

The groundcrew had plugged an accumulator into G-George which provided the aircraft with ignition power to avoid draining its own generators. Other erks hauled tarpaulins off the fat tyres. These protected the rubber from oil spills. In the cockpit the starter button was depressed and held. There was a strained set of wheezing thumps as a Merlin turned over, a detonation and the engine settled to a roar. A second, a third, then a fourth joined the chorus down the dispersal line at Waterbeach. The engineer took care of the run-up as the engines settled in around 1200rpm. One by one the crew announced their readiness over the intercom. The Lancasters, their engines roaring, lumbered from dispersal on to the perimeter track.

At 10.30pm flight control gave G-George permission to taxi to the runway. It was third in line. A green light showed and the skipper slowly opened the throttles. They picked up speed, the bomber vibrated through almost seventy feet of fuselage and the rear gunner reported 'tail up'. Below, from his house beyond the end of the runway, a retired general waved each crew off into the darkness. At 500ft the flaps clanked shut, the wheels folded away and G-George was already turning on course for the forming-up point over the Channel. The first leg was at 7,000ft, then up to 10,000ft where oxygen masks must be used, and finally a steady climb to 20,000ft. One by one the rest of 514's bombers followed.

Across the Channel, Luftwaffe officers waited for the first radar reports of approaching Allied bombers. At this time the Germans' Junkers Ju88 nightfighter carried three radar systems and was heavily armed with 20mm cannons, 7.9mm machine guns, and a flexible 13mm machine gun in the rear of the cockpit. The Lancasters had four .303in machine guns in the rear turret, another two at the front, and two .5s in the mid-upper position. Some

Ju88s were fitted from autumn 1943 with a pair of upward firing *Schräge Musik* (Jazz Music) cannons or machine guns, useful for firing into the Lancasters' meaty unprotected bellies.

G-George's course avoided the heavier concentrations of flak on the Dutch coast. In the front turret, Carter picked out the Dutch coastline. Burford, in the mid-upper turret, was suffering from a dry throat. He had taken to smoking heavily on base, hoping it would ease the nagging pain of a toothache.

Suddenly the intercom crackled with loud expletives and cries of surprise as a huge dark shape hurtled across their nose. Lawrie dived swiftly and all was well, but the unknown bomber pilot was roundly cursed by all the crew in G-George until they composed themselves again. Both gunners kneaded frozen condensation in their oxygen masks while sweeping the sky for German fighters.

Ahead, the horizon was brightening, the moon would be almost full. It had been called a bombers' moon when Germany used it to attack British cities. Now it was mostly a fighters' moon. It could light up a whole quarter of the sky, or cast an opalescent glow on a cloud field, so Luftwaffe pilots could pick up bombers and scream into the attack. In a great sweep south from Denmark the Germans had divided the air up into boxes through which the bombers must pass to reach the Fatherland. At the airfields serving these boxes the grey shapes of the Ju88s waited, the clumsy radar aerials on their noses marring their clean lines and upsetting their aerodynamics.

The Rhine passed slowly below the bombers. Thin pale beams of light swept across the sky, now and then converging, and flares drifted down. These were not the bombers' target indicators for Rüsselsheim. Perhaps the Pathfinders had dropped diversionary markers to keep the Germans guessing.

'I saw one of our planes being attacked, but my guns remained silent as we could not give our position away,' says Chester-Master. 'The other bomber was hit, losing height with one engine on fire. I watched it go down in the moonlight, saw two parachutes open and hoped the others made it. Suddenly our plane was shaken, straddled by anti-aircraft fire. The explosions were shattering. German searchlights probed the darkness, one caught G-George briefly as it passed over, stopped and came back, but lost us. We breathed more easily. Another aircraft was hit by flak and exploded. The crew had no chance. Flak intensified as we drew nearer the target. Navigator Reg Orth reported we were fifteen minutes from the target and we gradually descended to bombing height, our nerves starting to tingle.'

Searchlights probed the night sky, trying to latch on to one bomber in a cone so all the anti-aircraft guns could concentrate on a single target. A less experienced pilot might try to dodge every beam and burst of flak, spending more time than necessary over the flak belts and reducing the chances of survival. His navigator would then have to find their position and recover the course. Experienced pilots had learned a trick or two, like watching for novices who were coned by several searchlights so they could fly above the cone, beyond the vision of the gunners. Or tricks like the one John Lawrie used, a simple but effective turn, not away from the light, but into it, the last manoeuvre expected by searchlight crews. Carter, now prone in the nose, set wind velocity as the figures came to him from George Durland. Searchlights darted on the port side from Frankfurt and to starboard, from Mainz.

'Flares five degrees port, skipper,' Carter reported and the bomb aimer took over for the straight and level bombing run at 18,000ft. Shortly afterwards, he added: 'Bomb doors open. Master switch on. Bombs fused and selected.'

Smoke and dust rose from Rüsselsheim, photographic flares glared, and the leading bombers, their work done, turned for home. The Master Bomber remained circling overhead, correcting for flare drift, false indication and creepback of bombs from the target, his voice calm or cutting. Thumps of flak were intermittently accompanied by metallic pattering on the fuselage. Burford's throat was now as dry as a brick but he continued to scan the sky, pivoting his turret. In the tail, Chester-Master swung his four .303s back and forth. They had so far been lucky with fighters, but the flak was heavy and he watched the glowing balls of tracer which seemed to drift slowly up to meet them, then whooshed past. A bomber, trailing flames, was losing height as Carter, the bomb aimer, took over for the straight and level bombing run.

He rapped: 'Left, left, steady, right, steady – bombs gone!' G-George rocketed upwards at 12.15am, relieved of the weight of its bomb and incendiaries. The bomb doors were closed and they remained dead straight and level for the automatic camera to photograph their aiming point. As they passed over the target the rear gunner saw numerous fires and explosions. They set course for home. Lawrie put the Lancaster's nose down for speed and veered away from Rüsselsheim, leaving the German gunners more interested in the bombers holding course on their bombing runs. G-George was caught by a searchlight and the flak built up as German gunners tried to get their range, but Lawrie jinked the big bomber out of danger.

Engineer Tom Young began juggling figures for fuel expenditure. Navigator Reg Orth played with others, the ones which would get them home as quickly as possible. The shortest route to Waterbeach was north-west, over Belgium and Luxembourg. G-George's log entries were now made under a new date, the thirteenth.

The bomber stream turned to starboard, north of Mannheim. The moon was starboard quarter high, to east-southeast. There was little cloud, two/tenths, as they flew across western Germany with Rheinland-Pfalz below to starboard and Saarland to port. The gunners continued to force their weary eyes to be everywhere, searching for the tell-tale shadow of a night fighter. Height had been sacrificed for speed, the Lancaster dropping to 10,000ft, heading to where they could go off oxygen and open Thermos flasks of coffee or tea.

In Rüsselsheim there was only slight damage to the Opel factory. The powerhouse, tyre and despatch departments had been hit, but most bombs fell in open countryside south of the town. Nine people were killed and thirty-one injured.

The German night fighter control rooms assumed the bombers would take the shortest route home and directed their aircraft accordingly. In many bombers the bomb aimers, their more important work over, began dropping 'window' through a 'chute in the aircraft. Window was metallic strips used to confuse German radar. During the festive season in England and in Germany, it was used to decorate family Christmas trees. Wireless operators reached for pads, awaiting a group broadcast. One of them was George Durland.

At 10,000ft over south-central Belgium, G-George was flying above cloud. With the moon and a Ju88 in roughly the same quarter of the sky relative to the bomber, the German pilot had the benefit of maximum reflection from the clouds if he spotted a target. There was a German equivalent to the RAF's 'Tally-ho!' used to announce an engagement with a target. It was '*Pauke! Pauke!*' Any listener at the night fighter control room would know a bomber was under attack. It was 1am.

'The night sky was suddenly aglow with a dancing line of green tracer snaking towards me,' recalls Chester-Master. 'Immediately ordering "Corkscrew starboard!" I rotated my rear turret and returned fire with the four .303 Browning machine guns. As we corkscrewed down the Jerry pilot was forced to climb, which gave me the opportunity of raking him with murderous fire into his starboard engine and underside. Even in the darkness I could see bits breaking off the fuselage. The Ju88 went into a dive, trailing flames and smoke. He was mortally wounded, a kill for us. Now reaction set in. Was it fear? Probably, I don't really know as the adrenalin was still pumping. Everything had been so quick and the responses automatic. I had triumphed, but there was no time to gloat, we had our own problems.'

Sam Burford moved his turret from port beam to the source of the tracer which had swept overhead to rake across the wings and fuselage from right to left. He saw flames burst from the German fighter's starboard engine and his own red tracer fly towards the Ju88 and slam into it as the twin-engine aircraft dived away.

As the skipper swung G-George to port he wondered where they had been hit. He had heard shells slamming into his Lancaster. He wrestled with the control column, the kite didn't feel right. One by one the crew called in, at least they were all in one piece. As he panted into his mask, straining with the sluggish controls, he heard Burford cry: 'Skipper...starboard inner's hit, it's on fire.'

Lawrie glanced at his engineer. Young shook his head. 'That's not what my panel says.'

'Come up here, then,' retorted Burford. 'I can see fucking great flames shooting out of it.'

'Feather it, Tommy,' snapped Lawrie. 'This kite is flying like a bloody brick.'

'Feathered, skipper.' Young reached for the graviners to work the extinguishers.

'How's it look, mid-upper?'

'I can still see sparks, skipper. Some flames.'

Young fretted from one indicator to another. Lawrie continued to struggle with the controls. The starboard inner was damaged. What about the hydraulics?

Burford called in again. 'Skipper, I can see fuel flowing off the port wing.'

Young inspected his panel. 'It's not fuel as far as I can tell. We could be losing coolant.'

Lawrie nodded. It was still possible they would make it home, they had got back before with only two engines, but he ordered parachutes on all round.

Bob Chester-Master took another look round for the German fighter before setting his turret dead astern so he could slip into the fuselage for his 'chute and start clipping it on, but his fingers were icy cold.

G-George had taken hits across both wings. Luckily only one shot had struck the forward fuselage and it had not hit anyone. Lawrie was telling George Durland to radio for a course to the emergency airfield at Manston, Kent, when both port engines failed. Lawrie glanced at the altimeter which showed 2,000ft and falling. He tried to restart the port engines, but they remained silent and the hydraulics had gone.

Lawrie rapped: 'Skipper to crew! Bale out! Bale out!.'

In a village south of Ghent a boy, Jacques de Vos, looked into the sky from his bedroom window, listening to the drone of aircraft. He noticed a trail of fire.

In the nose, Carter twisted the latch of the escape hatch which fell away. He glanced back at the flight deck where Lawrie was trying to coax more height from the straining starboard outer engine. The entire aircraft vibrated and the nose dipped more steeply. Carter dropped out and was whipped away by the slipstream. Young passed Lawrie his parachute and scrambled forward into the nose. Orth patted the skipper's knee as Young baled out. The navigator swung his legs through the hatchway and followed him. In the rear of the fuselage the tail door had been opened and Burford tumbled out, followed by Durland. Chester-Master was last out. His freezing hands had fumbled over the parachute clips. The aircraft was at 700ft when the gunner rolled through the open doorway and immediately pulled the ripcord. He struck the ground with a jolt, intense pain shooting up his left leg. It was about 1.30am.

Lawrie remained at the controls, fighting for height, to give his crew precious extra seconds to get out. The time had passed for him to clip on his

parachute and jump out to safety. Like so many other brave Bomber
Command pilots, who put their crewmates before themselves, Lawrie died.

Jacques de Vos watched awestruck from his bedroom window as a trail
of sparks passed over his house and vanished. He heard a terrible detonation
and the sky was lit up. As the noise of the explosion faded the boy heard
again the drone of distant bombers going home.

G-George was one of thirteen Lancasters lost on 13 August, the night of
an almost full moon. Apart from Lawrie, this had been their thirteenth
operation. Their old kite, U-Uncle, flown by another crew, would be lost
over Frankfurt on 13 September. Little wonder so many otherwise rational
young men became superstitious in the course of a tour.

At Gavere, west of Brussels, people saw the flare of light and the glow
which followed G-George's crash near the church at Bavegem. The
deafening explosion shook and severely damaged several buildings and
houses, including the home of village shoemaker Nestor van der Heyden.
The aircraft became a fireball, Merlin engines hurtled across the ground.
Van der Heyden's family fled outside to find fruit trees ablaze, still tossing
in the shockwave. In that moment of horror he wondered if any of the crew
were still on board. He raised his hands against the inferno in the crater left
by the bomber's impact, but the fiery mass of burning fuel, exploding
ammunition and oxygen bottles and melting alloy was unapproachable.

George Durland hit the ground roughly, breaking a leg. Bob Chester-
Master badly sprained an ankle landing in a field of haystacks. He crawled
to one of them, dug his way in, wrapped himself up in the parachute and fell
into an exhausted sleep. Sam Burford landed safely in a tree. Tom Young
came down in a deserted area near Scheldewindeke. He moved quickly
away, running when he could, eventually collapsing from exhaustion into a
ditch and slipping into uncomfortable sleep. Reg Orth and Martin Carter
also landed uninjured. None knew how many of their crewmates were still
alive. One charred unopened parachute pack was found near the home of
Nestor van der Heyden. It had belonged to John Lawrie. Van der Heyden
found the pilot's body and buried it in his garden to hide it from the
Germans. After the war, Lawrie's body was moved to the military cemetery
at Schoonselhof, Antwerp.

George Durland was the only man from G-George who fell into German
hands. He was taken to Brussels where his broken leg was twisted into
position without anaesthetic. He was among prisoners in a coach with the
German Army retreating towards Aachen when American Thunderbolt
fighters strafed the road which heaved with enemy soldiers. Durland and
two Americans got out of the halted coach and escaped over fields, the
Englishman hobbling in his plaster cast. They were hidden by a Belgian
farmer and his wife in their hayloft and fed for three days until the British
Army arrived.

It was light when Chester-Master awoke in the haystack. He pushed his
flying gear further into the hay and crawled out of his hiding place. His

ankle hurt and he swallowed painkillers from his escape kit.

'What was I to do?' he says. 'Here I was a nineteen-year-old Australian flier in a foreign country, unable to speak their language, with an injured leg, cold, hungry, thirsty, deep behind enemy lines and feeling lonely. A feeling of apprehension flooded over me and I felt a surge of self-pity, but soon realised this would not help and I should adopt a more positive attitude.'

He undid his tie, took out the collar stud, scraped at the back and revealed a hidden compass. He saw a farmer crossing the field with his dog which came bounding and barking over to him. The farmer spoke only Flemish, but pointed to a wood, indicating the gunner should wait there. He spent the night on a bracken bed. In the morning, drawn to the edge of the wood by a low whistle, he stumbled out to find food and water which he wolfed down. The day and another night dragged by. Another whistle in the morning and more food. The third day two men told him in broken English they would be back.

Next morning the larger man hoisted the gunner on his back. After twenty minutes they broke into a clearing where three bicycles were waiting. One had a fixed wheel and his good foot was strapped to the pedal. It was a long ride to a village where his foot was bandaged and he received a splendid breakfast. Another long ride through the countryside brought them to a safe house, owned by Hector and Maria de Smet in the village of St Lievens Houtem. They could not speak English, but after the airman had washed de Smet gave him some of his own clothes to wear. His bed was a pile of straw in the loft and the couple shared with him their meagre rations.

Days passed until he was taken on another bike ride, this time 20kms to Brussels and another safe house at 18 Rue de la Surrere, which was owned by brother and sister Willy and Maria de Keyser. To Chester-Master's delight Martin Carter, the bomb aimer, was here. He had been picked up by the same cell of the Comète escape line. They exchanged stories, listened to BBC radio reports from London, watched Allied bombers fly over the city, and German fighters take off from a nearby airfield in pursuit of them.

Their attempt to join the escape line through Spain was cancelled after Germans caught and shot several Belgians. An abortive attempt was made to go north via Switzerland before the decision was made not to risk anyone and stay put. Boredom and lack of exercise forced the two airmen to risk a walk through Brussels, but they were never challenged by the Germans. Soon afterwards, the enemy retreated and British tanks came rumbling into the city. The two airmen were reunited with navigator Reg Orth before being flown back to England.

CHAPTER FOUR

HAUNTED BY A MEMORY

A few seconds often separated aircrews from survival and death on bombing sorties. One second their bomber might be roaring happily through the clouds and the next it could be torn apart by a German shell, spilling the corpses of young men into the sky.

Vic Tomei was granted vital seconds to escape his blazing bomber on 4 December 1944, but he has never escaped the guilt he feels for what happened that night over Germany. There is no reason for that guilt, but it continues to haunt him over fifty years later.

The crew of Lancaster NG145DX J-Johnny were no different to any other which was based with 57 Squadron at East Kirkby, Lincolnshire, near the end of 1944. They were young, fond of girls, having fun, drinking beer and scoring good-humouredly off chaps in 630 Squadron, with whom they shared the airbase. When they thought of it, they liked the idea of living to see Germany defeated and rejoining civvy street. The transition from dropping bombs on Germany to a normal peacetime job with girlfriends, shopping down the high street and Saturday night at the pictures would be difficult, but that is what they lived for. For the moment these seven young men were anticipating a happy and peaceful Christmas in three weeks, the chance to relax for a night or two.

Bomb aimer Flight Sergeant Tomei, twenty-one, and his crew had only been at East Kirkby a few days, eighteen miles east, as the Lancaster flies, from 106 Squadron at Metheringham. Their posting was not a happy one.

Tomei recalls: 'On 25 November we were involved in a Loran cross-country skyways synchronisation exercise from Metheringham. On 1 December we were doing fighter affiliation at East Kirkby. It was a cold miserable station, wet and muddy, none of us liked it. I wondered why the devil we'd left 106 Squadron to come here.'

Lieutenant Phil Becker was pilot of J-Johnny. Attached to the Royal Air Force from the South African Air Force, he was tall, well-built, bluff and genial. His future had been laid out by well-off parents who owned a farm near the Cape Province port of East London. Becker was a popular skipper with a crew who had great faith in his ability.

The second most important man in a bomber crew was the navigator. Twenty-year-old Flight Sergeant Bill Ching, of the Royal New Zealand Air Force, had taken them on eleven operations bringing them back successfully each time. He was hoping for a posting to the Far East to be closer to home.

Tomei remembers wireless operator Sergeant Charlie Lees for his initiative and doggedness in saving money. Lees took to pieces his watch which had gone wrong. He shortened the spring and put it together. It worked perfectly but every few weeks the watch stopped and Lees had to do it all again which he did happily, never thinking he might be better off buying a new one, for good watches were hard to find in wartime.

Flight engineer Sergeant Ron Osman, who was married, came from west London. Both gunners were Rhodesian, Flight Sergeant Norman Deacon in the mid-upper turret, and Sergeant Adrian Roselt, a slim nineteen-year-old six-footer, in the rear. Tomei, born in Beckenham, Kent, was a chirpy stocky blue-eyed rugby scrum-half, who also enjoyed cycle racing and photography. An insurance accounts clerk, he joined the RAF because he wanted to fly. His unusual name had been bequeathed to him by his Italian paternal grandparents.

Two nights before, a gardening (mining) sortie had been scrubbed. Everyone hoped tonight's operation to Heilbronn, north of Stuttgart, would get the same treatment, but no one dared make a bet on them having had their last bombing operation before Christmas.

The Heilbronn raid was on, shrugs all round and heads down as they left the meagre warmth of the crew hut, stepping outside where the cold snapped at their ears and made their eyes water. They were driven to their aircraft parked on the hard standing and soon the airfield vibrated to the sound of the Lancasters' engines building up power. Each aircraft carried a 4,000lb Cookie bomb and incendiaries. For the people of Heilbronn, going quietly about their business, it would be the night when the war suddenly turned vicious.

It was dark when they took off at 4.30pm, one of forty Lancasters leaving East Kirkby, booming over the lightly populated countryside, circling to get near to their operating height of about 16,000ft. Half the bombers came from 57 Squadron, the others belonged to 630 Squadron, which had been formed from B Flight of 57 Squadron. For the crew of J-Johnny it was their twelfth operation together, their first with the new squadron.

This was the only major raid carried out by Bomber Command on Heilbronn, a small town of little importance, with the supreme misfortune of straddling the main north-south railway lines. The communication link needed to be broken ahead of advancing Allied troops.

A total 282 Lancasters and ten Mosquitoes were sent to Heilbronn from 5 Group. A total 1,000 bombers were in action over Germany that night, attacking several targets which included Karlsruhe and Oberhausen. Fourteen Lancasters and a Mosquito were lost.

Tomei recalls shortly after takeoff, standing in the cabin, looking round inquisitively for other aircraft. 'I spotted 106 Squadron's P-Peter which used to be the wing commander's bomber. When I mentioned this over the intercom for the others to have a look at it, Phil said: "Shush! We don't want to know that," as if the sighting was wrapped up in superstition. I had thought it would be something interesting to be logged by the navigator.'

Tomei's mind had inevitably turned nostalgically to his old squadron which had sent twenty-two aircraft on this raid. Tomei spent most of the flight sitting at a bench with the navigator. Tomei was also the aircraft's radar set operator. 'We had H2S, Gee and Loran and there was enough to do to worry about these,' says Tomei. 'Times had changed since early in the war when bomb aimers had to lie in the nose and call out landmarks over the intercom to the navigator. On the way to Heilbronn we thought the winds were slightly wrong from what we had been told during briefing by the met officer at East Kirkby. We took a new wind reading and Bill adjusted our course and passed that to Phil Becker. I went into the nose when it was time to set the sight for the target. We kept our eyes skinned for the Pathfinders' flares and target indicators. We got over the target on time. It was dead on 7.30pm when the Master Bomber instructed us to come in and bomb on the markers. There was no cloud and visibility was good. I pressed the bomb tit.'

The Cookie and incendiaries fell on to the target which was already enveloped in flames. The operations record book for 57 Squadron reports:

'A successful attack on the Town Marshalling Yards, carried out to hamper the Germans in their efforts to reinforce and supply their forces between STRASBOURG and the SAAR. Marking was punctual and accurate, and bombing well concentrated apart from some scattering of incendiaries... Ground opposition negligible but very strong fighter opposition within twenty five miles of the target. Weather was clear below cloud with good visibility. Severe icing was experienced in cloud after leaving the target, and considerable difficulty in climbing out of it. Times of attack: 1929 1/2 – 1943 hours. Heights 7,300 – 15,000ft.'

It took only a few minutes for 1,254 tons of bombs to fall on Heilbronn which was devastated. A report from the postwar British Bombing Survey Unit believed that 351 acres, 82 per cent of the town's built-up area were destroyed, mainly by fierce fires. Over 7,000 people died, many in a fire storm which ripped through Heilbronn.

J-Johnny turned for home, its job done, and was immediately attacked by two German night fighters, which began spitting death into the Lancaster. Tomei, who was still in the nose, sprawled over the escape hatch looking at the target, saw a Ju88 fighter flying away from them and, fleetingly, wondered if it had been a British Mosquito. Then he heard Norman Deacon, the mid-upper gunner yelling into the intercom that he had shot down a Messerschmitt-410. There had been no time to shout for the pilot to corkscrew out of danger, the damage had been done. Revenge was sweet for the German pilots who had seen the incineration of Heilbronn.

'I heard the sound of our Browning machine guns firing,' recalls Tomei, 'but a German shell had struck the port wing and both engines were in flames. I don't know which fighter had fired the shell, probably the Ju88 with its upward firing machine guns. I will never forget the sight of those flames leaping across the top of the aircraft as I looked up from my position in the nose.'

In 1944 twin-engine 300mph Ju88s, in addition to their three 20mm cannons, three 7.9mm machine guns in the nose, and one 13mm machine gun in the rear of the cockpit, were fitted with two 20mm cannon mounted in the fuselage and firing upward and forward. These became known as *Schräge Musik*. The cannons enabled the Ju88s to attack from behind or the side, passing under the unprotected belly of the Lancaster into which it fired its shells. Many Lancasters perished in this way although some Ju88s, overcome by supreme confidence, ventured too close to the big bombers and were also destroyed in the explosion. Compared to the German fighters J-Johnny was punily armed with .303in Browning machine guns.

All time seemed to be compressed into a few seconds. Osman, the flight engineer, activated the fire extinguishers in the engines, but the flames grew even more fierce, licking hungrily over the cockpit. Becker suddenly flung the great Lancaster into a dive in a desperate attempt to snuff them out. It was a time to grit teeth, hang on and mumble a quick prayer as the bomber screamed towards the ground, flames pouring out of it. Roselt, in the isolation of his rear turret, clung to his machine guns. Deacon, with other things on his mind in the mid-upper turret, had almost forgotten the elation of shooting down a German night fighter. Tomei struck his head on the bomb sight as he was shot forward in the nose. The aircraft came out of the dive but fire was still consuming the port wing. Becker knew a hopeless situation when he saw it. When the flames reached the wing fuel tanks they would be goners for sure. Little time now separated them from death and survival. He ordered the crew to abandon the aircraft. Becker remained at the controls while everyone else scrambled into their parachutes.

Tomei believes he may have established some sort of record for clipping on his parachute. He threw off his flying helmet, for there was always a danger of being garrotted if its trailing wires and tubes caught in the hatch. Of all the crew he had the least distance to travel to get out of this deathtrap. When the Lancaster straightened up for level flight he had slid feet first back to the escape hatch, beside which he was now crouching. There was no time for dithering.

'The escape hatch had been released, all I had to do was drop out of the aircraft. You're on automatic by now. It was the first time I had baled out, but you don't wait to ask what shall I do? You just get on with it. It was all happening so quickly. There was hardly time to think, but discipline took over. I had to save my own life. Having dropped the cover I began to slide

feet first out of the hatch. Suddenly I was trapped half way out. I brought up
my arms and covered my face as I dropped out. You know you will hit your
head if you're not careful. That was my natural instinct. My head and back
still banged against the hatch as I went through into the sky. I wasn't hurt,
but I was aware of not wanting to hit the aircraft as I floated free of it.'

It was dry, dark, cold and lonely. The Lancaster, streaming great gouts of
flames, was soon out of sight. Tomei, cocooned in darkness, was suddenly
faced with an unnerving problem which prevented him from gazing after the
doomed bomber and watching in the diminishing glare of the flames to see
his crewmates follow him out.

'I didn't know which side the D ring (release toggle) was. I used both
hands to feel around for it on my chest. My right hand found it, then lost it,
but in that split second I'd already pulled the ripcord, so that was okay. The
small 'chute – which pulls out the main canopy – darted up past me. The
main canopy opened and I began to spin. That was bad news. The shroud
lines were not quite right. There were two, one over each shoulder but only
one of them was holding up the canopy which I was afraid would collapse.
I had heard this might happen from a lecture I'd attended.'

The memory of that lecture at Scampton in a hall of shuffling feet and
jabbering tutor, when useless information was often remembered while the
vital stuff forgotten, was from another world of polished floors and neatly
made beds and it floated chillingly into his mind as he struggled to release
the lines. The bomber had dived a fair distance. The bomb aimer reckoned
he had jumped out at between 10,000 and 12,000ft. What he knew for
certain was that the ground was rushing up to meet him.

Tomei again: 'Then I remembered being told if you put one leg up and
the other straight out I would stop spinning. But I couldn't remember which
leg was to be used for what so I tried both ways until it worked. I was very
relieved, but still afraid. I had never experienced fear in my life until that
moment. It was the fear of the unknown, too. I had stopped the spinning but
I didn't know what else was in store for me. The sky was totally black. I
could see and hear nothing. I couldn't see the ground and when that happens
you can't be so easily prepared for the impact when you land. I didn't know
if I'd be killed when I smashed into the ground, where I'd be, or where the
rest of my crew were. I hoped we would all meet up on the ground.'

There was no warning when the top of his parachute snagged in the
branch of a tree and he slithered to the ground so easily and painlessly he
might have spent months practising for such a landing. A few feet this
way or that and he could have been badly injured or killed. Lady Luck
had watched over Vic Tomei that night. As he touched ground he smacked
the buckle on his chest, releasing the parachute. He tried to gather up the
great swathes of silk but couldn't pull them out of the tree. He left the
parachute hanging there. It would be brought down by Germans in
daylight. It was then, with the relief of solid ground beneath his flying
boots, he heard the sound of the engines of the Lancasters returning to

England. It was around 7.40pm British time.

'I automatically looked up but of course couldn't see anything. I thought oh, they're going back to bacon and eggs, lucky buggers. I suddenly felt miserable. Oh God, I'm on my own now. I thought of my pals from J-Johnny and wondered if they'd all managed to get out all right and whether I might bump into them in the dark.'

Events had moved swiftly. Only ten minutes had passed between getting to the target, releasing the bombs, being hit by a German fighter, diving in a vain attempt to put out the flames, falling alone through the sky and landing in Germany. The drone of the Lancasters which Tomei could not see contrasted strangely to the loud squawking of the agitated chickens which he had roused as he cautiously explored the area around the tree he'd landed in. He assumed he was in a farmyard.

Tomei again: 'I looked around as much as I could in the dark, walking slowly in a circle. I remember seeing piles of wood and a fence which seemed to be surrounding the area into which I'd fallen. The chickens were making a lot of noise, disturbed by my arrival. I didn't want to move around too much for fear of attracting a lot of attention, although in retrospect, the chickens were as good as watch dogs. I was in shock, but managed to push my mae west underneath the wood. I stuffed my target map inside my shirt. I was still groping my way around the farmyard when I was suddenly surrounded by up to a dozen understandably hostile Germans, some of them armed, mainly with 12-bore shotguns. Some were young, others middle-aged, and I was told in German to put up my hands which I did. It was a bit unnerving.'

The Germans had seen the burning Lancaster and watched for parachutes. The nervous chickens had done the rest. Tomei, blundering about the farmyard, had fallen neatly into their laps. With the nearby town of Heilbronn on fire, the Germans gave a different meaning to the words 'welcome committee'.

Tomei recalls the horror of that moment. 'They propelled me along a road through a village then stopped beside a tall tree and some angry discussion was held under it. It seemed they were trying to decide whether or not they should hang me from that tree.'

It was clear to Tomei from the Germans' angry gestures at him, then to the tree and to their throats, that they wanted to kill him as a small token of revenge for the destruction of the nearby town of Heilbronn. Tomei was terrified, believing his life was in the balance, when one of them, Karl Bihr, who was a little older than the others, argued for the British airman's life to be spared. How would they feel if the British – swine though they might be – executed any German boys who baled out of their crashing aircraft? Not everyone was in agreement with Tomei's champion, but they stood aside as the burly German took the airman by the shoulder and led him to a nearby building.

After the war, Karl Bihr, then held by the Allies, would appeal to Tomei for him to testify that his intervention saved the airman's life after he was captured.

They went into an office where he sat down at a table and screwed up his eyes against the bright lights. Tomei told them he wanted to be put in touch with the Luftwaffe, whom, he believed, would treat him more kindly than the Gestapo. None of the Germans could speak English, but Tomei gave his name, rank and number and kept repeating the word 'Luftwaffe', which he hoped they would understand. Little progress was being made when the door was flung open and a man dropped Tomei's mae west on to the table. A discussion became heated and another man drew a revolver, pointed it at Tomei and, speaking in tortured English, made the airman understand that if the mae west had been booby-trapped he would be shot without any further preamble. Tomei, who possessed a quirky sense of humour, saw the funny side of this although, wisely, he swallowed a chuckle. The Germans obviously thought the cylinder of air which accompanied the inflatable life jacket was a bomb, but failed to understand that if it exploded, they would all be killed.

The door again burst open and a second German triumphantly dropped a blood-stained air gunner's yellow one-piece Sidcot flying suit beside the mae west. It had belonged to Adrian Roselt. 'I felt sick,' recalls Tomei, 'and feared the worst. I didn't know if he had been shot in the aircraft, or on the way down while on the end of his parachute, whether he had died in the crash, or if it was simply a German trick. The Lancaster had, apparently, crashed nearby even though I'd heard nothing of the explosion.

'I was put in a cell that night by the village policeman. There was no light, only a bench and a blanket. I spent much of the night wondering how I could get rid of my target map. It was printed on silk and could be rolled up very small. I snipped two stitches in my battledress collar and managed to push the map inside and flattened it out. I also needed to hide a tiny compass. In the bottom of my trouser fly there was a small 'V'. I removed a stitch and forced the compass inside. It stayed there for the rest of the war and I brought it home with me. Afterwards, I slept on the bench. I can sleep anywhere, even now, and I was pretty tired, I'd had a long day.

'Next morning I was brought two pieces of ersatz bread with a thin coating of margarine and a cup of black ersatz coffee. I got down a mouthful of that and nibbled a bit of the bread. It was revolting and I left it. The policeman made me understand that I should have both food and drink because some time might pass before I would get the chance of another meal. I still refused any more of it.

'I was put on an open truck which had Wehrmacht men aboard. It drove around for a bit and we picked up another RAF chap who had also been shot down. We tried to talk to each other, but the Germans made sure we didn't. The lorry was powered by steam. A wood burning boiler stood on the back. When we came to an incline they stopped to stoke the boiler. We pressed on and came to the wreck of an aircraft. It was a bit of a mess. The Germans made signs that it was my Lancaster. They said: "All is kaput. For you the war is over." I refused to believe my crew were dead. I thought it was another trick. I always was a doubting Thomas. Surely some of them had got out alive?'

Tomei and the other airman were driven to the town of Ludwigsburg and put in cells at the top of a building. Tomei saw dozens of dates and names of other prisoners which had been carved into wooden panelling. From here they were taken to the railway station to catch a train to Frankfurt-am-Main, and the Dulag Luft interrogation centre. They had to get off the train when the air raid sirens wailed, but wardens would not let them into the shelters. It was here Tomei saw his first friendly German face. It was a young woman, dressed all in black, in the entrance to the air raid shelter. His battered morale was lifted by her smile which, although fleeting, he has never forgotten. On the train the guards advised Tomei to remove his bombardier's brevet, the sight of which might enrage German civilians. Tomei unpicked the half wing with the 'B' of the bomb aimer and slipped it into his pocket.

Tomei spent two weeks in solitary confinement at the Dulag Luft, with nothing to do except pace up and down the small solitary cell and hum and sing to himself. His singing drew the attention of an American gunner along the corridor and they irritated the guards by repeatedly asking to go to the ablutions so they could exchange a few words. The Germans believed that solitary confinement would dull the senses of prisoners, forcing them to crack and give them the information they wanted. Tomei told them nothing they did not already know, but it was here he accepted that all his crew mates in J-Johnny had died. He dwelled on the horror of that knowledge in his small cell.

'The Germans knocked it into me, telling me repeatedly that they were all kaput. I had to believe it whether I wanted to or not. I suppose there was no reason they would tell me they were dead if they were alive. During my last interrogation I was told the names of my dead crewmates by a German officer. It was a terrible shock, but why didn't they get out? The Lancaster wasn't an easy aircraft to leave in a hurry, but I was so sure they were following me out. The plane was level when I slid out. It was on fire, but they would have been putting on their parachutes and running for the exits. I still feel guilty that I survived and they didn't. Why am I the only one alive?'

Tomei was haunted by various scenarios which he went through repeatedly in his mind while he was a prisoner-of-war and years later. The bomber might suddenly have been engulfed by flames, slipped into a dive and blown up shortly after he jumped out, but surely he would have heard the explosion? A crisis might have developed on board. Perhaps the rear gunner was trapped in his turret and the pilot had ordered the others to get him out, but by the time they had done so they were too near the ground to bale out. Becker might have decided at the last moment to try a crash landing. The answer will never be known. Whatever prevented them from getting out safely was no fault of Tomei's, yet he continues to feel guilty because he was the only survivor.

His six crewmates were buried in the cemetery of Obersetenfeld in the district of Ludwigsburg. After the war their remains were reburied at Durnbach War Cemetery for Allied airmen. Navigator Bill Ching had a brother who was a pilot in the RAF. Shortly after the war, and due to meet Tomei to talk about his brother, he too was killed in an air crash.

After he had endured many privations including a forced march of 150 miles over nineteen days in a bitter January, followed by dysentery, Tomei's delighted family welcomed him home on 11 May 1945.

CHAPTER FIVE

SAVED BY THE BELL

Europe was in the grip of the worst winter for fifty years when, on 7 January 1945, the last major raid on Munich was mounted by Bomber Command.

A force of 213 Lancasters and three Mosquitoes from 5 Group was briefed for this raid on the central and industrial areas of the German city. A further 384 aircraft would attack two hours later. Sixteen of the Lancasters in the first force came from 106 Squadron, based at Metheringham, Lincolnshire, where snow lay on the frozen airfield. One sortie would be abandoned, with one squadron bomber posted missing.

Flying Officer Jim Scott, twenty-three, was at the controls of PB724 M-Mike, which stood at the head of the runway, its four Rolls-Royce Merlin engines building up to a bellowing crescendo. The green light flashed from the control hut and the great bomber surged forward, rapidly increasing speed. Huddled ground crews and well-wishers waved as the Lancaster thundered past to climb heavily into the clear sky. It was 4.50pm.

This was the eleventh trip for the crew in M-Mike who felt more comfortable than on their previous visit to Munich on 26 November 1944, only their fifth sortie. At briefing they had been reminded that Munich was Hitler's favourite city, the Nazi movement had been founded here.

In the crewroom, before takeoff, the normally cheerful Sergeant Harry Stunell, twenty-one, had been wrapped in gloom. He stood in front of the kit lockers with his long standing friend Bill Winter, also a wireless operator and said: 'Bill, I've got a strange feeling about this bloody Munich job.'

Winter, the placid son of a policeman, replied: 'We all get those feelings sometimes, Harry. You'll be okay.'

Stunell replied: 'Tonight feels different, I don't feel happy at all.'

It was Stunell's father's birthday that day. Perhaps his melancholy had been generated by the wish to be celebrating with him in a Sussex pub.

The rest of the crew did not seem to share Stunell's uneasy prescience. For Scott, the popular and intuitive pilot, it was another job, another sortie to be marked up towards the completion of his first tour. Scott was born in Musselburgh, on the Firth of Forth, in Midlothian. Going prematurely bald, he had intense blue eyes which sparkled when he smiled. Women found him irresistible. Flying Officer Ken Darke, the twenty-two-year-old navigator, from Muswell Hill in north London, was a well-built 6ft 2in, with a shambling walk. His adeptness with figures honed by his prewar work at a bank, together with dogged precision, served him well in the unreal world of Bomber Command.

From Edinburgh, Flying Officer Bob Dunlop, twenty-three, the bomb aimer, stocky, handsome, with dark wavy hair was always the optimist, even in the hairiest situation. Like all good bomb aimers, he was forever in pursuit of the perfect aiming point.

Sergeant Les Knapman, from Surbiton, Surrey, the flight engineer was, at twenty-six, the oldest member of the crew. Married, he was tough and resolute, with a twinkling smile and wry sense of humour, and capable of piloting the Lancaster in an emergency. Nineteen-year-old Sergeant Jack Elson, the vigilant mid-upper gunner, from Godalming, Surrey, was quiet and reflective, but could raise everyone's spirits with a hearty laugh. Also nineteen, the rear gunner, Sergeant Ron Needle, was one of eleven children, a former butcher's apprentice. Good-looking, dark hair, energetic, and sharp-witted, he spoke often of his close-knit family in Birmingham.

Harry Stunell, from Brighton, was a seventeen-year-old railway coach upholsterer when he joined the Home Guard to help protect the Lancing factory from invading Germans. Stunell's decision to join the RAF was motivated by an incident he witnessed early in the war. A Heinkel bomber flew low over Brighton and dropped its bombs on the Odeon cinema which was packed with children for a special matinée. Many were killed or crippled.

Enveloped in darkness as they crossed the French coast, the bombers entered southern Bavaria at 19,000ft around 7.45pm. There was a thin stratus cloud with good visibility. Forty minutes to Munich.

Stunell recalls: 'Tension was now at concert pitch, reaction speeds intensified. Here we were, young lads who not long ago feared our strict headmasters. Now we were flying into the Third Reich, which was presided over by one of the biggest bullies of all time.'

The first wave of bombers was seen attacking red and green markers. The measured cool voice of the Master Bomber offered words of satisfaction. The attack was going to plan.

'Route marker ahead,' reported bomb aimer Bob Dunlop. Pathfinder Force aircraft were busily dropping marker flares.

A moist dewy sheen coated the upper surface of the vibrating wings, silvered by an eerie light. Vibrations became uncomfortable jolts, caused by the back wash from the propellers of a bomber grinding through the sky just ahead of them. The bomber stream narrowed and they prepared to enter the gateway of the bombing run. Scott held the Lancaster steady in the left hand orbit of the circuit for the start of the bombing run, following the target markers which were a close concentration of glowing red and green blobs.

At 20,000ft the sky was aglow from fires which were sweeping Munich, illuminating the bombers in staggered layers above and below as they moved in for the kill. There appeared to be little resistance, apart from some flak and a few searchlights.

The pilot called out: 'Keep a look out for fighters! This is where they strike.'

The Master Bomber reprimanded aircraft whose bombs were overshooting or had bombed cancelled dummy flares. Target marking aircraft swept low over the burning city, replenishing spent flares and cancelling dummies.

M-Mike's bomb doors were open, yawning wide. Dunlop peered down, his thumb on the bomb release tit.

Stunell recalls: 'Looking down it was like a bloody great coloured nightmare of stark proportions. The whole wild scene resembled a contorted Turner skyscape daubed with deft fiery brush strokes. Within it there was a huge sea of boiling red broth, emitting thousands of surface bubbles. Cavorting flashes of the most startling brilliance waxed and waned in accordance with the savagery being inflicted from above. Closely jostling Lancasters, some almost in line abreast, singled themselves out into much narrower air lanes, their crews requiring even more vigilance.'

Dunlop, lying prone in the nose, called: 'Target coming up, skipper. Steady Jim. Steadeeee! Keep her right there.' Then: 'Bombs gone! Keep her nice and steady for the photo.' It was about 8.25pm. Bombing was concentrated and intelligence later reported a successful raid.

Seconds after the bomb load of one 4,000lb Cookie and 954 four-pound incendiaries had added to the swirling maelstrom of devastation below, the small world of M-Mike was plunged into madness as another Lancaster hurtled towards them.

Stunell again: 'The rogue Lancaster seemed to be making a premature exit from the starboard flank of the stream, as if being pursued by a night fighter, but more likely it was attempting to make a swift getaway from the target area. It came like a bat out of hell, in a sky bathed in a weird greyish light, its engine nacelles thrust belligerently forward, closing fast. A shit or bust situation. Then, at the last moment, it attempted correction, as did Jim Scott, but it was too late. It appeared to feather flick our upturned avoiding starboard wingtip. That, combining with a powerful blast of slipstream, turned us over.'

M-Mike, flipped on to its back, dropped with the speed of a released guillotine blade. G-force rendered the crew incapable of movement although Dunlop had managed to jettison the front escape hatch and rear gunner Ron Needle moved his turret to beam position, but he was unable to bale out.

Scott cried: 'Prepare to abandon aircraft.' But no one could move.

Stunell had floated out of his radio compartment and was pinned to the inverted floor. His reserve trailing aerial flew past, unwinding from its reel, lead weights rattling against the fuselage. Navigation charts, maps and

miscellaneous papers, together with Very cartridges which had been forced
from their rack, cascaded through the fuselage. Scott and his flight engineer
Les Knapman wrestled with the controls. The Lancaster remained upside-
down in an oblique gut-wrenching dive, just short of the vertical, the gasp
of every crewman transmitted through the intercom.

Stunell recalls: 'I was enveloped by a feeling of complete powerlessness,
but was not afraid because I knew I was going to die. The fire-ravaged earth
loomed closer.'

The sound of the roaring wind plunging through the open escape hatch
rose above the tortured scream of the four engines. The continuing drop
seemed without end, although approaching oblivion could be measured by
heartbeats.

Then, the miracle. Scott and Knapman dragged the aircraft out of its
violent dive. God was thanked for saving seven lives. Scott found the
bomber handling in a dead and heavy fashion, but they ploughed on towards
England. The burning city of Munich was left behind, its heart and
industrial areas severely damaged.

As the crew of M-Mike prepared to abandon their stricken aircraft,
Stunell was in a spot of bother. His parachute had disappeared and he cursed
himself for not placing it into the correct stowage position, by the wall
opposite his radio compartment. He searched the entire fuselage, dragging
himself over the main spar, then came forward in desperation to navigator
Ken Darke who squatted near the open escape hatch, ready to jump. Stunell,
rather than search for the intercom socket, pulled up the side flap of Darke's
leather helmet and yelled: 'I've lost my 'chute, Ken. I'll have to go with
you. I'll hang on to your harness straps, OK?'

Stunell looked into Darke's stricken staring eyes and knew it was
impossible. He scrambled wretchedly back to the mid-section as the aircraft
lurched and stumbled over the missing parachute. It had jammed against the
generators which powered the radio. With a great sigh of relief, he clipped
it on and there was time to consider the possible damage to the aircraft.
Rivets might have sprung on the wing panels, which could have sustained a
rippling effect during the dive. The tail plane assembly, twin fins and
rudders, could be badly strained, reducing the Lancaster's chances of
getting home. It was a pity the engineer could not hop out to make a few
temporary repairs; perhaps that would be possible in another war.

Scott coaxed the aircraft slowly up to 10,000ft, but the cold intensified
and the pilot had to reduce altitude because of icing on the wings. Ice
granules shaken free by the vibrations, spewed backwards like a road
gritting machine. A torrent of icy air poured through the rectangular hole
where the escape hatch had been. The Lancaster shuddered as it began
fighting its way through a worsening snow blizzard.

Darke visited the Elsan toilet, located near the rear turret, to relieve his
bladder. On his return he stood briefly beside Stunell, smiled and patted the
wireless operator's parachute pack, which was now strapped to his chest.

They shook hands, cheerfully acknowledging they were still alive. Darke's hand, Stunell recalls, was like ice.

Darke had planned a new route home, away from the briefed course over the soaring Alps and the impossible difficulties which the great mountains would impose on their hobbling aircraft. They headed, instead, for Juvincourt in France, an emergency landing airfield, now in Allied hands, about twenty miles due south of Rheims. They entered France, north of Strasbourg.

Stunell, monitoring his radio, harbouring feelings that all was not well, stood with head and shoulders in the perspex astrodome. 'I looked round, full circle. The visibility was appallingly bad. A driving spume whipped across the vibrating wings. There were signs of hoar frost appearing on the interior of the aircraft.'

He soon learned, over the intercom, that both air speed indicator and altimeter could no longer be trusted, yet Juvincourt could not be far ahead. Stunell listened intently for the voices of the controllers at the emergency landing strip.

Jim Scott had to cope with a continuous blast of freezing air from the nose sweeping across his feet. Accurate plotting on the charts was difficult for Darke whose bare fingers were numb. He preferred to work without gloves which he found restricting. Everyone was affected by the cold, particularly the two gunners, whose specially heated flying suits could not cope with the conditions. The pilot told Needle to leave his refrigerated turret, let Darke have his gloves, then sit at the tail end of the aircraft, plugged into the intercom.

Stunell raised his helmet ear flap to listen for ice granules breaking away and smashing against the aircraft, but heard nothing except the roar of the engines. He wondered if ice was building up on the wings. This would not only add weight to an already troubled aircraft but also alter its aerodynamics.

The pilot aired further doubts about the accuracy of the altimeter as they trundled through the blizzard. It was almost 11pm British time when he called: 'Captain to crew – can anyone see signs of the deck?'

Jack Elson, the mid-upper gunner, replied calmly: 'Yes, skipper, it's right below. I can see some trees.'

'Can't be,' snapped Scott, 'we're showing 5,000ft.'

Stunell recalls: 'Those few words seared through my brain. "Bloody trees!" I thought. "Christ, we must be bloody low." I braced myself for the impact. The usual emergency drill for the wireless operator in an impending pile-up was to sit on the floor with back braced hard against the main spar between the two wings, but there was no time for that. I shoved both feet hard against the edge of my wooden table and forced my body into the back rest so I was fixed and rigid.'

Seconds later the Lancaster struck the snow-covered tops of tall densely packed forest trees and raced along them in a series of gigantic crunching thunderclaps, a great clumsy sledge, bucking, roaring in pain as it was ripped to pieces, lifting momentarily, then plunging to the ground, igniting the trees, snuffing out the lives of five crewmen, ripping some of them to shreds.

The Lancaster came to a shrieking shuddering halt, blazing like a giant blow torch. Behind stretched a flaring avenue of smashed trees. More trees piled up at the front of the wreckage were already sending sheets of flame leaping high into the sky, crackling like gun fire, fanned by a high wind.

Flames shot up between the legs of Stunell who realised that escaping petrol had flowed against the generators under his desk, igniting as it caught sparks from a still rotating armature. Fuel tanks in the wings had been ripped open sending a flood of petrol surging into the fuselage. Stunell was surrounded by a fire storm, with molten perspex from windows dripping on to him. He acted instinctively, yanking out the flex lead from the radio socket to his helmet as flames devoured his trousers and ate into both legs. He stood on his seat and dragged himself agonisingly slowly through a hole in the melting astrodome, cursing the metal bar which had been designed to hold rigid the portable navigational sextant, but multiplied the problems for escaping aircrew. He reached out with his bare hand which became glued to the scorching surface of the fuselage. Hauling himself through the hole into the open air, his head met the fire which was sweeping the fuselage.

The whole of his body seemed to be on fire, the pain was unbelievable and his strength ebbing fast. It would have been easy to give up and drop back. Death would have been swift inside that inferno, but he drove himself on. He wanted to live, there was no future in death.

Stunell recalls: "'Oh God!" I shouted. "Get me out!" I managed to place my buttocks on the outside surface. My backside was burning, I was in terrible pain. I drew up my knees, dragged my feet through the hole, then dropped them over the curved side of the outer fuselage. I was now free to jump down on to the port wing. Unfortunately, the wing had gone. I fell heavily to the ground, severely jarring my ankles. The ripped away port wing was burning to the rear. I crawled like mad away from the overpowering heat, then rolled furiously over and over in the snow, across a tangle of brambles, to extinguish the flames in my clothing. I must have looked like a roll of smouldering carpet. When I was clear of the flames, I looked back at an awful scene. The nose section had been crushed by piled up trees. Flames were consuming the front two-thirds of the aircraft to a point past the mid-upper turret. The rear turret was battered and unoccupied. A tide of molten aluminium moved downwards, reducing the height of the fuselage.

'Ron Needle, the rear gunner, also survived that terrible night. We had crawled away from the bomber in different directions, each unaware of the other's existence, believing he was the sole survivor. My neck had been severely jarred by the impact. I had torn flesh at trouser belt level. I felt very confused. My trousers had gone except for the crotch area, thanks to the protection afforded by stout harness straps which girded my thighs. I was suffering torment from embers still glowing inside my flying boots. Fuel tanks and ammunition continued to explode and there was a pungent smell of cordite. Occasionally a great crackling burst out as flames surged upwards from the forest floor to the topmost branches of the tall trees.'

Needle was in a bad way with a smashed leg, broken ribs, punctured lung, dislocated shoulder and suffering from smoke inhalation. He had been flung forward by the impact of the crash and remembers regaining consciousness in an upright position, hanging by his harness which had been caught in part of the fuselage, saving his life. The inside of the bomber was on fire, bullets were exploding on the conveyor rack. He pressed the harness release disc and dropped to the floor. In agony, he could not stand. He summoned up the last reserves of strength to open the rear door and drag himself from the burning aircraft in his heavy flying suit, resting briefly against a tree before crawling to the forest edge, where he lay down exhausted in the snow.

Stunell struggled to his feet with the stench of his own roasted flesh and rubber-impregnated smoke assailing his nostrils. There was a darting pain in the right hip where the flesh had been ripped open. He had first degree burns to his forehead. His face had been reasonably spared, protected by leather helmet and oxygen mask, but third degree burns had eaten into legs, hands and buttocks. He found that M-Mike had come to rest about eighty yards from the fringe of the forest. A fierce wind drove the blustering snow into his face. Having been frozen on the flight home, then exposed to terrible heat, he was now shivering with cold, in danger of dying from exposure. He fell into a three-foot deep ditch which skirted the forest and glanced down the hillside through a thick curtain of snow. He believed he was alone in that bleak featureless landscape.

He recalls: 'I was freezing cold, stumbling along aimlessly, with tattered strips of skin flapping about in the high wind. I craved rest but could not stop. I had to keep my central engines running, my life blood circulating. I was naked from the waist down, collapse from fatigue could be fatal in such arctic conditions. I was about knackered when I stood still and looked in all directions from my elevated position and saw the merest pinprick of light. It was about 2am, three hours after the crash.'

Stunell, hardly daring to blink, set off for the winking light, which he judged was probably one and a half miles away. He tried to run, afraid the light might disappear, but kept falling over, hauling himself out of deep snowdrifts, then tumbling into barbed wire. Fighting to extricate himself, he realised the wire was attached to a long line of fence posts and allowed himself to think he was near a hill farm. He struggled on, falling heavily down a steep embankment into what seemed to be a lane, filled with deeply drifted snow. Ahead he saw a square smudge in the gloom, a house. With gasps of joy he staggered towards it, his damaged ankles sending stabs of pain through him at every step.

It was an ancient rugged two-storey stone building, with wooden shutters at the windows reinforced with metal bars. He touched a stone wall and shouted: 'Hello! hello!' There was no sound from within and with his less burned right hand he pummelled the shutters until they rattled, still calling. It was then he wondered if the Germans still occupied this part of France.

Stunell recalls: 'I kicked and kicked again with alternate feet at the base of a very stoutly timbered door. My feet felt like two lumps of frozen meat. The falling snow seemed to mock my predicament and I was dismayed by the silence, but where was the light? I found a huge barn door, swinging in the wind, held open by a drift of snow. Inside, a single low wattage bulb hung from the rafters winking as if powered by a generator, but there was no sound. I was then startled by movement, sheep huddled together, unnerved by my approach. I was flaked out, trembling with cold, afraid of frost bite, and considered snuggling in with them to get warm, but they fled into the night. I lay down in the deep straw, the ends of which poked painfully into my fire-ravaged legs, and drifted off into a restless sleep.'

He was wakened by the slap-slap of the swinging stable door and saw light streaks of dawn infiltrating the sky. He stood up with difficulty and tried stamping life into his deadened feet, before flopping wearily back into the straw. The snow-covered sheep waited patiently outside like a silent patient queue of anxious shoppers clutching ration books. Suddenly, an unexpected sound penetrated the sighing wind.

Stunell again: 'It was a bell, I presumed a church bell. It rang and rang, its sound fluctuating in the wind. I shuffled outside. The wind had dropped. Snow was still falling, but less heavily. It was freezing cold. There was no movement from the house, still shuttered and barred. I was at the end of a lane deep in snow. I walked along it, falling repeatedly. I looked up towards the featureless rising ground topped by the forest which stretched out of sight. There was a "bite" in the trees near the far end where the Lancaster had crashed. Wisps of smoke were still rising. The bell continued ringing for several minutes, giving me time to work out where it was coming from.'

Ron Needle knew he would die if he stayed in the snow. He had dragged himself to a path which passed a woodman's hut. Hearing the same bell as Stunell, he crawled in agony towards the sound until, exhausted, he leaned helplessly against a tree and began calling for help.

Stunell staggered past a few scattered stone cottages contained in fenced enclosures and the lane broadened. He saw a man of about fifty driving a small herd of cattle followed by a horse and turned eagerly towards him, falling over a low wall, concealed by drifting snow. The man was not smiling. He carried the slim branch of a tree to swish the flanks of the cows. He pointed for the airman to walk ahead towards a crossroads.

Stunell recalls the moment clearly: 'I slithered and fell and became aware of a closing circle of men. Two stood me upright and held me fast by each arm. Another showed me a long handled pitchfork, which he jabbed towards me. Clearly, it was not the hay-making season. They growled: '*Deutsch! Deutsch!*' and were not impressed when I called out '*Anglais!* Not *Deutsch!*'

in a flat Brighton accent. They were understandably suspicious. I could have been anyone. They looked at me without pity. I had left my dog tags on a shelf above my bed at Metheringham, a chargeable offence. I nodded down towards my breast pocket. A man stepped forward and retrieved two blackened coins, a florin (10p) and a shilling (5p). The coins were passed round for inspection and gradually their expressions changed.'

The British bomber had crashed high above the little village of Meligny-le-Grand, home to about 120 people. It lies fifteen miles from the small town of Commercy which is about twenty-eight miles due west of Nancy, an industrial town in the province of Lorraine. The angelus bell had been rung by twenty-year-old farmer André Fromont who was calling villagers to prayer at the old Roman Catholic church of St Evré.

Stunell was carried in great style to the home of the man who had found him, farmer Lucien Giroux, and laid on a huge ornately carved oak bed. Family photographs adorned the walls. The ground floor room was separated from the cattle by a wide timber door, the top half of which was open. The cattle, peering in at him, provided the ancient two-storey farmhouse with a crude form of central heating. Giroux's wife, Genevieve, a tiny woman of about forty, with a noble face and gentle dark eyes, picked fragments of straw and sheep's wool from Stunell's raw wounds and bruises, which she dabbed with a damp cloth. She caressed his burned forehead and gave him sips of water.

After ringing the church bell and before Stunell appeared in the village, Fromont had met his grandfather who told him he believed an aircraft had crashed near the village. During the night he heard bullets exploding and saw flames leaping above the woods. Fromont, his cousin Albert Agner, the deputy mayor André Bouchot and other villagers set off towards the wrecked aircraft, carrying a stretcher.

Fromont, whose ancestors have lived in the village for over 200 years, recalls: ' We heard someone crying out and found a wounded airman (Ron Needle) leaning against a small tree. He was cold, shivering, suffering from frost bite, making signs with his hand to tell us he was a comrade. We had thought the aircraft was German and that the crew might shoot us. I gave him my velvet muffler which had been made by my mother then laid him on the stretcher.'

They fortified him from a flask of the potent spirit Mirabelle, distilled locally from white plums, before carrying him carefully to the village and the house of Madame Mariette Bouchot, wife of the deputy mayor. She cut away the flying boot to help ease the agony from his foot before giving him a boiled egg. His foot, affected by advanced frostbite, turned gangrenous and was later amputated. Eventually, surgeons would be compelled to remove his leg.

Fromont and his cousin followed Stunell's footsteps in the snow to find the crashed aircraft. They found the wreck in a V-shaped clearing, created by the great fire.

Fromont again: 'What a sight! It was horrible! The cockpit was still there. The wings were torn to pieces. There were no more survivors, we saw only mangled corpses. We could do nothing but turn back.'

Late that afternoon two United States Army trucks arrived, one each for the injured airmen, who were driven fifteen miles to Commercy, now occupied by British and American troops. On the way Stunell, after receiving a morphine injection, learned that the low-flying M-Mike had come very close to being shot down by Allied radar-assisted anti-aircraft guns. Stunell and Needle were taken to the town hospital, which had dealt with a flood of casualties from recent battles with the Germans in the north. Several weeks later Stunell was transferred for extensive plastic surgery to the burns unit at an American Army hospital in Cirencester, Gloucestershire. Ron Needle was admitted to Royal Air Force Hospital Wroughton, Wiltshire.

In civvy street, Harry Stunell and Ron Needle worked for handicapped people of all ages. They return regularly to their friends at Meligny-le-Grand where André Fromont still rings the angelus bell of St Evré. They also visit the graves of their five crewmates at Choloy military cemetery, near Toul. A memorial stone marks the Lancaster crash site, where fragments of the bomber are still found.

When the two Bomber Command veterans want to revive the more poignant memories of their miraculous escape they switch on the audio cassette tape which Fromont has given each of them. The tape contains the sound of the angelus bell ringing out over the lovely undulating French countryside, the same bell – rung by the same man – that helped save their lives on that terrible morning of 8 January 1945.

CHAPTER SIX

EMERGENCY LANDING

Seven men, their faces grey and strained, clambered down wearily from the Lancaster after a flight which had lasted nine hours and ten minutes. The pilot, Flying Officer Ross Gray, nodded cheerfully at each of them as they joined him, smoking and quietly chatting, waiting for the van which would take them across Metheringham airfield to the debriefing hut, free fags and a cup of tea. It was a little after 2am on 8 January 1945.

A biting cold wind whipped spitefully across the flat Lincolnshire countryside and the men huddled into their flying suits beside the Lancaster whose cooling engines crackled in the frozen air. An airfield dispersal was not the best place for standing around in the middle of a wintry night, but they were dying for a smoke and the skipper, although himself a heavy smoker, had banned cigarettes from his aircraft. A few hours before they had attacked Munich and were thankful to survive another gruelling operation, their fifteenth.

Gray's wireless operator, Flight Sergeant Bill Winter, looked around for his best pal Harry Stunell as they were being debriefed, but there was no sign of him. Later he learned Stunell's Lancaster had not returned from the Munich raid. Winter went to bed with a heavy heart.

They had been together since meeting at 10 Air Gunnery School on Walney Island, Barrow in Furness in November 1943. Theirs was a friendship which had endured despite all the appalling odds, and they had even started to feel lucky. Last night Winter had tried to reassure the apprehensive Stunell, but now his friend had gone. Winter knew he must try to make his own luck last until the war was over.

Winter was twenty-two, blue-eyed, an inch under six feet, born at Pooley Bridge on the edge of Ullswater in Westmorland, a county of rugged hills and lush valleys. There it was like living in a miniature Switzerland compared to this part of Lincolnshire, which resembled a green tabletop. He had been a clerk with the Ministry of Labour before joining up and though he loved the comradeship of the RAF it was not easy to accept that some young chaps who flew jauntily off into the night might never be seen again.

His pilot, Manchester-born Ross Gray, good-looking and a keen sportsman, had worked for a textile agency. He was a year older than Winter who considered him a good skipper, occasionally nervous, but fair-minded. Only once did Gray show any degree of irritation with his crew and then it was entirely justified.

'We were told from time to time not to go out in the evening in case we had a late briefing,' Winter recalls. 'We got tired of staying in for nothing and one night, on 26 November 1944, went to a pub in Martin, the village nearest the airfield. We were drinking merrily when Ross came in and said: "I thought I told you bastards to stay in tonight, there's a briefing shortly." We knocked back our beer. Briefing was after 10pm and we took off later for our first trip to Munich. We saw the lights of Switzerland, and the Alps, and flew round Mont Blanc. I had a terrible headache during the journey. I'd had a skinful as had the rest of the lads, except Ross and the bomb aimer who were in the officers' mess and wouldn't have drunk anything. This incident impressed on us that too much beer and flying didn't agree.'

The bomb aimer was Flying Officer Jack Aitken who, at twenty-nine, looked on himself as the father of the crew. He had already sailed twice round the world in the Merchant Navy, and served in the Metropolitan police, before joining the RAF. The crew were always prepared to listen to him and heed his advice.

Flight Sergeant Pete Adams looked too big at 6ft 4in to squeeze comfortably into his cramped navigator's position. A former clerk at a sawmill, he lived with his mother in Birmingham. His one passion was classical music and he listened to it whenever he could on the mess radio.

Sergeant Bryan Hewitt was married, a Barnsley lad, dour but, at twenty-one, a reliable flight engineer. Mid-upper gunner Sergeant Harold Pickersgill, from Thorne, near Doncaster, worked in a draper's shop before going to war. He was pleasant, tall and slender, and regarded every meal as if it would be his last, shovelling it in rapidly, much to the amusement of his crewmates who nicknamed him Piggy. The rear gunner, Sergeant Wilf 'Shorty' Sharman, had given a false age when he joined up to escape working in a Northamptonshire ironstone mine and in early 1945 was only seventeen and looked it.

Metheringham was a wartime airfield with everyone living in scattered Nissen huts. Although most airfields accommodated two squadrons, only 106 was at Metheringham. In winter it was cold and bleak, starved of fuel for the hut stoves. Australian crews, who felt the cold more than most, were adept at stealing anything which might help keep their stoves blazing. By the end of the war few lavatory doors remained at Metheringham.

The morning of 1 February 1945 was cold but clear. They hadn't been up since a training flight five days ago. Few were bothered by their inactivity, which had the advantage of keeping them alive, but tonight they had to get back into the swing of things. They were briefed to attack synthetic oil manufacturing units at Siegen, east of Bonn.

Winter, as usual, carried a newly charged two-volt battery for the intercom to the aircraft which stood at dispersal, as the crew checked it over. The intercom batteries were rotated each day, whether or not they flew. Winter had a box of spare valves for the receiver and plenty of different coloured cartridges for the Very pistol. His hoarding habit could have led to him being put on a charge, but he liked to be prepared. It was the wireless operator's duty to fire the Very pistol, which was a fixture in the Lancaster roof near his position. Sometimes it was possible to learn the German colours of the day and when being attacked by ack-ack or a fighter the appropriate cartridges could be fired in an attempt to fool the enemy into thinking they were part of the Luftwaffe and calling off their hostile gunners and pilots. Winter kept his extra cartridges tucked behind cables which swarmed along the fuselage.

That afternoon Gray and his crew carried out the pre-flight checks on their Lancaster LM215 F-Fox. This would be their nineteenth operation together, the seventh on F-Fox, a reliable bomber, veteran of sixty-seven sorties. This Lancaster had become their lucky charm, like a well worn scarf or a favourite pair of socks. Afterwards, in good weather they would stand outside the aircraft smoking for a while. In January they trooped into their ground crew's nearby ramshackle tin hut, which had the luxury of a hot stove.

'We talked about anything to relieve the tension,' Winter recalls. 'In that hour before takeoff it built up. It was caused by fear. I defy anybody to say they weren't frightened. You've been told at briefing what the defences are at the targets, you've got umpteen night fighters after you, anti-aircraft guns firing at you and searchlights looking for you. If you're unfortunate enough to bale out you will end up in an entirely foreign environment. Anything can happen and, of course, it did to a lot of fellows. This could be your last trip, although we didn't talk about that. Once the engines were started the tension eased a little for there were things for each of us to do. It's like a football match; once you start playing you just concentrate on your job.'

A Metheringham aircrew and ground crew once argued heatedly at dispersal about whether a figure in an adjacent field was a man or a scarecrow. The rear gunner said it would be a simple matter to resolve. He climbed into his turret and fired a burst from his four Brownings above the figure, which ran off at high speed. Questions were asked, but the gunner claimed he was testing his guns, the safety catch slipped off and it was an unfortunate accident. His explanation was accepted.

F-Fox's ground crew, with thumbs up, waved them goodbye from dispersal, as the heavily laden bomber trundled to the perimeter track. They returned gloomily to the warmth of their hut to wonder if they would see the seven aircrew again. A group of a dozen or so loyal WAAFs stood shivering outside the mobile control cabin at the head of the runway, with several airmen and a few officers who regularly saw off each bomber, waiting until the roar of each aircraft had been swallowed up by the gathering darkness. The green light showed from the control cabin and F-Fox lurched forward.

It was carrying one 4,000lb Cookie bomb and a load of incendiaries. It was 4.15pm as it took off, a ruthless surge of power rippling through the big bomber.

Wheels were up and locked at 500ft and Winter unwound his 100ft trailing aerial, which was fed through the floor of the Lancaster. Without this aerial it was doubtful they would receive any of the messages transmitted every thirty minutes from base.

F-Fox was one of 271 Lancasters and 11 Mosquitoes of 5 Group despatched to Siegen. Three Lancasters and one Mosquito would be lost. Most of the bombs would fall in the countryside outside Siegen after markers had been swept away by a strong wind. Some bombers were deceived by dummy markers and a decoy fire. The raid killed 128 people.

The bombers rendezvoused at Reading at 5.10pm, still climbing, turning south-east to cross Beachy Head, pointing towards the French coast which they crossed south of Boulogne. Cloud had thickened and it remained 9/10ths until they drew near the target. A few miles into France they changed course to almost due east, droning over Luxembourg. Each change of course was made deliberately to confuse the German ground controllers, to make them wonder which of their cities had been targeted. Maximum confusion was created among the enemy that night for other heavy raids had been mounted on Ludwigshaven, Mainz and Berlin and there were several other minor operations, in all 1,273 sorties. The puzzled Germans, it was hoped, would not know which way to turn. The force heading for Siegen flew north-east over Germany at 6.37pm and again, more sharply at 7.01pm. They had avoided all known defended areas and so far this had been a comfortable ride.

Long before they got to the target Winter undid his harness for comfort. 'I always put the shoulder straps over the bulkhead, just where I was sitting,' he recalls. 'The leg harness dangled between my legs. The harness was in position but not connected. I kept my parachute on a ledge behind me. We never wore the parachutes, they were just there in case of emergency.'

It's impossible to say how many aircrew took a similar view. Certainly, many died because there was no time to find and clip on their parachute when the aircraft was mortally wounded or blown apart. To survive a devastating explosion you needed a decent slice of luck and a parachute. A select few lived with a massive amount of luck and no parachute, but luck was fickle and indiscriminate.

They flew across the Fatherland while below the Germans scanned their radar screens, scratched their heads and surmised this bomber force could be heading for Cologne, Essen, Dortmund, or Kassel. Then the invading aircraft made a short stabbing turn to the north-west, and the sirens started blaring in Siegen.

Five minutes from the target, as heavy cloud gave way to broken layers of cumulus, nobody in F-Fox saw the German fighter which darted towards them, cannons and machine guns blazing. Gray, the pilot, spoke later of a shadowy movement at 2 o'clock, and some of the crew heard a metallic clang before the port inner engine caught fire.

'I instructed the engineer to feather the prop and use the fire extinguisher button and this he did,' Gray recalls. 'The fire went out. I retrimmed the aircraft, opened the bomb doors and approached the target on the correct height, course and speed. Suddenly the port outer was on fire and again the engineer put it out. I told the bomb aimer to get it right as we would not be going round again on two engines. All the time I was fighting the aircraft to keep it straight. It was 7.22pm when we bombed at 8,800ft on the glow of red target indicators. When we turned for home I noticed we were down to 7,000ft and found I could not maintain height. Luckily, we were descending at the same rate as the land.'

When his crew realised they were in danger the parachutes were quickly clipped on. Soon after leaving the target a nauseating stench of 100 octane petrol infiltrated F-Fox and the pilot was told fuel was sloshing about in the cabin. Breathing became difficult and Gray ordered everybody to wear oxygen masks warning that a single spark could cause an impressive explosion.

'We were all frightened before taking off,' Winter recalls. 'We were more scared now flying home over Germany. We were in a hell of a precarious position. We had been shot at when we were sitting on a load of bombs. Two engines had caught fire and were u/s. Now several inches of petrol were swilling about on the floor. It was an inch or two below the generator which was sparking inside a metal case under my table. If a spark had touched the fuel we would have exploded. It was nerve-wracking. Petrol had soaked into my trousers and the tops of my flying boots from my kneeling down to ascertain where it was coming from. There was no question of mopping up the petrol. There was nothing to mop it up with. We didn't think of it at the time but if we'd taken off the little bomb inspection panels running down the aircraft the fuel might have seeped away. At this point we were wondering what to do next.'

F-Fox continued to lose height as petrol swirled over the feet of Bill Winter and the navigator Pete Adams nearby. A fragment of shrapnel had blown out a petrol cock, which released fuel contained in the port wing tanks. The fuel poured through the wing into the cabin, streaming towards the rear turret, saturating the aircraft. Bryan Hewitt, the engineer, aided by Bill Winter, attempted unsuccessfully to transfer fuel from the starboard tanks to port. Studying the gauges, Hewitt made a swift calculation and announced there was not enough petrol in the starboard wing tanks to get across the Channel.

The skipper offered his crew two alternatives. They bale out or try to make for Juvincourt, the emergency landing airfield in France, south of Rheims, now in Allied hands. There was a brief discussion, but the decision was made suddenly by Jack Aitken, the bomb aimer, who said, in a gruff tone that brooked no argument: 'We'll stay.'

And so they stayed, aboard a limping two-engine Lancaster dripping with petrol, which might explode at any second. It was clear that if they did bale out they would be condemning their skipper to certain death. He would have to remain at the controls, keeping the aircraft steady and level as they dropped out, one by one. Once he took his feet off the rudder bar the bomber would flip over. Under those circumstances escape was impossible for Ross Gray, and he was secretly proud of his crew's loyalty.

F-Fox slipped uneasily away from the security of the main stream returning to England. The crabbing Lancaster was alone, at the mercy of any prowling fighter. A single bullet or sliver of shrapnel passing anywhere through the floor of the fuselage would score an easy kill. The navigator produced a new course to Juvincourt and Gray persuaded the disgruntled Lancaster on to it. The straight-legged pressure necessary to keep on a heading became increasingly painful. The pilot's right foot had to turn the rudder into the engines to stay on even keel. It was three days before his leg was back to normal.

Both gunners, who remained in their cold turrets, were now, more than ever, the eyes of F-Fox. The eyes of Piggy Pickersgill and Shorty Sharman ached agonisingly from the endless toil of peering into the unfriendly chasm of darkness which surrounded them. Not for the first time they thought there was far too much sky to poke around in, although it was a job for which they had both been trained. They searched for the jolting hint of a swiftly moving night fighter, the merciless killer shark of the skies. They looked for shifting shadows which might not have been a harmless swirl of cloud or an aircraft fitter's smudged fingerprint on the perspex turret, and they watched for the red glow of alien exhausts, while trying to subdue imaginations which remained lively and innovative, even though both men wanted, more than anything, to sleep. And then, if they did see a blurred something out there, would they be alert enough to gasp instructions for the skipper to dive out of trouble?

Chugging over Germany, an emergency corkscrew was a grim prospect with only two engines, both on the same side. They were now under 5,000ft, still drifting down, with little sky between them and the ground which could be used up in a dive. And then to have time to pull out of it. All of this was a worry and a grave responsibility for the two young gunners.

The crew spotted occasional distant flashes of flak, but had no time to think about possible stragglers who had strayed too near an enemy gun emplacement. Germans, restless in their beds, heard the fearful overhead grind of the Lancaster's straining engines, and fervently hoped the aircraft was one of theirs. F-Fox dragged itself painfully across the river Rhine, threatening nobody but themselves. Cruising speed for a Lancaster with four healthy Rolls-Royce Merlin engines was around 200mph. Now, with only two, going like the clappers, they shuffled along like an arthritic old man in a pair of shabby carpet slippers, not much faster than 100mph.

It took some time for wireless operator Bill Winter, using the W/T, to make contact with the emergency airfield at Juvincourt, a former German fighter base. When he got through he explained their difficulties and requested permission to land. Then the pilot took over, using the radio transmitter. Gray, battling to keep the Lancaster aloft, was not pleased to hear discouraging noises from Juvincourt. They didn't want F-Fox to land there and refused to switch on the landing lights. The Lancaster was fifty miles from the airfield and a decision had to be made, but Juvincourt continued to be obstructive. The airfield was only twelve miles from the front and Gray detected a certain nervousness and whining reluctance that they should continue to be used as an emergency landing ground until the Germans had been pushed farther back. Naturally, they were worried about the enemy seeing the runway lights switched on, realising an Allied bomber was in trouble, and sending a fighter or two to shoot it up and make a mess of the airfield. After a lot of haggling the pilot wheedled Juvincourt control into putting out three flares beside the runway, milk bottles containing kerosene and wicks. It was a bit pathetic, but it would have to do.

'I could not hold my height until nearing Juvincourt when it became stable at about 1,400ft,' Gray recalls. 'I got the crew into crash positions beside the main spar and now had the problem of the undercarriage and flaps. These were both operated by the port inner engine, but there was an emergency air bottle which I used. The wheels went down with a whoof and the two green lights came on. So far so good. I then made my only mistake. I was approaching a bit too fast because I had no flaps and decided, as I held off at about twenty feet, to use them as an air brake. I told the engineer to select flaps. I had forgotten they were on air bottle. They went down with a whoosh and the Lanc leaped up to about eighty feet. What happened next is a bit of a blur, but I wrestled it down. Just after landing we passed the last flare. We were in complete darkness doing over 80mph. I had no idea what was ahead of us, it could have been anything, from a hangar to a hill.'

They were still hurtling along the ground when they struck something with a great clatter and crunching, and pieces of metal flew along both sides of the bomber. Whatever they had struck served usefully as temporary brakes for the Lancaster, which left the runway, bumped and bounced over grass, tore through a wire fence and came to rest in a waterlogged field, the two over-heated engines sizzling like an enormous pan of frying sausages. While practising aircraft evacuation at Metheringham their best time had been seventeen seconds. Wearing parachutes, they beat that easily at Juvincourt, their haste driven by the awareness that the bomber might still burst into flames. As Gray followed his crew out of the rear door, he turned aghast to see an American Lockheed P-38 Lightning twin-engine fighter spinning miserably on its nose wheel, demolished by his Lancaster. It was 9.15pm.

A fire engine and ambulance followed them swiftly through the hole in the wire fence and as they piled out they were greeted by an American serviceman, his teeth clamped on a lighted cigar. 'Anyone hurt?' he drawled. The disadvantages of smoking a fat cigar beside a bomber heavily impregnated with fuel were quickly explained to him and the Yank backed off smartly. No one was hurt, except Piggy Pickersgill, who had bumped his head in the fuselage when the Lancaster struck the ground and took off again rather smartly. Not surprisingly, the gunner's appetite was undiminished and he later demolished the meal that was put in front of him. Gray and Aitken were invited into the debriefing room where they helped reduce a consignment of good champagne which had been hidden from the Germans.

Next morning they went to look at F-Fox and found four jagged holes in the port wing, each about a foot wide, all close to the engines. The bomb doors hung open, which was normal after landing. An American was peering curiously into the bomb bay. He pointed. 'Hey, what's that, fellers?'

Someone said, casually: 'Oh that's a bomb that hasn't gone off.' The American paled and retreated at a gallop. The hung up 'bomb' was, in fact, a case of incendiaries. These were welcomed by RAF groundcrew who explained how useful they were when Juvincourt was greeting shot up bombers.

One said, exuberantly: 'It saves switching on the runway lights. When we know a bomber in trouble is coming in two or three of us run beside the runway throwing the incendiaries which go off producing a miniature flarepath.'

Foolhardy maybe, but they claimed the idea worked perfectly and were delighted to add F-Fox's incendiaries to their store of special runway aids.

Ross Gray discovered to his horror that the Lancaster had passed over a five-foot deep bomb crater in the dark, its big wheels having no more than six inches to spare on either side. He admitted it would have been impossible to taxi over the crater in daylight.

'The wreckages of several crashed German aircraft, some spattered with bullet holes, were strewn about the airfield,' Bill Winter recalls. 'There were German bombs, painted a duck egg blue, with casings made of concrete. They must have been very short of steel, a concrete bomb would just disintegrate on impact.

'Some of the RAF groundcrew were disappointed when we told them we did not intend making regular journeys between England and Juvincourt. They wanted to get a supply line going. A twopenny bar of soap, unobtainable in France, could be sold for ten bob (50p) and anyone could name their own price for a packet of ten Players.'

They left France bearing gifts: grapefruits which they had not seen for years, and a bottle of champagne each, scrounged from a warehouse in Rheims as they heard the heavy thud of guns at the front.

They flew back to Lincolnshire in a patched-up Lancaster after being advised to leave the undercarriage down on the flight home because there was no guarantee it would come down for landing. They flew without parachutes and most of the helmets which had been taken by souvenir-hunting Yanks at Juvincourt. As they were getting out of the aircraft at Metheringham, Piggy Pickersgill was dismayed when he dropped his bottle of champagne, which smashed on the runway. Later ground staff officers prepared to launch an inquiry into the loss of the helmets and parachutes.

Winter explains: 'After we got out of the aircraft at Juvincourt we threw our helmets and parachutes back inside. The Yanks, who got there before us next morning, decided that anything which had not been removed was worth pinching. Ross told our officers the Americans only wanted the pilot's name after we had smashed up their fighter and we heard no more about it.'

After completing their tour Ross Gray was awarded a DFC, Bill Winter received a DFM. Winter was pleased his war was over, but sad that he never discovered what had happened to his friend Harry Stunell, who was lost on that second Munich raid.

One evening in the spring of 1989 the telephone rang at Bill Winter's home in a village near Carlisle. It was answered by his wife Nancy who told him a man called Stunell wanted to speak to him. Winter shook his head, puzzled.

He says: 'I could not bring him to mind, but before reaching the phone I began to remember. My first blurted words were: "Your name is Harry and you were with me as a wireless op at 106. Your locker was next to mine."

'Harry said: 'That's right. I saw your name on a 106 Squadron Association reunion list and was wondering if you were the same Bill Winter.'

'I said: "That's me."

'From that moment we have become very close again, discussing our service lives, and what has happened since. On that night when Harry called it was like hearing a voice from the dead.'

CHAPTER SEVEN

A FIELD TOO FAR

Don Farrington woke one chilly March morning in 1944 to find his skipper sitting on the edge of his bed in the sergeants' quarters. He yawned wearily, rubbing his eyes in surprise.

Flight Lieutenant Frank French gazed down at his wireless operator and grinned, cheerfully. 'Come on, Don, let's be having you. It's time we got moving, we're on operations again tonight.'

Farrington regarded him ruefully through eyes which struggled to stay open. The pilot, dark-haired and handsome, looked disconcertingly wide awake. It took Farrington a while to assemble his thoughts. French stood up, looking at his watch. 'We have to be ready for briefing this afternoon. I'll see you there.'

It was 10am as Flight Sergeant Farrington watched his skipper walk smartly out of the cold Nissen hut and slam the door without a backward glance. He yawned and reluctantly threw back the bed covers, gasping as the cold struck. The fire in the black coke stove had died during the night. He collected soap, flannel and towel from his locker and slouched to the end of the hut into the washhouse where ice had formed on the windows. Shattered from a succession of late nights, he'd been looking forward to a quiet night with a good book and drink in the sergeants' mess, or a couple of hours relaxing at the camp cinema.

Farrington was twenty-two, from Stockport, Lancashire. He was a slim trim man of nine and a half stone, standing 5ft 7in. Less than four years ago he had a safe plodding job as a junior clerk with the Co-operative Society in Stockport. That was another world, as much a part of history as Henry VIII and the dissolution of the monasteries. Farrington filled a sink with hot water, took off his pyjama jacket and began a hurried wash. The unheated washhouse at RAF Tuddenham, Suffolk, was no place to linger in winter. The wireless operator was a bit of a loner, not often going out with the rest of the crew, although they all got on well together. He was a keen footballer and played for 90 Squadron's team, but he did not care for pubs. He neither drank nor smoked, an unusual trait for wartime aircrew, most of whom lived for the moment and to hell with tomorrow.

Four-engine Short Stirling bombers were based at Tuddenham where 90 Squadron was part of the Special Operations Executive early in 1944, dropping arms, ammunition, clothing, money and food into France. These operations only took place at full moon periods and were flown at low level to the dropping zones. Farrington slapped water over his face and thought of the previous night when they had flown into a blizzard. They were on their way to a field in the south of France where, as usual, they looked for a torchlight flashing a code at the dropping zone. The entire operation depended on their spotting the light which was no more easily picked up at 500ft than a cluster of glow-worms. By some miracle they had seen it through the driving snow.

Farrington and the mid-upper gunner, Flight Sergeant Graham 'Buck' Buchanan, an Australian, muffled up in warm fur-lined Irvine jackets and plenty of underclothes, heaved two huge containers a short distance along the fuselage to the escape hatch. The hatch cover was removed and the two men grunted as they struggled with the infuriatingly awkward containers. It was a tight squeeze and they reported their problems over the intercom to French. The pilot patiently circled low three times over the field as the two men manhandled the containers into the right position and shoved them through the hatch, making sure they didn't lose any fingers. A flickering light of thanks reached them from the ground, the hatch cover was replaced, and the Stirling headed immediately for England. They had an easy flight home, without encountering flak or fighters, and touched down at Tuddenham at 2.32am. They had been in the air for seven hours.

The seven-man crew stood shivering on the wind-swept airfield waiting for a truck to take them to briefing, looking forward to the bacon and egg breakfast which would follow in the mess where cooks remained on duty to feed homecoming aircrews. They got to bed, hoping for a day or two off to relax, sink a few drinks and chat up a few pretty girls. No such luck, now there was another night of it ahead of them. Well, they were all volunteers. None of them believed fighting the Germans would be a picnic, but it was tough all right. Farrington wondered how his family would react if they knew just how tough it was flying a bomber over enemy-held territory. Fighting was something young men did at time of war but few back home were aware of just how much luck was needed for aircrews to survive in Bomber Command.

Farrington dressed and strolled to the sergeants' mess, gazing about him. He had been posted to Tuddenham in November 1943 shortly after it had been built.

'Everything was so basic, it was unbelievable,' he recalls. 'We washed, shaved and showered with cold water. It was obvious the camp was not finished. Eventually, we did get hot water and the food was good and plentiful, but there was nothing salubrious about Tuddenham, especially at the height of winter. No doubt those who survived and lived there during the summer will say it was quite a good camp, but for us, it wasn't.'

That afternoon, 4 March 1944, Frank French and his crew were briefed to drop supplies to the Resistance who would be waiting in a field south of Lyon. It was much later they learned that their skipper had volunteered them to take the place of another crew whose pilot had reported sick. Volunteering for anything was usually regarded as an act of utter recklessness by wartime aircrews. It might lead them into situations which could make life uncomfortable, or worse. French's decision, together with a few other incidents which occurred that day, combined to make Farrington later believe his twelfth operation had been cluttered with bad omens. One of them came after briefing when they found their normal aircraft, J-Jake, had been declared u/s and they were transferred for the first time to another one.

'That night as I sat in the mess in front of the coke stove waiting for the call to go out to the aircraft, I remembered some advice I was given at one of our briefings when going on these SOE operations,' Farrington recalls. 'This was that we should always carry a copy of that day's newspaper. The idea was if you were shot down and eventually managed to contact the Resistance, this would give them the proof needed that you were indeed serving in the RAF. At this time the Resistance was losing many men due to betrayal, and Germans had infiltrated the organisation in the guise of RAF aircrew. I put a copy of that day's *Daily Express* into an inside pocket. There was a photograph on the front page showing our latest bomb, the 12,000lb Blockbuster. I thought if I was shot down at least I could show this to the Resistance people and they would be highly delighted.'

The other NCO members of French's crew were sitting around sombrely in the sergeants' mess waiting for the hands of the clock to crawl nearer to the time of takeoff. The waiting was always the worst part of an op. As they waited, talking among themselves, their imagination paraded any number of horrifying scenarios for that night's trip. Thoughts turned to home, loved ones and friends. One of the crew was the bomb aimer, Flight Sergeant Murray Hoffberg, a Canadian, with a wicked smile which drew girls to him like moths to a lighted candle. He enjoyed himself off duty, putting the stress of operations to the back of his mind.

The flight engineer was Sergeant Joe Cashmore, a twenty-two-year old from Birmingham. He was quiet and studious and wrote most days to his wife. Flight Sergeant Graham 'Buck' Buchanan, was the mid-upper gunner. A bachelor from Murwillumbah, sixty miles south of Brisbane, he ran a farm with his sister. A short man, he had a prominent backside which waggled so much like a duck as he walked the others pulled his leg about it. An extrovert, who lived life to the full, he was the same age and best pal of rear gunner Flight Sergeant Steve Bulmer. Bulmer, blond and good-looking, from Thirsk, Yorkshire, had an angelic look about him even when riding his powerful Norton motorcycle. The two gunners often drank the night away in Cambridge or Newmarket, returning in the small hours to deliberately rev the bike up noisily outside where the others were trying to sleep. They were not popular. Once offered a lift into Cambridge by the ebullient pair, Farrington was hoisted on to the handlebars and found bouncing along quiet country lanes at 40mph more frightening than flying at night in a bomber.

The navigator waited with his skipper in the officers' mess. Flying Officer Harry Yarwood, tall and well-built was, at thirty-three, known by the others as 'Grandad'. Before the war he had been employed as a private detective looking after members of the Royal Family.

When the red glow faded from the stove in front of him Farrington gave it a stir with a poker. Suddenly, the front of the stove gave way, spilling red hot ashes on to the stone surround. Fortunately, nothing caught fire, but Farrington remembered this incident later, adding it to the short list of dark omens as superstitious aircrew did each time they flew into the unknown. They climbed with reluctance into the Stirling EH906 XY T-Tare, but after a moment they forgot they were in a strange aircraft.

'It was the last thing you thought about,' says Farrington. 'You had your own duties to perform and you're concentrating on them. It wasn't our normal aircraft, but the wireless set was exactly the same as the one I usually had and I don't think Frank was unduly concerned. He was always cheerful, always optimistic. It was going to be just another trip, although we were going further south than we'd been before."

T-Tare took off at 8.30pm on a clear crisp moonlight night, the Stirling's four Bristol Hercules 1650hp engines roaring. The Stirling was the first four-engine bomber to go into service with the RAF. Short, the designers, had been restricted by Air Ministry specifications to a maximum 100ft for the aircraft's wingspan, so it could get through the doors of the prewar hangars. As a consequence, the Stirling's 99ft 1in wingspan struggled to get it above 14,500ft with a full bomb load. This was hopeless for attacking heavily defended targets in Germany, but the Stirling continued being part of Bomber Command's offensive until it was withdrawn from all bombing operations in September 1944. The Stirling's low ceiling did not create any disadvantages for the men flying for the SOE. They would not have seen a torch flashing on the ground from 15,000ft.

T-Tare crossed the English coast alone at 8,000ft over Selsey Bill and climbed to 14,500ft to get above heavy cloud which had built up over the French coast. They experienced icing in the cloud, but this did not present any problems. The navigator obtained a Gee fix at Cabourg and left the cloud behind.

'The Stirling descended to 1,500ft as I kept a watch through the astrodome,' Farrington recalls. 'It was a beautiful night, almost full moon, and the reflection from the snow on the ground made it feel as though we were flying in daylight. The first turning point on the River Loire was encountered at ETA and we were well on track. Gee was now being jammed by the Germans, but Murray, our bomb aimer, was able to map read quite easily in the bright moonlight. Both gunners were watching out for fighters, or any sign of resistance from the ground. I had to maintain wireless silence while we were over enemy territory. At this point I was mainly observing. When we got nearer the dropping zone, Murray and I watched for the signal from the Resistance. It might be no more than a pinprick of light. We had to maintain our alertness.'

Bombers were usually part of a vast operation, involving hundreds of aircraft and coloured marker flares being dropped usefully on to the target for the benefit of the bomb aimers. There was safety in numbers too and while German gunners had so many intruders to shoot at there was a good chance that most of the bombers would escape unscathed. T-Tare was different. It was a solitary aircraft and soon after crossing the French coast it came down to 500ft, a mouth-watering sight for any alert German gunner. Its target, or more accurately, the dropping zone, would not be marked by coloured flares or the leaping flames caused by the bombers which were ahead of it. T-Tare's mission was a one aircraft job, involving seven men in the air and any number of people from the Resistance ahead, standing patiently in a farmer's field.

At this time the French were waiting quietly, listening and watching for the British aircraft. They checked they had not been spotted and followed by Germans. It was not unusual for the Resistance to be betrayed by their own countrymen. Their job was a dangerous one. The Stirling, arriving low, and circling the area would attract every German within several miles. After the drop, the Resistance must quickly unpack and hide the containers, distribute the supplies and conceal them from the prying eyes of the Germans.

'About twenty minutes from the turning point Harry Yarwood, the navigator, picked up a Gee transmission and asked Murray for a visual check of our position,' says Farrington. 'This was not possible at the time because the ground was covered in snow, but he believed we were flying to starboard of track. Five minutes later at 10.50pm the navigator was able to get a Gee fix which showed we were eight miles starboard of track. Everything was running smoothly at this point and the navigator had just called through to the skipper to alter course ninety degrees port when the aircraft was suddenly enveloped in a blaze of blinding light. We had been caught by a master searchlight which locked on to our aircraft and was quickly joined by more searchlights. Unwittingly, we had strayed over the edge of the airfield at Camp D'Avord, near Bourges.

'At this point we were suffering from shock. The searchlight had been instantaneous, so unexpected. It was as if we were in daylight. Flak began pouring up at us, the gunners replied, aiming for the searchlights but the aircraft was badly hit, mainly in the port wing. Steve Bulmer, the rear gunner, cried out for the skipper to dive and weave as we were right over the German guns. Frank took evasive action, but because of our low altitude we were a sitting target. I was standing in the astrodome watching the tracer bullets coming towards us from all sides. We had almost got out of the range of the guns when I saw the leading edge of the port wing tip hit and catch fire. I immediately reported it to Frank. It was a small flame, but it spread rapidly snapping up the outer engine and closing in on the port inner and Frank began having great difficulty controlling the aircraft. Staying on board and trying to save T-Tare would have meant certain death, but Frank managed to drag the bomber up to around 800ft to give us all a chance. The skipper didn't mince his words. As he hung on to the controls, trying to haul it up another few feet, he cried: "Bale out! bale out!" It took only a moment for us all to reply. I said: "Wireless operator, received, understood." I snatched out my intercom plug. It was every man for himself.

'Now came the moment to bring into operation the parachute drill we had rehearsed on the ground so often. On this occasion speed was essential due to our lack of height. Murray Hoffberg, our bomb aimer, was first to go through the escape hatch in the nose, followed by Harry Yarwood, the navigator. Joe Cashmore, the engineer had gone back to the emergency hatch in the fuselage from where he and Buck Buchanan, the mid-upper gunner, jumped.

'Meanwhile Steve Bulmer, the rear gunner, had problems. The rear turret hydraulics were not working, so he had to rotate the turret manually to the central position before he could get into the fuselage. He put on his 'chute and jettisoned the rear escape hatch. Unfortunately, as he was going out head first through the exit, the slipstream whipped him round so his left leg was caught below the knee against the step. By holding on to the side of the exit he managed to get back against the slipstream and threw himself into space.

'My turn came to sit on the escape hatch and I can remember vividly seeing the ground below rushing by at a tremendous speed, but terrifyingly close. However, when one's life is at stake you do not hesitate to take whatever option may be open to you.

'As soon as I had left the aircraft at little more than 500ft, I pulled the ripcord of my parachute. There was no time to go through the normal count of one to ten. I experienced a sensational feeling of floating in space and after rolling over several times I received a terrific jerk on my shoulders as the parachute opened. I had only just got over that shock when my feet hit the ground. I had made a perfect landing in the middle of what appeared to be a potato field. I was safe. I was not hurt, not even bruised. Some of the furrows were filled with snow and had helped break my fall. What a marvellous feeling. But if the parachute had taken another two seconds to open it would have been a different story. I shivered as I realised how close to death I had been, then offered up a prayer of gratitude.

'After unfastening my harness, I looked at my immediate surroundings which were virtually in daylight for a full moon was shining. When I checked my watch, it was just turned midnight. I was surrounded by fields, and in the distance I could see what appeared to be a farmhouse. I made my way to one side of the field where I buried my parachute, mae west and some wireless notes and codings I had with me which might have been useful to the Germans. I tried to find a sheltered spot in one of the hedges, but it was far too cold to sleep. I opened my escape kit and sucked a couple of Horlicks tablets. A dog barked incessantly. As I had no idea of my location I decided to stay put until daylight and then review the situation. I wondered how the rest of the crew were and if, by some miracle, Frank had managed to survive.'

Frank French was dead. After gaining height and unselfishly allowing his crew to bale out safely, the pilot had only one option: to stay with the aircraft. He would not have enough height for his parachute to open if he baled out. T-Tare refused to gain more altitude, and no wonder for the port wing was well ablaze. French was staggered the fuel tanks had not exploded. There was no time to think about family and friends. Nor even regret the decision to volunteer himself and his crew on this tragic operation. The pilot's mind was totally focused on survival, but with one wing on fire and the other pointing towards the ground he knew how slim his chances were.

Looking around he was encouraged by the open farmland, but there was no time to search for the perfect site. He aimed for what appeared to be a flat field, with trees at the far end. He tried to coax T-Tare down, but ran out of space and the Stirling plunged with a tortured bellow into the trees which stood on the edge of a forest. Frank French, an only child from Midhurst in Sussex, was killed instantly. The aircraft blew up and there wasn't much left of the pilot. The twenty-one-year-old French had heroically given his crew a slim chance of survival by dragging the crippled Stirling up a few more yards into the sky. It was the last act of a brave man, but his courage went unrewarded. The Air Ministry did not consider Frank French's valiant efforts deserved a posthumous award.

The crashing aircraft was seen by the Chappellier family who lived nearby in the village of St Hilaire de Gondilly. Helen Chappellier was ten when she and her parents watched with horror as the bomber came out of the sky trailing flames and exploded in the trees. Her parents did not go to the wreck to help any injured airmen because they knew Germans would shortly be on the scene and civilians would not be welcome. The Germans put a cordon round the aircraft, removed the pilot's body and handed it over for the villagers to bury three days later. After the war, French's mother was asked for permission to remove her son's body from the village graveyard to a military cemetery. Mrs French requested that he should be left undisturbed in the village.

As T-Tare was consumed by flames a group of Resistance men waited anxiously, stamping their feet, in another field some miles away. Eventually, they trudged home, cursing the Germans, whom they believed were probably responsible for the failure of the British aircraft to turn up with precious supplies.

Don Farrington buried himself into a small copse where the hedges from four huge fields met. He was wearing an Irvine jacket and fur-lined flying boots which were good protection against low temperatures, but not the bitter cold of the French countryside in March.

'I felt pretty miserable,' says Farrington. 'I surveyed the area from my hiding place. All I saw that day was the farmer who was cutting up logs outside the farmhouse. Then he disappeared. That night I decided to go to the farm. I knocked on the door and crossed my fingers. A woman appeared and I tried to tell her that I was an English aviator. I was invited inside and given a chair beside the fire. It was so good to feel warm again. She reappeared with a plate of bread and chicken. Two young children were also at the table. The farmer told me with signs and odd words he knew about our aircraft crashing and that one of the crew was dead. This was the first indication I had of Frank's death. I pulled a map of France from my escape kit and he showed me where I was. I decided to head south by night, trying my luck at farms en route, hoping eventually to make contact with someone from the Resistance.

'Afterwards the farmer took me to a barn where there was plenty of straw which was to be my bed for the night. As I lay there, my thoughts were back in England, to the eggs and bacon that I would miss in the mess, and to my parents who would eventually receive a telegram: "We are sorry to report that your son is missing on operations." Then I thought how lucky I was. At least I was alive and well and still not captured. Who knows, I might be able to make a home run back to England.'

Next morning was brighter and much warmer. Farrington breakfasted on two fried eggs in the farmhouse where he learned the farmer was Polish and his wife came from Belgium. She made up a pack of four hard-boiled eggs, butter, cheese and bread and he set off into the French countryside, consulting his compass.

Farrington spent four days and nights evading the Germans before he was picked up by the Resistance and passed through several safe houses. The *Daily Express* he carried speeded up his acceptance as a genuine RAF airman. His freedom lasted until 11 June when he and five other British servicemen were captured in woods at Taille de Ruine, near Romorantin, after they and the Resistance were surrounded by a force of 2,500 German troops, tanks and artillery. He still feels he owes a debt of gratitude to the Maquis freedom fighters.

He says: 'Many of those involved were ordinary families who gave us shelter and fed and clothed us, despite their own shortages. They knew if they were caught it would mean being shot or sent to a concentration camp. A farmer who helped me died in one of those camps. I was sent to Stalag Luft VII at Bankau, which was evacuated in January 1945 due to the Russian advance. I was moved to Stalag IIIA at Luckenwalde in appalling conditions. I arrived home on 16 May.'

Yarwood and Bulmer made contact with the Resistance, sheltering in Paris for a while before making their way to the Spanish border and climbing over the Pyrenees. They came home via Gibraltar.

Murray Hoffberg was having a reviving drink at a French farmhouse when his host phoned the local gendarmerie. He was handed over to the Germans and suffered rough treatment at the hands of the Gestapo. Joe Cashmore linked up with the Resistance and reached the Swiss border, but was betrayed to the Germans. Buck Buchanan spent a while with the Maquis before walking south on his own. He found an airfield near Marseilles and was amazed that the first aircraft he saw was a Stirling bomber. The airfield had been captured from the Germans and the RAF were now in control. He was back in England on 20 September.

CHAPTER EIGHT

THE NIGHT OF THE STRONG WINDS

Eddie Davidson was eighteen early in 1941 when he told his mother he was joining the Royal Air Force to fly in a bomber. Maisie Davidson laughed with disbelief, telling him bluntly: 'You used to be sick on the garden swing and long bus trips, how would you cope in a bomber? I'll give you a month before they send you home.'

Davidson was not sent home. With grim determination, after filling hundreds of vomit bags, he conquered the terrible travel sickness which had plagued him since childhood. Plying instructors and pilots with sweets and cigarettes, hoping they would not report him to higher authority, he had learned to control the vomiting by the time he was posted to an operational training unit. A wireless operator, he would fly on thirty-two operations, none of them worse than his sixteenth, a raid on The Big City, Berlin, on 24 March 1944.

This would be the seventh raid on Berlin that pilot Tommy Farmiloe and his crew had endured, including three in four days at the end of January. An earlier sortie that month could not have had a more horrifying start, guaranteed to tear at the spirits of young aircrews. A Lancaster, ahead of Farmiloe, was pounding down the runway at Coningsby when it suddenly collapsed and burst into flames, killing all its crew. A red Very signal went up immediately to halt the following bombers, but five minutes later a green set them moving again. The bombers, including one from 61 Squadron piloted by Farmiloe, were illuminated by the burning Lancaster as they flew a few feet over it, not knowing if the aircraft, with a 4,000lb Cookie in its bomb bay, would explode.

Pilot Officer Farmiloe had been christened Howard, which he hated, and was always known on the squadron as Tommy. The only child of his father's second marriage, he had been brought up by his stepbrother outside Birmingham and educated at a boarding school in the Cotswolds. Farmiloe was blond, quiet and shy, but once he got into a bomber he was the boss. On earlier trips, however, his short legs created what seemed to be a serious problem not covered by Air Ministry Regulations.

Davidson recalls: 'When he sat with his parachute on he could fly a

Lancaster unloaded. But when it was fully loaded with bombs and needed a pilot's brute strength at full revs to get airborne, his feet slipped off the rudder bar. He nearly killed us a number of times on takeoff. The navigator and bomb aimer in the original crew refused to fly with him. It was ironic that those of us who stayed with him survived the war, while those who joined other crews went for a burton. Tommy's problem was solved by one of the ground crew who screwed racing cyclist pedal clips on to the rudder bars which held his feet firmly. We had special loops made to fit over the bars. They were put on and taken off each aircraft he flew. It was a brilliant idea because he was a first class pilot with the clips on.'

When bomb aimer Flight Sergeant Vowe joined Farmiloe, after losing his own pilot, friends said he was mad, considering his new skipper's reputation. This was before Farmiloe was introduced to cycle clips. A prewar bank clerk, Vowe was a pleasant slow-speaking Lancashire lad. Navigator Flight Lieutenant Stan Halliwell had already been awarded a DFC, but he was not popular with the crew. In his late twenties, he was older than the others, except the rear gunner.

Davidson again: 'He was tall and slim with dark hair. He fancied himself. He was a former schoolmaster and in his eyes we were a shower of NCOs, except Tommy of course who, like himself, was an officer. He treated us disdainfully and never went out with us. We all piled into Tommy's car and went to Boston or Nottingham and shared beds overnight in cheap lodging houses. Halliwell disappeared when he got off the aircraft.'

Sergeant Davidson, like the pilot and the bomb aimer, was twenty-one. Born on the outskirts of Glasgow, where his father had a small tailoring factory, he was brought up with his younger sister Pat as a boarder at the Methodist College, Belfast. He was trainee manager at a food canning factory in Belfast when he volunteered for aircrew. There was no conscription in Northern Ireland, although many young men wangled their way to Ulster to avoid being called up. Tall, slim and attractive to women, Davidson lost count of the number of WAAFs he took out. He dropped them all when he met Leicester secretary Joyce Simpson and they were married in April 1945.

Sergeant George Gerry, of King's Lynn, never had his leg pulled about his surname. If it had been, the twenty-year old would have blushed scarlet for like his pilot he was very shy, but went about his work as flight engineer with quiet efficiency. The engineer was so diffident he didn't have the courage to tell his crewmates he was getting married until he returned from his honeymoon.

Mid-upper gunner Flight Sergeant Pat Patchett had already been a gunnery instructor at Jurby on the Isle of Man when he joined the crew. He loved cards and occasionally played all night in the mess or Nissen hut where they slept.

Sergeant Ray Noble moved from the mid-upper position to the rear turret, replacing the regular gunner, Frank Ellick, who had been killed after he was picked as a spare bod for an operation with another crew. 'Ray was six feet tall, very well built and very well endowed,' recalls Davidson. 'He walked round the hut naked, like a bull. He was very proud of it.'

The previous month 61 Squadron had been moved to Coningsby from Skellingthorpe where they were so crowded they often queued an hour in the rain for breakfast. They returned to Skellingthorpe after a new squadron base had been built there.

The night of 24/25 March 1944 became known in Bomber Command as 'The night of the strong winds'. The met men's forecast of 'light to moderate winds' was wildly inaccurate as pilots of the 811 aircraft sent to Berlin had to cope with powerful gales from the north which buffeted the bombers south throughout the flight. Different methods used to warn crews of wind changes did not pick up the enormous strength of the gales which ruthlessly scattered the aircraft. On the return flight many crews blown into the Ruhr were picked off by radar-predicted flak batteries. Casualties were high. Forty-four Lancasters and twenty-eight Halifaxes were lost. It was to be the last major RAF raid on Berlin, although the city would still be attacked many times by small forces of Mosquitoes.

Farmiloe was at the controls of ME596 H-How, known by the crew as 'Hell's-a-Poppin'. The Lancaster, with a grinning red Devil painted on its nose, was one of sixteen aircraft from 61 Squadron briefed to attack Berlin. H-How took off from Coningsby at 6.52pm, carrying a Cookie and incendiaries. They were familiar with the northern route, across the North Sea making a good landfall on the coast of Denmark, despite the blustery winds.

'The "light to moderate winds" we had been promised at 20,000ft steadily increased to 125mph,' says Davidson. 'When we turned south-east for Berlin this terrific wind was on our tail so we flew towards the target at over 300mph. Every half-hour on each flight the wireless operator had to switch off from the intercom and listen out for winds or any other encoded messages coming from 5 Group. During that time I was isolated from the rest of the crew. When I decoded a message it was usually about the winds, which I gave to the navigator. Selected aircraft in the main force estimated their wind speeds and sent them back to Group, who averaged the velocity and direction and released what they assessed as the mean average every half hour. Invariably they were completely wrong. That night was no exception.

'So far things were going well for us despite the bomb aimer and the gunners reporting heavy flak, searchlights and tracer being very close on the port side, and the explosion of a Lancaster. Your stomach started churning as you saw one of ours go down.'

Their reasonably comfortable trip did not last. They were attacked by two German fighters before reaching Berlin. Each one was picked up by Davidson on his Monica radar set giving them vital extra seconds' warning. Some aircrews dismissed Monica (an early warning device against fighters) as useless, but Davidson was not one of them.

He says: 'When we were given Monica I had confidence in it but remember having rows with the skipper when he refused to call out the heights so I could calibrate it. Eventually the flight engineer called them out for me every 100ft on takeoff. At first, it was impossible to get the crew, particularly the gunners, to trust me using Monica. They soon changed their tune when we were attacked by German fighters.'

Monica was later withdrawn after it was discovered that German fighters could home in on its signals.

They were at 20,000ft and three-quarters of an hour from Berlin when Davidson saw the blip on his screen coming in from starboard at 2 o'clock. He roared a warning and the rear gunner yelled: 'I can see the bastard! Corkscrew starboard!' All six Brownings started firing as they plunged. The fighter shot over the top of them, guns and cannons blazing. The shells and bullets missed and the fighter was going so fast the Lancaster was out of sight before the German pilot could return to the attack. H-How's corkscrew was sharp and steep and seemed to last forever. Davidson's head cracked against the roof and his code books, maps and memo pads were scattered.

'We were in the second wave,' Davidson says. 'They already knew we were bombing Berlin, so the fighters were waiting for us. The lucky ones were in the first wave who had bombed and were able to get away. The second and third waves were the ones who caught it.'

Farmiloe was given a new course by the navigator and they began climbing as Davidson sorted out his papers then realised it was time to listen out for the half-hourly met report which showed no change in the wind velocity. They were at around 19,000ft thirty-seven minutes later when he saw a blip on the Monica screen 600 yards out at 11 o'clock. As he opened his mouth to yell, Ray Noble, the rear gunner, shouted: 'Enemy at 11 o'clock! Corkscrew starboard!'

This time Davidson had strapped himself into his seat and heard the gunners open up. He saw the blip following them down, but from the port side. He yelled: 'Corkscrew port!' They heard the Lancaster shudder as the skipper tried to level out and George Gerry, the engineer, screamed: 'For Chrissake Tommy, you'll tear the wings off.' They lost the fighter and tried to regain height.

Ken Vowe, the bomb aimer, said he could see a glow ahead which must be Berlin. There was a sigh of relief all round when Farmiloe said: 'We're early, but I'm going in.'

Davidson again: 'It was time to listen out once more. I had missed two wind reports so, as normal, I disconnected myself from the intercom.'

Ill fortune was flying in formation with H-How that night and as the bomber nosed into the illuminated area near the target things began to happen with a malignant suddenness that called for all the reserves of alertness and determination that the crew could muster. The first indication of trouble was a high-pitched whine which could be heard above the roar of the engines. A hurried look by Gerry at the instrument panel showed that the revs on the port inner engine had increased to 3,800. The captain ordered the engineer to feather the engine but although the correct procedure was carried out there was no response, and now the temperature was rising quickly. Within two minutes flames were streaming from it and the whine was so loud the undamaged engines could scarcely be heard.

Immediate emergency action was taken to put out the fire by employing the graviner switch, but this had no effect. Luckily, the windmilling propeller caused a draught throwing the flames up to two feet over the wing. Farmiloe manoeuvred the bomber into a sideslip, hoping this might bring the fire under control, but the flames continued to pour in a torrent from the engine, reaching beyond the rear turret. Farmiloe told the crew to prepare to abandon the aircraft.

The pilot held the aircraft on course for the target hoping the fire would go out but his problems increased when the revs and temperature soared in the port outer engine. It was feathered by the engineer and didn't catch fire, but with two engines unserviceable on the port side the aircraft became difficult to control. Full rudder trim and full opposite rudder plus a little banking were necessary to get the bomber back on course.

Meanwhile Davidson, hunched over his wireless set, knew nothing of the latest drama. He decoded the message from base, saw there was no change in the wind, switched the set off, and leaned round to hand the navigator the wind report.

'I saw he was not at his desk but standing behind the pilot and engineer with his parachute on,' says Davidson. 'At the same time I heard a screeching whine and looking out of my window saw flames pouring past it. In a panic I switched back into the intercom and shouted to the pilot, asking what the hell was happening. He said: "An engine's on fire, we're standing by to bale out." After a brief discussion it was decided to drop the bombs and then bale out. I was frightened and angry as it was the navigator's responsibility in an emergency to tell the wireless operator to reconnect into the intercom. I could have been left alone in the aircraft if they had baled out. I stood in the astrodome and was hardly able to hear the sound of the starboard engines over the whine and scream of the port inner. I believe the two engines failed after the strain put on them by corkscrewing at high speed out of trouble.'

Shouting over the whine, Farmiloe said: 'Stand by, let's go in and drop the load and get out of the target area, then we'll bale out.'

Although the crippled aircraft was rapidly losing height, and becoming increasingly difficult to control, Farmiloe ordered the bomb aimer to direct him through the defences and on to the target. Molten metal and flames surged from the port inner engine, but the Lancaster went in, escaping flak and searchlights by gentle evasive action. Ken Vowe, the bomb aimer, got into position and started his patter as they ran through the first of Berlin's defensive searchlights. Red target indicators were going down about five miles ahead and in the glow of exploding bombs and waving searchlights they saw flashes of tracer as other British aircraft were being attacked. Incredibly, H-How, which could be seen more clearly than any other intruding bomber, trailing a stream of flames, was ignored.

They heard the voice of Vowe calling out calmly in his quiet distinctive Lancashire accent: 'Left, left. No, right, left again.' With a target indicator in the bomb sight, H-How bombed at 10.35pm.

It had been difficult in the strong winds for accurate marking over Berlin and bombs also fell on 126 small towns and villages away from the capital, although five military establishments were damaged. Altogether 180 people were killed and 20,000 bombed out of their homes. Fourteen bombers were shot down by fighters over Berlin.

Leaving the target area Farmiloe turned on a course of 208 degrees, heading south-west. After consulting the navigator he decided to head on a direct course for Coningsby and turned the aircraft on a heading of 300 degrees. He found the fire and engine whine were at a minimum if he flew just above stalling speed. The aircraft continually pulled to the right and the pilot had to press heavily down on the rudder bar in an attempt to maintain course. Ken Vowe helped ease the strain on the pilot's foot by wrapping his arms around the rudder bar and holding it against the drag of the two useless engines. The engineer manually pumped petrol from the port wing tanks into the starboard side in an attempt to prevent the bomber being enveloped by flames. He also watched the instruments for any sign of over-heating in the two remaining engines. It seemed impossible they could drag the Lancaster back to England without any further drama and they talked uneasily over the intercom about baling out.

'We were scared stiff that if we baled out over Berlin the civilian population would tear us to pieces,' says Davidson. 'I suggested we should try to get as far away as possible from the city before leaving the aircraft and that's what we agreed to do. All this time no flak had been directed at us and no fighter had attacked us. The engine was on fire, the flames still being forced over the wing by the windmilling prop.'

They watched the flames anxiously. The wing could catch fire at any moment. The lack of full power had forced the aircraft down to 9,000ft and the skipper told them to jettison equipment in an effort to maintain height. Then Davidson noticed the accumulator dial registered zero.

'Not believing it, I tested my receiver. It was almost dead, even the "static" was faint. I told the skipper the bad news. I said: "Our electrical power is almost gone. I can't use the wireless transmitter. Only the generator on the starboard inner is working, the port inner one is dead. If we switch off everything except the essential equipment we might build up enough power to send out an SOS." This meant the Gee radar equipment was u/s and the gunners would have to leave their turrets. If they tried to rotate them the accumulators would be completely exhausted. Their heated suits were also draining the power.'

The gunners were reluctant to lose their guns, leaving the Lancaster unable to fight back if attacked by fighters. Grudgingly, they agreed that if the turrets could not be rotated their guns would be virtually useless. But the guns were their babies, they had lavished a lot of care and attention on them.

Davidson and the two gunners dragged open the rear door, then he helped them dismantle the Brownings and heave them overboard, together with all the ammunition. Before the guns were flung out Davidson attacked them with an axe to make sure the Germans could not make use of them. They all believed their chances of making it back to England were slight. The odds were stacked against them living through another day. Such a tense situation was not conducive to clear thinking, for it was unlikely that anything dropped from a height of 9,000ft could be of value to the Germans. But Davidson wielded the axe with gusto. Being busy avoided fretting with nothing to do except watch the aircraft sink lower and lower. Not even the rest bed and the Elsan toilet escaped Davidson's fury. He stood beside the open door holding a strap with one hand while expendable equipment was slid across the floor to him by one of the gunners. The second gunner kept a tight hold on the wireless operator to prevent him being sucked into space, although they all had their parachutes clipped on.

'Everything went out that we could lay our hands on,' says Davidson. 'Out went the Gee, the IFF (Identification Friend or Foe) set, even the oxygen bottles. I took the pins out of the flame floats and hoped that when they started smoking the Germans would think they were a new type of bomb. The floats were used in the sea for practice bombing. It took the three of us to shut the door when everything had been chucked out.

'Unbelievably, we were still flying with that horrible whine in our ears and the engine continued to burn. We all had a feeling of nakedness. Why were we not being attacked by fighters? Why as we managed to crawl round the heavily defended areas did the flak and the searchlights ignore us? All the time we fully expected to be shot at, but no one opened up at us and no fighter came near. Perhaps they thought we were goners anyway, why waste valuable ammunition?'

The stumbling aircraft, with a dramatic twenty-five degree list to port, inched round the flak which they saw spitting up at bombers ahead of them. The Lancaster was like a great disfigured crab disgorging flames which might yet destroy them, while acting like a self-illuminating searchlight, as if daring the Germans to deliver the coup de grâce.

With nothing to do the gunners sat on the main spar near Davidson who was watching the accumulator build up. It was then they discovered the Lancaster wireless operator's terrible and highly guarded secret. With a warm air vent and the controls beside him, his position was the only one in the aircraft which could be regarded as cosy.

It was soon obvious H-How was still losing altitude. Davidson again: 'Apart from the loss from the weight of the guns I don't think anything we threw out contributed all that much to us maintaining our height. It was the psychological effect of our thinking we were lightening the weight of the aircraft that was important.

'The radio direction compass was unserviceable,' continues Davidson, 'but a pin-point was obtained by the bomb aimer at a river east of the Zuider Zee and an alteration of course was then made. The skipper asked me to try and get a fix. I switched on the wireless set, tuned into the emergency frequency and sent out an SOS. At 1.20am I logged into a second class fix and a request came through for details of our situation, all in code. Nine minutes later I was given a first class fix and a further request for information. Half-way through my reply the power went, but this fix showed we were going south down the Belgian coast, heading for France. We were now at 4,000ft and as the skipper turned across the North Sea, heading for the Norfolk coast, he said: "Put your mae wests on, lads." We put them on, praying we would not ditch. I didn't fancy drowning.'

Everything electrical was switched off so the starboard generator could build the voltage up from nine to twenty-four. Everyone listened anxiously for the slightest change in pitch of the over-worked starboard engines.

Sergeant Ted Wood, a 61 Squadron wireless operator pal of Davidson, who listened out for distress calls, picked up Davidson's signals and told his skipper that Tommy Farmiloe's aircraft was going down.

England was covered by a blanket of cloud when H-How limped over the Norfolk coast at 500ft. They saw the flicker of a few searchlights and Davidson worried about their own gunners shooting at them because he had thrown out the IFF equipment.

The pilot used his RT to send out a Mayday call. He received the usual reply: 'Give details.'

Farmiloe replied politely: 'Look up and you will see. We are on fire.' There was a pause, then a voice said: 'Follow the searchlights.'

A searchlight was immediately switched on to their port side and made a circle on the clouds. It then laid a beam along the ground. As they reached the end of it another searchlight pointed them forward. This happened three times until the runway lights at Little Snoring airfield came on, told them to circle and asked what was wrong. Farmiloe snapped: 'For God's sake, we are on fire. I am at 150ft, I'm coming in.'

Davidson, Halliwell and the two gunners took up crash positions on the floor with their backs against the main spar. Farmiloe, fighting to neutralize the aircraft's list ready for landing, told the bomb aimer and the flight engineer to join the others, but they refused.

Davidson again: 'Ken Vowe would not leave his position holding the rudder bar and George Gerry, the flight engineer, insisted on standing by to help his skipper. They were both very brave men. This was the ultimate moment of truth. We were home, but would the wheels lock and could the skipper keep the aircraft on the runway? It took immense confidence and ability to control and prevent the aircraft from swerving off the runway, tilt up and burst into flames. Would the wheels lock and the brakes work? So many ifs and to make matters worse the runway lights went off before we ran out of runway. It was pitch black when we stopped and the aircraft tipped up on its nose. The engines were switched off and the fire in the port inner went out. None of us was hurt and when we climbed out on to the fuselage we saw the nose was embedded in a water-filled dyke. We were puzzled that no fire engine or any other vehicle had followed us. I climbed back in, found the Very pistol, stood on the wing and started firing it. When we climbed down from the aircraft, we all kissed the ground. It had been a life and death struggle all the way back from Berlin. We didn't think we would make it. We were kept waiting for half an hour before a waggon drove up and we were taken to flying control. Two squadrons of Mosquitoes were based here. The skipper and navigator were driven to the officers' mess for a hot meal and bed. A corporal took the rest of us to a cold dormitory where we were given mattresses and bedding. No food was available for us.'

Tommy Farmiloe was awarded an immediate Distinguished Service Order. Halliwell received a bar to his DFC. Davidson and Vowe were each decorated with the DFM, as well as being told to apply for their commissions, which were granted three months later.

Ted Wood had spread the news at Coningsby that Davidson had crashed in a burning aircraft. When Davidson went into the sergeants' mess next day, a WAAF who was serving collapsed with a scream and a clatter of crockery. One of his girlfriends, she had believed he was dead.

CHAPTER NINE

THE NIGHT WE LOST THE NORTH SEA

Navigator Alex McKie's most celebrated operation was bombing the German battleship *Tirpitz*, which was berthed near the Norwegian port of Tromsö when it was attacked by 9 and 617 Squadrons on 29 October 1944. The 617 Squadron aircraft, piloted by Australian Flying Officer Bill Carey, flew out from Lossiemouth, and dropped its 12,000lb Tallboy deep penetration bomb, before being badly shot up. It limped to Sweden, having lost two engines and most of the fuel, and did a wheels-up crash-landing into a bog. Everyone survived and a fortnight later, after having a whale of a time in Stockholm, wearing expensive new civilian clothes paid for by the British Embassy, they flew triumphantly back to England in a Dakota to carry on with the war. Although they had set fire to their Lancaster in Sweden, only the front was destroyed. The rest of the wreck is still there in the bog, a unique tourist attraction, stripped clean of souvenirs, reached by a special walkway. One of navigator McKie's 47 operations which is less well known, took place one night, early in 1944, when he inexplicably lost the North Sea.

In January 1944, Sergeant Alex McKie was stationed with 106 Squadron at Metheringham, Lincolnshire. He was twenty-one. He recalls: 'We'd gone to Metheringham in November 1943 from Syerston, which was a peacetime aerodrome with all the facilities. Metheringham was all mud, which became worse in heavy rain during the wet period when we arrived. The aerodrome was still being built, it was like a vast building site. We all had bikes to get around, although that was sometimes difficult in the mud which was quite horrendous, and we got pretty dirty. The Nissen accommodation huts were okay; there was a stove in the middle which we got red hot. There was always a fight to get a bed near the stove. Two crews shared each hut. Three times while we were there the other crew didn't get back from operations. The military police moved in and cleared out their kit very quickly and before long there'd be another crew in. You didn't dwell on this, it was just one of those things. We lived for today, not for tomorrow. We were professionals doing the job we had to do.'

McKie's pilot was Pilot Officer William 'Bunny' Lee, a tall broad

Australian from Toowoomba, about sixty miles east of Brisbane, Queensland. He worked in his father's joinery business before joining up. Lee liked having fun away from the bombing and enjoyed his beer, but in the air it was quite different.

'He imposed a strict discipline on the crew in the aircraft,' says McKie. 'Some aircrews occasionally smoked as they crossed the English coast on the way home. We never did, nor did we use first names on the aircraft. It was always "pilot to navigator", "bomb aimer to pilot," and so on. It was different on the ground, but in the air discipline was very tight, it had to be and I believe that was a major reason why we survived.'

Lee's crew agreed he was a superb pilot, although not the best at putting down a bomber, usually landing after the second bounce.

Navigator Alex McKie was brought up at Alsager, near Crewe. Long before he joined the squadron he knew what discipline was about for in January 1938 he became an apprentice at Halton, where he was yelled out of bed at 6am and marched briskly on to the freezing square thirty minutes later. He trained to be an engine fitter, but after qualifying he remustered to aircrew, realising there was more to the RAF than working on the ground. He was looking for excitement and wanted desperately to get into the war. Keen to be a pilot, he was thrown off the course in Lakeland, Florida, for dangerous flying. McKie didn't look like a young tearaway, yet flying solo in a Harvard he beat up a train for a bit of fun. Unfortunately, the senior flying instructor was travelling on the train and, purple-faced with anger and embarrassment, he took the number of McKie's aircraft and dispensed with his services a few days later. The dismissal acted as a brake on further high spirits when McKie joined a navigators' course in Canada.

The wireless operator, Sergeant Frank Richards, twenty-three, a stocky man, from Staines, Middlesex, floated through life, unruffled by difficult situations. He married a WAAF whom he met after finishing bombing operations. The wise-cracking dark-haired Sergeant Gus Hoyland, from Liverpool, was bomb aimer. Sergeant Alan Hebbes was one of three flight engineers who flew with Lee. Hebbes was smaller than his crewmates and rarely mixed in with their lively pub crawls, possibly because he had not been with them from the beginning of their tour. Sergeant Doug Pooley, a tall man with fair wavy hair, occupied the mid-upper gunner's turret, and Sergeant Peter 'Red' Hunnisett, from Dover, Kent, who had worked at a local engineering works before joining up, was the cheerful rear gunner.

They sometimes cycled to a pub in Metheringham on nights when they weren't flying. The whole crew went one evening, parked their bikes and went inside. When they emerged later they found a black Wolseley police car standing on the other side of the road. The policemen shouted at them to put their lights on. The seven men, glumly aware they were without pumps or lights, pretended to switch on non-existent lights and pedalled furiously, but the police car followed slowly.

They darted round the next corner, threw their bikes into a ditch and

started walking back to the airfield, but a policeman grabbed Frank
Richards and an airman from 83 Squadron as the other lads fled gleefully at
high speed.

'Look here,' the constable said, pompously, 'You're all riding around on
bicycles without any lights. If you're not careful you could get yourselves
killed.'

It was a supreme moment of irony which was lost on the deadpan
constable. He knew the two young men were stationed at the airfield down
the road. He was, perhaps, less aware that they flew unlit Lancasters to
bomb Germany night after night. Richards was fined 10s (50p) and received
a rollicking from the station adjutant for bringing the RAF into disrepute.
The other lad was fined the same amount, but the local magistrates did not
collect his 10s. The airman was lost in a raid over Germany on the night of
the court hearing.

There was no time to celebrate New Year's Day at Metheringham in
1944. There was little to suggest 1944 would be any less grim than 1943 for
British bomber aircrews. Two nights before, Bunny Lee and his crew had
been to Berlin. Tonight they were returning to The Big City in the same
aircraft on their fifteenth operation.

Bomber Command chief Air Chief Marshal Sir Arthur Harris launched
his main battle against Berlin on 18 November 1943, hoping that a
persistent heavy bombardment of the city would crush the German people's
spirit and lead to an early surrender by Hitler. The last major RAF raid on
the German capital was on 24 March 1944, by which time the Allied bomber
losses had been severe and Harris's forecast of a German surrender by April
was clearly wide of the mark.

On the morning of 1 January 1944, Lee took Lancaster JB562 M-Mother
across the Lincolnshire coast for a routine air test, its engines purring
serenely. The gunners fired bursts from their Brownings over the North Sea
and everyone returned to Metheringham, all expressing satisfaction with
their equipment. Alex McKie in particular found that all his navigational
gear, including the radar instruments, was in good nick. After leaving the
Lancaster at dispersal to be bombed up later by the armourers, they went
their separate ways. Some returned to the billets to snatch a few hours'
sleep, others went to the mess to talk about anything but the war. The last
minutes of the day were ticking away as a van dropped them off at dispersal.
They stood around for a bit, enjoying a last smoke before climbing into M-
Mother. It was a bitingly cold night with a lot of winter ahead of them, and
summer an impossible dream. It was then Alex McKie discovered the Gee
radar set was not working.

'We got the instrument people round to have a look at it,' he recalls. 'In
the meantime we'd missed our slot to taxi round the perimeter track and get
on to the runway. The radar mechanics were still in there shaking their heads
when a car came hurtling round the perry and our squadron commander,
Wing Commander Baxter, jumped out and made his way through M-Mother

and spoke to the pilot. Bunny told him our problem and the CO asked: "Is everything else all right?"

'Bunny said it seemed to be and the CO added: "Can you go without a Gee?" Bunny turned to me and I said we could. I wasn't particularly worried at that stage. We had the radio and the wireless operator could tune into signals coming in from the UK and give us a magnetic bearing from which you can convert to true bearing. That could take you back to base. We also had the H2S radar equipment which as far as I knew was working okay. Of course, by this time we'd missed our slot and were thirty to forty-five minutes late taking off.'

The aircraft's engines were kept running as the mechanics struggled with Gee and the fuel tanks had not been topped up when M-Mother was the last bomber to leave Metheringham. Briefed to bomb in the first wave, there was no chance of that. They would have to join the main force wherever they could. It was twenty-five minutes after midnight as they climbed into a clear star-twinkling sky. A stiff wind was blowing from the south. There was no time to circle above the station, gaining height. Bunny Lee set off straightaway after the main force. Normally if an aircraft developed a fault before takeoff its crew were switched to the squadron spare, which was normally standing by. But that night, as with all the Berlin raids, Bomber Command was on maximum effort and another crew had taken the spare. A total 421 Lancasters were heading for Berlin where civilians would have another desperately miserable night but their defences, the toughest in Germany, were waiting.

They made up some time, crossing the Wash, climbing steadily to 15,000ft.

McKie again: 'Normally, once you'd set course over England you used the Gee set to home in on your aerodrome. You worked like mad while going over the North Sea finding out which way the winds were blowing because you couldn't use Gee before you got to Denmark as it had been jammed by the Germans. The idea was to get as much information as you could to check the winds you had been given by the met officer at briefing. Without Gee I couldn't do this.'

They switched to a northerly course over Denmark, moving east, north of the Zuider Zee and beating across the Baltic, thankful of turning points which had been marked with flares by the Pathfinders. They turned south to Berlin, fingers crossed. No one relished a trip to the German capital, for the reception committee always turned out in force to provide the unfriendliest of welcomes. Anyone who returned to base from Berlin unscathed deserved accolades from his peers and an extra fried egg for his breakfast. Nothing was more sacred to aircrews early in the morning than their bacon and egg breakfast on return from a particularly nasty sortie.

British bombers were now attacking Berlin with such regularity that Intelligence was continually striving to provide new routes and doglegs to persuade the German controllers that they were heading elsewhere.

'We had been given a different route to Berlin than two nights previously,' McKie recalls. 'The idea was to take us north over Denmark to give the impression we weren't interested in Berlin but were, perhaps, heading for Leipzig. Hopefully the German night fighters would then be diverted away from Berlin. The H2S was useful for me, especially when crossing the Danish coast because the contrast between the sea and the land showed up well on the screen and I was able to get a pinpoint on the coast and work out the wind.'

The German controller was not fooled by the diversion raids of Mosquitoes on Hamburg, Witten and Duisberg and unleashed his fighter dogs early in the proceedings. The fighters were especially busy between two route markers en route to Berlin. Two Lancasters were shot down over Berlin by fighters, with the flak probably being restricted to a height above which the German pilots could operate safely. The twenty-eight Lancasters which were lost on the raid represented 6.7 per cent of the force.

Over the target 10/10ths cloud reduced bombing efficiency and the Pathfinders' marker flares soon faded. Bombing was scattered, mainly in the south of the city and the heavily wooded area of Grunewald. Only one industrial building was destroyed, but a bomb struck a lock on a key canal which halted shipping for a few days. Seventy-nine people were killed.

'An FW190 attacked us before we reached the target,' recalls McKie. 'Red Hunnisett, the rear gunner, called out to the pilot and we corkscrewed out of danger. The idea was to corkscrew towards the fighter, making him turn so tightly he was unable to follow you round. As the fighter went away Red fired at it.'

Hunnisett remembers the moment. 'The FW190 dived straight down on us. I put the gun up in the air and fired. He blew up and we carried on. We were lucky.'

The wind had become a problem, a good deal more blustery than the met man had told them at briefing, but there was nothing new about that. They had been told to expect gusts of 90mph.

'I had a reading of 154mph for the wind and thought this must be wrong,' recalls McKie. 'When I checked again I found the H2S had packed up, so I reverted to using the met man's 90mph, but the wind appeared to be stronger than this and it had changed direction.'

M-Mother was late getting to the target, and Berlin was already in flames. M-Mother bombed from 21,000ft at 3.16am, adding its 4,000lb Cookie, 32 thirty-pound and 900 four-pound incendiaries to the devastation below. The flak was heavy and within seconds they were caught by the blue master radar-controlled searchlight. Other searchlights switched on to them. It could not have been so many, but to McKie it seemed as if thousands of lights were pouring up at them. It was the first time they had been coned and although they had seen other unfortunate crews caught in this way and some shot down, it was an even more horrifying experience than they had imagined. Almost immediately they heard the flak banging against the aircraft like a squadron of frenzied ghosts knocking to get in. The cabin was lit up as if it were daylight and as the pilot flung the big bomber into a violent corkscrew, everyone knew they were close to being shot down. The diving Lancaster was chased by the searchlights and flak. As Lee twisted and turned the shells screamed into the empty piece of sky behind them and though they got alarmingly close they were not close enough. It would only take one piece of red hot metal in a vital part to cripple the Lancaster or blow it apart in a brief storm of shattered metal and pulverised bodies.

Wireless operator Frank Richards, who was holding on to his desk, which was bolted to the floor, recalls: 'It was like being on a funfair roller coaster, only worse, and there was nothing exciting about it. I was pressed down into my seat. I stuck there and there was nothing I could do. As we came over the top to do a roll we were flung to the top of the fuselage, clinging on, it was hair-raising. Even so I had every faith in Bunny who was one of the best pilots. Bunny never let us down in all the hairy operations we were involved in.'

It was mayhem inside the aircraft as Bunny Lee tried to shake off the lights which exposed them to the pursuing whiplash of death.

'The only one of us working as we went down was the pilot, and he was strapped into his seat,' recalls McKie. 'Everyone else was just hanging on and hoping we were going to escape. I was trying to keep my instruments together. I lost my dividers and never did find them. Everything was flying and sliding all over the place. I remembered thinking: "Do I know where my parachute is?" There was a chance I would need it in a hurry. I glanced over my shoulder and saw it clipped behind me on the fuselage wall. It crossed my mind that if we did get hit while we were diving and corkscrewing like this, how the hell was I going to get out anyway, because of Gee force? We wondered afterwards why the wings had not come off because being thrown about must have put an enormous strain on the aircraft. It was a magnificent demonstration of flying by Bunny because the Lancaster was not a small aircraft. He dived and corkscrewed and dived again and eventually we got out of the cone at 5,000ft. Bunny maybe couldn't land an aircraft very well, but he could certainly fly one.'

M-Mother was riddled with holes; luckily, none found a vulnerable spot, although later an unexploded cannon shell from a fighter was found lodged in the root of the starboard wing. They were able to contemplate that unnerving sight more comfortably from the ground. Had it exploded their flying careers would have been suddenly and messily terminated.

They had escaped the cone somewhere south of Berlin and the idea was to climb to around 19,000ft. McKie set course for home.

He says: 'I was again having to rely on the winds that had been given to us at briefing. You always worked out your course to the target and back based on these winds. I set a course, but had to guess where I was setting it from, because it certainly wasn't from the centre of Berlin.'

It was the rear gunner who spotted another German fighter and yelled for his skipper to corkscrew.

Hunnisett recalls: 'The Bf109 must have had a brand new pilot. He did what was called a curver pursuit. They started at the rear up, flew past the bomber's tail to starboard, turned up their nose, and as they did this they should be aiming at the front of your aircraft. As they turned up their nose you call immediately for evasive action and go down so he misses you. As this one came in I fired first and hit him all along the belly. He turned away sharply and didn't come back.'

McKie again: 'We flew for a considerable time on various legs and Bunny said: "Pilot to navigator. Christ! there seems to be a hell of a lot of flak in front of us. We certainly can't go through there. Where do you think we are?"

'I looked at the map and knew there was only one place we could be and that was heading for the Ruhr, Happy Valley, where there was an immense amount of flak being put up. I said: "Navigator to pilot. It's the Ruhr. We'd better steer north and then go round it."

'We were not alone among bombers being blown into the Ruhr that night. We saw a tremendous amount of flak that was pumped up at them and could be seen from miles away. We were supposed to turn south after leaving Berlin, then turn west, but a lot of bombers ended up ploughing through the Ruhr. We flew north for a considerable time and in the meantime I was in the astrodome trying to take some star shots with my bubble sextant, but it was a poor night, with a fair bit of cloud and we were being bumped around by the wind. I couldn't get the stars I wanted, but I decided where we were from my shots and set us on a westerly course for home. We saw a lot more bursts of flak in different places but it was impossible to identify where these were.'

They ground on and eventually the pilot spoke to the navigator: 'Where are we? We're running low on petrol, we should be approaching the coast by now.'

They had passed their ETA for Metheringham. McKie returned to the astrodome trying to take more star shots through drifting clouds as they rumbled along at 19,000ft, but it was difficult. The navigator told his skipper he believed they were south-west of Paris.

The pilot said: 'We'd better do something about it, we haven't much petrol left. If something doesn't happen soon we'll have to put the plane down or bale out.'

Lee immediately began losing height and McKie gave him a course back to England from where he believed them to be. The wireless operator could have obtained more accurate bearings but an Allied aircraft flying south of Paris was still under signal silence. It would be suicidal to attempt to get a fix with all the German fighter airfields in the area. Several minutes passed as Alan Hebbes, the engineer, monitored the fuel situation which soon became critical and they contemplated the misery of spending the rest of the war incarcerated in prison camps. The pilot said they would never make it across the North Sea and decided to take a chance by switching on the IFF (Identification Friend or Foe) set which transmitted a coded blip to radar screens in England. Time passed, nothing happened, then as they were around 12,000ft, a searchlight came snaking out of the darkness and they braced themselves for a belly full of flak. But the light appeared friendlier than those which they had encountered over Berlin. It dipped, waved and pointed.

Runway lights came on and Lee said anxiously he would go down to take a look. They saw the runway and buildings huddled in the darkness. It could have been anywhere.

The pilot said: 'We have no choice, chaps, we're nearly out of fuel, I'll have to land.'

M-Mother touched down and, after the normal Bunny hops, they hurtled along the runway. The four engines cut out, one by one before they came to a standstill. It was 8am, their flight had lasted nearly eight hours.

'We'd cut it a bit fine,' admits McKie. 'There's no doubt that if we'd stayed up a little while longer we would have fallen out of the sky. It was a sobering moment. We might have been on foreign territory, but all we knew was that we were safely down on a runway and alive. Before we had stopped a car drew up beside us. We were surprised to see it was an RAF car and in it was the airfield's duty controller. Bunny, somewhat relieved, yelled out: "Where the hell are we?" The officer replied: "Wing."

'Well, we knew where Wing was,' recalls McKie. 'Then somebody said: "What the hell happened to the North Sea, Mac?"

'I felt very guilty. People very often say to me: "Were you frightened when you were flying?" The answer to that is yes, but what frightened me more than anything else was not knowing where I was. If I didn't know, certainly nobody else did. In fact we were damned lucky to escape without a single injury between us on that trip to Berlin. We were given a meal and put to bed, greatly relieved.'

Later that morning they inspected the battered Lancaster and were shocked by the amount of damage it had sustained. Dozens of holes had been smashed into the wings, fuselage and tailplane. They grimaced at the cannon shell crumpled in the wing root, and found one of the aileron arms was badly damaged and needed repairing.

'The Lancaster was my favourite aeroplane,' says McKie. 'It was a superb aircraft in which you had a lot of confidence. It could take a lot of punishment. Even on two starboard or two port engines it could fly, and on one, although it would lose height it could remain airborne. It was, of course, a difficult aircraft to get into, clambering over that great main spar, particularly when you had all your gear on and lugging my navigator's bag. It was always sensible to go to the toilet before getting into the aircraft. When you were in the air and wanted to go, the Elsan toilet was at the back behind the rear turret. You knew where it was but in the pitch darkness it was a drag.'

The engineering officer at Wing, 26 Operations Training Unit, decided that M-Mother was not fit to be flown back to their squadron before extensive repairs had been carried out. A call was put through to Metheringham and a Lancaster flew across the Midlands to Buckinghamshire to pick them up. On the whole it was not an entirely discouraging start to the New Year, at least they were alive.

In April 1944 they had finished their first tour with 106 Squadron and were waiting for a posting to an OTU on an instructors' course, when Bunny Lee and Alex McKie heard that Leonard Cheshire, commanding offficer of 617 Squadron, was looking for a Mosquito crew. Lee and McKie went to Woodhall Spa to offer their services, but when Wing Commander Cheshire heard they had been flying Lancasters he said he wanted the entire crew. Six of them joined Cheshire in a squadron where everybody had done one tour and he encouraged an eager press-on attitude. Many tough raids lay ahead, including the long trip which ended up in Sweden. The flight engineer did not join them at Woodhall Spa. Perhaps he had had enough of operational flying and was pleased to go to a training squadron. Ironically, it was the wrong move, for he was killed.

'The discipline of the crew was tremendously important,' says McKie. Each man, whatever the task he had in the aircraft, was really very good at it. That made all the difference. Looking back, I don't know how we got through it night after night but then, we were young.'

Bunny Lee was later awarded a DFC, Alex McKie and Gus Hoyland each received a DFM.

CHAPTER TEN

NAVIGATOR'S AGONIZING DECISION

The Lancaster was in a shallow dive, its four engines dead, heading for oblivion. The crew, parachutes clipped on, began piling out into the night. Navigator Flight Sergeant Don Feesey was following them when a hand suddenly gripped his shoulder. He looked back into the white face of pilot George Lee. 'Oh God,' Feesey thought bleakly, 'George is trapped in his seat.' The two men were the last remaining aboard. The navigator was overwhelmed by a moment of agonizing indecision. Should he ignore the pilot, bale out and save his life? Or should he help Lee, and risk them both running out of time to escape the doomed bomber?

The 1,000-odd mile round trip to bomb a synthetic oil plant at Leuna, near the German town of Merseburg, just west of Leipzig, had been horribly jinxed from the start. It was 6 December 1944. The crew's regular mid-upper gunner, Sergeant Ron Hales, had to miss their fourteenth operation together after hurting his leg. He had fallen backwards from a Lancaster's fuselage door after some twerp had removed the ladder. They had been given a spare bod, a situation which was guaranteed to summon up all the available forces of evil and misery to condemn the trip to a sticky end. Almost as bad, unable to use their usual Lancaster I-Item, they had been allocated E-Easy. There was worse to come.

Feesey recalls: 'On checking its registration number I discovered to my horror that it was ND707. We were not in E-Easy but W-Willie. The real E-Easy had been shot down over Karlsruhe the previous night and Willie had been re-christened. A short trip in Willie was bad enough, but this was to be a long one. Another morbid thought was racing through my mind. The identification letters of 166 Squadron were AS and painted in large letters on the side were the letters AS E. I found myself humming "The Death of Ase" from Grieg's Peer Gynt Suite No 1. Willie was the squadron spare, the old hack, used for the odd training flight and occasionally operationally by newly arrived crews who had not been allocated a regular kite. We'd been in Willie on a short trip and found it vibrated and shook alarmingly, a shattering experience. Chaps hated it although she always came back. It was a rotten night. There was a threat of thunder about and thunder, more often than not, caused me to have a migraine. I had one that night.'

At least Buck would be fighting on their side. Buck was a stuffed toy rabbit given as a lucky mascot to Australian wireless operator Flight Sergeant Max Leversha by a young family whose land was on the other side of a hedge which enclosed the airfield at Kirmington, Yorkshire. A hole had mysteriously and illegally appeared in the hedge alongside their dispersal point through which Max and his crewmates occasionally disappeared to enjoy the generous hospitality of the Stanleys, friendly pig farmers, whose bacon and pork pies were delicious.

After the war Kirmington became Humberside Airport. In 1944 it had little appeal for aircrews.

'The main camp was a ramshackle place built inside the grand estate of Brocklesby Park,' recalls Feesey, 'We were in Nissen huts about half a mile up the road from the sergeants' mess and then another good half mile from the mess to the airfield.'

Aircrews were a superstitious lot and the chaps who flew with Flying Officer George Lee were no exception. All aircrews occupied an unreal world in which they could be wiped out at any time. For that reason they did not mix too closely with other crews.

'This was largely because there was this fear that tomorrow they might not be with us,' says Feesey. 'Chaps were being shot down so often we didn't want to get attached to them because of the loss if they didn't come back. We stuck with our own crew. I lived on a day to day basis, writing a letter each free night to my fiancée, Daphne Orchard. If I was still alive tomorrow it would be a bit of luck. After each op a sort of black curtain came down in my mind, shutting virtually everything out that had happened.'

The skipper, George Lee, was short and plumpish, a fine pilot yet at times, curiously indecisive, habitually relying on his navigator's advice. Ten years older than Feesey, a car salesman in civvy street, he was proud of being an officer and was never seen without wearing the brown gloves, which were an indisputable trademark of his commission. His wife Anne was expecting their first child.

Feesey, a civil servant, with pacifist inclinations, had not wanted to go to war. His father was gassed in the First World War. He had fought with bayonets hand to hand with the Germans and was awarded a Military Medal for capturing an enemy machine gun post. Feesey was proud of his brave father, but believed it was morally wrong to kill young Germans whom he presumed were as innocent and indifferent to the war as he was. Then the death in 1940 of two close friends, both fighter pilots, who lived near his south London home at Catford, made Feesey reconsider. Although Feesey had previously argued that war was no way to settle a dispute, he believed he had to join the RAF to help defend his country against a cruel dictator.

He trained as a pilot in Canada but was let down by his eyes which did not adjust to a change of light. On a bright sunny day the glare forced him to level out too high. Tinted goggles and a green film across the windscreen did not help and he turned to navigating. All the crew called him Fizz. He was twenty-two.

Leversha, a well-built cheerful fellow was, like most wireless operators, mad keen on the Morse code, and went about Kirmington muttering 'did-a-did-did-did-a-did-did – ' using it even when asking for the marmalade to be passed at breakfast.

Flight Sergeant Ray Forbes, the bomb aimer, was an outspoken Australian in his late thirties. He had no time for petty rules or officialdom and expressed his views without inhibitions or respect for rank. He always argued with reason and logic and if rebuffed, he said: 'You can't argue with ignorance.' He was a fine bridge player and taught his crewmates.

'The rumour was that we played bridge on the navigator's table when we were flying,' says Feesey. 'I think everybody believed this, including the wing commander but, of course, it wasn't true.'

At twenty, Sergeant Ray 'Nobby' Clarke, the flight engineer, from Leicester, was the youngest man aboard. Slim and tall, he took his job very seriously and displayed inordinate concern about the others, always making sure they had all their kit and that everyone was okay. He was a pillar of strength for the much older pilot.

Peter Turley, the rear gunner, came from Grimsby. He was brought up in a children's home with a younger brother and a sister. The brother was once smuggled into the airfield, given a uniform and shown over a Lancaster. A ruddy-faced man, Sergeant Turley was the crew comic, keeping up their spirits during tough situations. He suffered from eye trouble and in later years started going blind.

Their stand-in gunner, the tall and stocky Canadian Flight Sergeant 'Scottie' Scott, whom they had never seen before, stood waiting for them self-consciously beside the Lancaster at dispersal. He knew they would regard him as a bad omen, nothing he said could change that. He could only get on with his job and hope the gremlins would leave them alone, but they were dispensing their first dose of mischief even before takeoff.

W-Willie's takeoff was delayed nearly forty minutes when the aircraft displayed its usual irritating threat of engine trouble during the run up of its engines. It was just after 5pm when W-Willie took off, part of Bomber Command's first major attack on an oil target in eastern Germany. Five Lancasters would be lost from the force of 475 which set off from their bases in England with 12 Mosquitoes.

It was cold, dark and rain was falling as W-Willie climbed sluggishly into solid cloud. The engines were already vibrating. The noise was a fearful grating mixed in with what sounded like a multitudinous swarm of angry bees. Fingers were crossed and prayers softly mumbled, but at 8.15pm, the starboard generator failed. Lee decided to keep going. Then, just before they bombed, the port inner engine cut and had to be feathered. The flight engineer adjusted the other three engines to maintain even thrust.

Feesey again: 'At the target there was solid cloud below and the target was obscured. The marker flares were not easily seen, but there was a tremendous glow coming from beneath the cloud, indicating that bombs dropped by earlier arrivals had found their mark. We bombed at 8.46pm from 17,000ft. Other Lancasters were around us bombing at the same time and there was flak. Unusually, we had bombed from the far side of the target on a north-westerly course, so we did not have to make a turn after dropping our load.

'We continued on this heading for some time, then made a sharp turn to port, taking a south-westerly course to go over the Rhine some way south of Cologne and then on to a westerly heading to cross into Belgium. At this point my migraine was getting worse. We were in thick cloud with lightning flashing all around us. Ray Forbes, our bomb aimer, came back and offered to take over the navigation. He had done a navigator's course and liked to keep his hand in. He frequently sat beside me to assist on the homeward legs of our trips. On this occasion I handed him my navigator's watch and let him take over completely. I gave him the course to take us from near Trier so we would cross the coast between Ostend and Dunkirk and settled back, confident that he could get us safely back to Kirmington. But none of us would see Kirmington again that night.'

W-Willie juddered its way across Belgium on three engines then, at about 10.50pm, after running into a fierce electrical storm the port outer engine cut. There were excited discussions between pilot and flight engineer when another engine caught fire. They were on the point of abandoning the wretched aircraft but the flames went out almost at once. The Lancaster limped on, unable to climb above the storm. With thick cloud below and jagged flashes of lightning above W-Willie had become the unwilling filling for an unpalatable sandwich.

Feesey says: 'With still some forty miles to go before reaching the coast the starboard inner engine cut and, with only one engine working, we began losing height. This time the pilot warned us to prepare to abandon the aircraft and we clipped on our parachutes. The 'dead' starboard engine occasionally spluttered back to life, then it would cut out again. We struggled on. Then we suddenly lost all power. None of the four engines was working, the judders stopped immediately and we began to dive. George at once gave the order "Abandon aircraft!" We were near Courtrai in Belgium. Ray Forbes, who was sitting beside me at the navigation table, was up and away to the front. The flight engineer opened the escape hatch in the nose and dropped out, followed by Ray. Max, the wireless operator, handed me my parachute and I clipped it on. He held Buck up for me to see then stuffed him into his flying suit. He gave me a thumbs up and went towards the back door. We had taken off our helmets with their oxygen connections and intercom leads. The aircraft was quiet, with just the swish of air rushing through the open front hatch and out of the back. It was hellish cold, but there was no time to think about that, it was a matter of quickly fitting on your parachute and going to your position. The pilot, bomb aimer, flight engineer and navigator were supposed to bale out through the escape hatch in the nose. The wireless operator and gunners normally went out through the back door.

'Rear gunner Peter Turley had his turret on the beam. He only had to open the rear doors and fall out into space. But he became caught up in something, probably the oxygen suppy lead or electrical leads. Instinctively, he stood on his seat and threw himself out over the top of his two .5 Browning machine guns. He didn't have much room. I don't know how he didn't get caught up on the gun sights or the scanner handle. His wedding tackle must have had a remarkable escape. As I went forward to the floor hatch beside the pilot, I heard someone hit the underside of the fuselage. I learned much later it was Nobby Clarke, who was caught by the H2S radar bowl which projected underneath the aircraft. Max and Peter actually collided in mid air before their parachutes opened, but none of them was hurt.'

Scott, the mid-upper gunner, opened the rear door and tried to jump out but was slapped back by the slipstream. Leversha indicated they should roll out and this is what they did.

Leversha recalls: 'I could hear the engines spluttering as I descended and realised at that point how bad the situation was. It then occurred to me that Don and George were still in the plane and a quick prayer went out for their safety. Then a jerk from the parachute made me realise I was alone, not knowing where I was. It was pitch black. I was talking to myself to make sure all the masculine bits were still intact. That was because you stop with an almighty jerk and you are strapped in at all the wrong places. A lifetime of thoughts went with me as I heard the last of the plane. Did they get out okay?'

Feesey says: 'We were losing height rapidly and I wondered how far off the ground we were and if there would be time for a 'chute to open. George had the aircraft in a gentle sort of dive, nose down attitude. If you've no engines you automatically put the stick forward and go into a dive, otherwise the aircraft would stall and drop out of the sky. We were in a spin, not a serious spin, but I could feel a sideways motion as well as the dive. It was going to port. We were not falling swiftly enough to create G-force.

'We were supposed to go out of the hatch feet first, but the plane was diving and screwing about and having heard one thud I was concerned about getting hit myself. Going out feet first I might get cut across the neck. I decided to go out head first reasoning that it would be better to risk having my feet knocked. I kneeled on the edge of the hole.

'Just as I was about to fall out, I felt the frantic pulling on my shoulder from the pilot. It was pitch dark and without my helmet I had no intercom. I could only think that George's seat belt or harness had somehow got caught up and he could not get out of his seat. I shall remember forever my agonising thoughts over the next two or three seconds. Should I go back and try to free him? Or with the ground so close, would we both be killed if I went back? Should I try to save myself by jumping and hope we were high enough for my 'chute to open?

'I thought of my mother's grief if I were to be killed. I also thought of Daphne, my fiancée. They knew I could get the chop at any time. Daphne and I had decided not to get married until the war was over, in case something happened to me. Paramount in my mind was loyalty towards George. We had been through a great deal together. Whenever we flew we knew that our lives very much depended on one another. The whole crew were a team and we had obligations to each other. I had to go back and try to get him out. Inwardly, I felt there would be no chance of doing so before we hit the ground. By going back I would almost certainly be killed. By jumping I might be able to save myself, but we might already be too low. But I couldn't leave George trapped in his harness to die alone in a crashing plane. I went back.'

Feesey fumbled around in the dark to find out why the pilot couldn't move. Lee was shouting and gesticulating but with the sound of the air rushing through the aircraft and no intercom they could not communicate. Feesey found the flight engineer's helmet and put it on. 'Why can't you get out?' Feesey yelled.

Lee shouted back: 'I've got an engine going. We're too low to bale out. Let's see if we can get back to England.'

'I'm not sure where we are,' said Feesey. 'I'll go back and have a look at the chart.'

'No, Fizz, stay here and help me with the engines.' Lee was struggling to keep the Lancaster level and working on the throttle levers.

Feesey says: 'I knew the coast, I knew where Manston was. This was the nearest emergency airfield, high on the cliffs near Margate. I didn't need the charts. I could get us there if the aircraft managed to stay airborne. Besides, the charts had probably been swept out into the night. We pressed on with the wind sweeping through from front to back. It was cold and I still had a migraine, but I tried to push that out of my mind. I helped with the throttles and occasionally we got one of the other engines to fire. After a bit we seemed to have coaxed a second one into permanent life. We maintained our height, even climbing to around 1,500 to 2,000ft over Belgium and then ahead we saw gunfire coming up at us. At this time in the war France and Belgium were almost totally free of the Germans, but they were still holding out at Dunkirk, which was in a direct line between us and Manston. The Germans had extremely accurate radar predicted anti-aircraft guns and shells began to be fired in our direction.'

The navigator gave Lee a course to avoid the guns. It meant he had to go into a turn and they were not too happy about how the engines would react. The starboard inner engine cut again and they staggered round Dunkirk, losing height to between 500 and 700ft, but away from the guns. The aircraft limped like a monstrous mortally wounded crab across the Strait of

Dover on a single engine. Their steady fall was only halted when a second engine was bullied into working. It cut again when they were low over the water and Lee had difficulty in keeping the aircraft level and on course. The white cliffs loomed above them in the half light. They fiddled frantically with throttles and petrol tanks. Shortly before Lee tried to swing round the cliffs the starboard inner engine coughed into life. It was not a moment too soon. They managed to stagger over the cliffs with little distance between them and the ground.

Feesey again: 'I had feared we might have to ditch in the sea, and with the bottom hatch gone we would soon sink, but luck was with us. We cleared the cliffs by about 200ft. It was then we saw other aircraft in trouble heading, like us, for Manston. Some were badly damaged. There was a Stirling with a split in the fuselage near the tailplane which seemed to be hanging as if partially disconnected from the rest of the machine. I could see the sky through the split. I don't know how it kept going. George fiddled with the radio and sent out a Mayday call several times. We could hear others doing the same. Everyone was in distress and trying to get priority to land. We were instructed by ground control to go round again as we approached the airfield and saw another aircraft only a short distance ahead of us preparing to land.'

The starboard inner engine was intermittently dying and restarting and Lee had no intention of trying to make another circuit. He told the control tower in clipped tones: 'We can't maintain height. We're coming in.'

Feesey again: 'We came round to within sight of the lit-up runway. The control tower were concerned about us trying to land on the runway with other aircraft coming in. George told them: "I'm going to put it down on the grass." He told me to get behind the bulkhead, between the pilot and navigator positions. I sat in a doubled up position with my back against the bulkhead and my hands behind my ears. He now had two engines going, one on either side. Without them both it would have been impossible to land. As it was, I expected to be thrown about and turned over, but I was amazed by the softness of the landing, absolutely perfect. As soon as we were on the deck the starboard inner cut yet again and a small vehicle drove out to us and switched on a large illuminated sign in red letters, reading "FOLLOW ME". It is nigh impossible to taxi a Lanc with only one engine and we had to give up. Eventually, after explaining our problem an airman arranged for us to be given a tow. We had managed to come back with one engine and another one coming on in fits and starts. I'd never heard of it happening to anyone else.

'I salvaged what papers were still in the aircraft for the draught had whipped my charts out through the back door. When George and I got out of the aircraft we put our arms around each other and he thanked me for staying with him. It was an emotional moment and we were concerned about the fate of our crewmates. George and I were taken to a debriefing room where we told our story. The debriefing officers were puzzled when they saw just the two of us, believing we had been flying a two-man Mosquito, although they had not heard of one landing there that night. They actually went to the office window to look for W-Willie. For a moment I believed they thought we were German spies.

'After that we were taken for a meal and given a place to sleep. But not together. Together we had been close to death. Together we had struggled to bring the aircraft back. And together we had won through. But it would never do for a flying officer and a humble flight sergeant to eat together or sleep in the same quarters. It was about 2am when we went our separate ways.

'I didn't see George until later that morning when we went out to look at W-Willie. A ground crew worked on all four engines so it was fully serviceable for the flight back to Kirmington late that afternoon, although the judders had not been smoothed away. Another front hatch had been put on but they hadn't got a rear door, so it was a cold and draughty trip. Once again W-Willie had maintained its record of always coming back, despite the odds against it.'

George Lee was quite rightly awarded a DFC for his outstanding night's work. He had dragged what seemed to be a dead bomber out of an impossible situation back to England. Don Feesey got nothing, although he admits that the story of that heroic flight to Manston was not fully explained during briefing.

Leversha, Clarke, Turley and Scott, who all landed safely near each other in the liberated Belgian countryside, were taken to an Allied army depot and flown home within a few days. Ray Forbes was not with them. The bomb aimer, fearful of hitting trees or a house, had missed them all and dropped into a cesspit. He emerged, highly aromatic and a little shaken, to find that the cesspit was attached to the house of the Mayor of Courtrai. The Mayor's daughter was getting married next day. Forbes was welcomed, cleaned up and as a heroic member of an RAF aircrew, invited to be her best man. He accepted with alacrity, enjoyed the wedding, together with the meal afterwards and was feted for a day or two before returning to England.

He enjoyed some unofficial survivor's leave in London before going back to the squadron, with a ready-made excuse. He had needed extra time to get his filthy clothes properly cleaned. Feesey was especially pleased to see him because he had loaned his watch to Forbes when the bomb aimer took over as navigator. The watch was RAF property which Feesey had signed for before taking off from Kirmington. He had been worried he might have to pay for a new one.

They next flew together as a complete crew in a brand new Lancaster, ME296 B-Baker-2, on Christmas Eve, bombing railway marshalling yards in Cologne. One of the 1,000lb bombs got hung up on the release wires in the bomb bay. On the way home Forbes climbed into the bomb bay and tried unsuccessfully to free the bomb which was resting on the bomb doors, making them bulge. Lee closed the bomb doors as tightly as he could and

oud Austin 7 owner George Riley, now on 617 Squadron, and bomb aimer Lew Hazel,
mbed *Tirpitz* on 12 November 1944, a few days before this picture was taken. Hazel
imed a direct hit.

(Riley)

ONE STEP FROM ETERNITY

Top: Stratford-upon-Avon, where Bill Belton did his square-bashing. His is in the centre rank, third from left. *(Belton)*

From left: Sgt Myers, Sgt Thompson, Sgt Brook, Plt Off Watts and Sgt Belton. *(Belto*

Bottom: Spare bod Bill Belton with an earlier Wellington crew at Alconbury.

Opposite page: Bill Belton's problems started when he left his rear turret. *(Belto*

Australian Bob Chester-Master spent an uncomfortable night in a haystack.

(Chester-Mast

Top: This fake identity card was produced for Bob Chester-Master when he was on the run from the Germans. *(Chester-Master)*

Above: They could not fly their usual Lancaster, U-Uncle. *Standing, from left*: George Durland, Tom Young, John Lawrie, Reg Orth and Martin Carter. *Kneeling*: Sam Burford and Bob Chester-Master. *(Chester-Master)*

Left: On leave in Falkirk, after liberation. From left: Reg Orth, Bob Chester-Master, Sam Burford and Tom Young. *(Chester-Master)*

HAUNTED BY A MEMORY

Top left: Bomb aimer Vic Tomei: 'I will never forget the sight of those flames leaping across the top of the aircraft.' *(Tomei)*

Top right: Cheerful nineteen-year-old Rhodesian Adrian Roselt obligingly poses outside his rear turret. *(Tomei)*

Bottom: Three weeks before Christmas 1944, these men went to bomb Heilbronn. *Back row, from left:* Charlie Lees, Phil Becker, Bill Ching and Adrian Roselt. *Front:* Vic Tomei, Ron Osman and Norman Deacon. *(Tome*

SAVED BY THE BELL

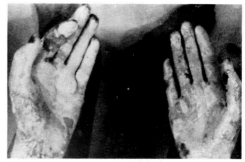

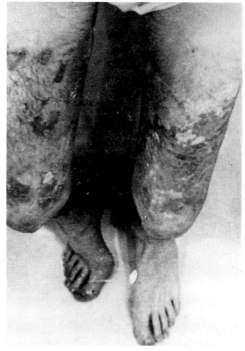

Top left: Harry Stunell: 'I crawled like mad from the overpowering heat'

(Stunell)

Top right: In hospital at Cirencester, Harry Stunell's severely burned hands were given skin grafts by leading American plastic surgeon Colonel Kenneth Lewis.　　　(Stunell)

Above: Harry Stunell's legs suffered when he escaped his burning Lancaster. Here he has a saline bath prior to skin grafts.　　　(Stunell)

Left: This crew picture was damaged and later stuck inside Harry Stunell's logbook. From left: Ron Needle, Les Knapman, Jimmy Scott and Bob Dunlop.

(Stunell)

Ron Needle knew he would die if he stayed in the snow.

(Stune

No. 106 Squadron,
Royal Air Force,
Metheringham,
Lincoln.
9th January 1945.

Dear Mr Stunell,

    I am writing to give all the details I have of the circumstances in which your son, Sergeant Henry Stunell, has been injured.

    On the night of 7/8th January 1945, my Squadron took part in the heavy and successful attack on Munich and your son was the wireless operator of one of the aircraft detailed for the raid. The aircraft did not return to Base at the scheduled time and after the petrol endurance limit had expired, I had no alternative but to assume it as lost, and I notified you accordingly.

    On Monday afternoon I received a message to the effect that the aircraft had crashed in France and that five members of the crew had lost their lives and the remaining two, including your son, had been injured. I telegraphed this news to you immediately.

    This morning I have been given further information. The reasons are not yet known, but the aircraft, when on the homeward journey, crashed at Meligny-le-Grand, south west of Commercy, which is about thirty miles from Nancy.

    Your son has been admitted to the 50th General U.S. Hospital suffering from burns - the extent of which I do not yet know - but his general condition was satisfactory. The Hospital is presumably near Commercy and information may not be available as readily as one would wish, but you may rest assured that that you will be kept informed of news of the condition of your son as soon as it is received.

    If there is any way in which I can be of assistance please do not hesitate to write and I will do my best to help you.

            Yours sincerely,

            W. W. J. Stevens

            Wing Commander, Commanding,
            No. 106 Squadron, R.A.F.

Mr. H.J. STUNELL,
18, Carlton Place,
Brighton.

Harry Stunell's father carried this letter in his wallet for years until it fell apart and was roughly stuck together.

(Stunell)

EMERGENCY LANDING

Winter in Metheringham and, (*from left*), Bryan Hewitt, Pete Adams and Bill Winter are ready for takeoff aboard this Lancaster in which they flew to Juvincourt.

(Winter)

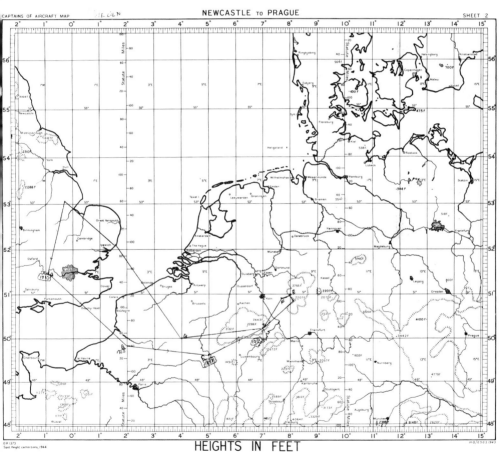

HEIGHTS IN FEET

Top left: Ross Gray in 1943. Many months must pass before this young pilot sits in the cockpit of F-Fox for the seventh time for the bombing raid on Siegen.   *(Gray)*

Top right: Bomb aimer Jack Aitken (*left*) and his skipper Ross Gray pause in the

Metheringham snow beside old faithful F-Fox.   *(Winter)*

Above: This flight plan took Ross Gray and his crew from Lincolnshire to Siegen, marked 'E'. They did not follow the briefed route home. 'G' is Juvincourt.

Don Farrington models the flying kit being issued at Yatesbury in 1941.   (Farrington

Top: Don Farrington and three other wireless operators at Jurby, Isle of Man in 1942, are waiting to be posted to a squadron. All four ignore the rude airman behind them. *(Farrington)*

Bottom: Stalag IIIA, Luckenwalde. Two prisoners face a German firing squad.

(Farrington)

Eddie Davidson was commissioned shortly before his wedding day.

(Davidson

Top: Most of 61 Squadron's ground staff gather beside Lancaster H-How with Tommy Farmiloe's two gunners on the extreme right in the third row from the front. *(Davidson)*

Above left: Eddie Davidson the Ladykiller with (*back*) Mary and Marjorie and (*front*) Mona and Nancy, who describes them all as The Five Stooges. *(Davidson)*

Above right: Outside the billet at Skellingthorpe are (*left to right*): Ken Vowe, Pat Patchett, Eddie Davidson and Ray Noble. Note the whistles in the lapels for helping to find each other if they baled out. *(Davidson)*

Left: This tree stands on the edge of Coningsby airfield and Eddie Davidson considered it a very fine place to briefly escape the war. *(Davidson)*

THE NIGHT WE LOST THE NORTH SEA

Top: Two months after losing the North Sea they find Lancaster JB 562 M-Mother at dispersal. *From left*: Frank Richards, Gus Hoyland, Alex McKie, Bunny Lee, Alan Hebbes, Doug Pooley and Red Hunnisett.

(McKie)

Right: Navigator Alex McKie found Berlin without radar. It was coming home when the real problems started.

(McKie)

NAVIGATOR'S AGONIZING DECISION

Top left: George Lee might be thinking of his hair-raising flight home across the Strait of Dover in December 1944 as he plays with his son David at the seaside. *(Feesey)*

Top right: Their bombing sortie to Leuna, near Merseburg, was jinxed from the start. *From left*: Ray Forbes, Nobby Clarke, Peter Turley, George Lee, Don Feesey, Ron Hales and Max Leversha. *(Feesey)*

Above: Flight engineer Nobby Clarke looks out of the cockpit above the Invincible Isles insignia of Lancaster I-Item. *(Feesey)*

Above right: Peter Turley relaxes in his rear turret for a change, with (*above*) Ray Forbes, who has almost lost his head, and Max Leversha, with (*below*) Don Feesey, Nobby Clarke and Ron Hales. *(Feesey)*

Right: Ron Hales is secure in his mid-upper turret, while below (*from left*) are Ginger, the servicing engineer, Max Leversha, Peter Turley and Nobby Clarke. The H2S radar cover is seen as a pregnant lump to the left of Ginger. *(Feesey)*

CLARRIE PUTS OUT THE LIGHTS

Top: Grounded for a few minutes congenial gossip are, *from left*: a photo section sergeant, Australian pilot Clarrie Woods (*nearest the camera*), Bunny Wilson, Doug Handbury and Max O'Neil, with Jack Beaumont in the doorway of W7527. *(Handbury)*

Bottom: They were coned over Munich. *From left*: Doug Handbury, Clarrie Woods, Jimmy Callister, Max O'Neil, Don Beale and Jack Beaumont, reaching for his matche *(Handbur*

Top: They flew many operations in Stirlings together. *From left:* Jack Beaumont, Clarrie Woods, Max O'Neil, Jimmy McAllister and Doug Handbury.

(Handbury)

Bottom: Clarrie Woods' conscientious ground crew worked hard to keep his aircraft in the air.　　　*(Handbury)*

THREE BRIDGES TO CROSS

Back Row   SGT. DAVIS   SGT. FOREMAN   SGT. BLAKE   SGT. SCOTT   SGT. PORTER   SGT. AME

Centre Row   SGT. HORNE   SGT. SHARPE   SGT. WALKER   SGT. WARDLE   SGT. HAMILTON   SGT. LUDLOW

Front Row   F/LT THYER   LT. FAIRWEATHER   F/O HURLBURT   P/O FAIRNEY   LT. COUTTS   F/O MACRAE

Above: These men, from three crews, were all killed and of the three bomb aimers, then away on a course, only one, Lloyd Lyne, survived. Among Lyne's crewmates on the Warsaw raid were: *Back, fourth from left:* Dick Scott; *fifth from left:* John Porter; *middle, second from left:* Buff Sharpe; *front, fifth from left:* Gordon Coutts; *and sixth from left:* Dougald MacRae.

Right: Cornishman Lloyd Lyne remembers the anti-aircraft shells were like 'flaming cricket balls'.

(Lyne)

ROLLER COASTER OF DESPAIR

op: Before Linz. *From left*: Norman orling, Jimmy Hilton, Johnny Morrison, es Matthews and Johnny Higgs.

(Matthews)

ottom left: Behind barbed wire at uckenwalde POW camp are Des Matthews *ight*) and Pete Notton. *(Matthews)*

Bottom centre: Norman Capar (*left*) and Des Matthews (*right*) struck up a friendship with a Norwegian POW at Luckenwalde.

(Matthews)

Bottom right: When these Russian officers arrived at Luckenwalde they made life difficult for the Allied prisoners. *(Matthews)*

NO ENGINES AT 1,000FT

The day after attacking Varese Dick Morris (*left*) and Bill Montgomery contemplate their lucky escape beside the torn fuselage floor of Wellington A-Apple. *(Morr*

Top: Pilot Victor Jackson (*extreme left*) explains to Squadron Leader Boxall (*fourth from left*) the buzz you get by running out of fuel at 1,000ft. Contributing their twopenn'orth are Bill Montgomery, Ted Hook, Dick Morris and Geoff Ward.

(Morris)

Bottom: Pampered in Turkey. *From left*: Dick Morris, Ted Hook, Geoff Ward, Victor Jackson and Bill Montgomery.

(Morris)

THE LONG DROP

Top: On 26 June 1943, Neil Scott received his wings at Carberry, Manitoba. Scott is fourth from left on the front row.
(*Scott*)

Above: The gutless M-Mike stood brooding at disposal hours before the flight to Brüx in western Czechoslovakia.
(*Scott*)

Above right: Amazingly only one man died in M-Mike which fell out of the sky at Oulton, Norfolk.
(*Scott*)

Right: In August 1944, pilot Neil Scott and the crew he flew with in this Stirling III at Shepherd's Grove, a heavy conversion unit. *Back, left to right:* Dick Willing, John Smith, Neil Scott and Bob Houston. *Front:* Rick Hardman, John Chalk and Bernard Lunn.
(*Scott*)

THE WRECKAGE THAT 'FLEW' TO EARTH

arry McLean, a prisoner of the Third Reich at the end of September 1943.

(McLean)

Top: A few days before the Munich raid part of the crew stayed at Jack Elliott's home in Leeds. *Left to right:* Jack Elliott, Harry McLean, Billy Biggs, Alf Richards and Les Moyler.

(McLean)

Bottom: Flight engineer Jack Elliott walked out of this wrecked rear cockpit area after it had 'flown' to earth.

(McLea

p: Another view of the cockpit area.
ese pictures were taken after the
ftwaffe had cut into the wreckage to
move the unexploded bombs.

(McLean)

Bottom: This shows the tail end of the
Halifax. The remains of the tail plane are
sticking up into the air. Two of the rear
gunner's four machine guns can be seen
pointing at an angle towards the ground.
The rear wheel is on the right.

BLOWN UP – AND LIVES

Top: Bob Burns (*Front, standing*) struck the right chord when he started his orchestra at Stalag Luft VII, Bankau. *(Burns)*

Above: Canadian mid-upper gunner Harold Brad joined the Royal Canadian Air Force straight from college. *(Burns)*

Right: G-force flung Bob Burns to the fuselage floor as his blazing Lancaster dived towards the ground. *(Burns)*

THE HORROR OF NUREMBERG

Top: Stan Bradford's first and last trips were to Nuremburg. *(Bradford)*

Left: The crew for the second operation to Nuremburg were (*Back, from left*): Fred Simmonds, Tony West, Stan Bradford, Douglas Lightfoot. *Front*: Taffy Evans, Ron Munday and Dennis Bracher.

Tom Wingham never met the owner of the house in Belgium where he was sheltered after baling out in April 1944.

(Wingha

p left: Stan Somerscales ordered his
:w to bale out after his aircraft was hit
a fighter. *(Wingham)*

Bottom: Gunner Jack Rowe had a tough
time getting out of his rear turret.

(Wingham)

p right: Engineer Sid Stephen tried to
al with the fire which spread into the
:elage. *(Wingham)*

THE WRATH OF PFORZHEIM

Top left: Mauritian pilot Gerry Ythier was trusted and respected by all his crew.

(Horrax)

Top right: Bert Delieu was trapped by a mob of Germans armed with pitchforks.

(Horrax)

Bottom: The trip to Pforzheim was much worse than could have been imagined. *Back row from left:* Ron Lewis, Bob Conning, Bert Delieu, Gerry Ythier, Ted Buckley, Nobby Clarke and Leo Horrax are pictured in February 1945 with their ground crew.

(Horra

they were diverted to Horsham St Faith, near Norwich, a base for American Liberators. They parked the Lancaster with its bulging belly far away from other aircraft or buildings. The NCOs spent a miserable night with straw palliasses on the concrete floor of a derelict hut. Snow blew through holes in the roof and broken windows.

On Christmas morning the crew rigged up sacks and planks below the plane, while Ray Forbes and Nobby Clarke went inside and down into the bomb bay, with George Lee operating the bomb bay doors. They freed the bomb, lowered it gently to the runway, rolled it to the side and left it. Fortunately, it was not fused. These days, such an act of heroism would merit front page headlines. In 1944, it was considered part of the job.

Turley was later awarded the DFM for shooting down an ME-262A-1, a German jet fighter, and Leversha received the DFC.

CHAPTER ELEVEN

CLARRIE PUTS OUT THE LIGHTS

Clarrie Woods looked more like a hard-nosed truck driver than a bomber pilot. He was about 5ft 8in with long arms and broad shoulders, and a thick mop of black hair, which sprayed out untidily from one side of his forage cap. He was an Australian, from Lismore, New South Wales, and unlike so many of his fellow countrymen, was quiet and, if he had a sense of humour, rarely showed it. Unprepossessing, he was nevertheless a brave and courteous man, who on nights off might be found drinking in the sergeants' mess, but never to excess. Woods looked older than his twenty-seven years for there was a weary gauntness about his dingo-like, occasionally sour features which proclaimed that he had, more than once, been to hell and back. Yet his intense dark darting eyes sparkled with intelligence, for Sergeant Clarrie Woods was a fine natural pilot who loved flying, going to war and the warm companionship he found with the lads of 214 Squadron at RAF Stradishall in Suffolk. Friendship with Clarrie Woods, however, was not easily earned as Doug Handbury learned when he joined the Australian's crew who had lost their navigator.

There was no compulsion for Handbury, a Lincolnshire farmer's son, to go to war. He was in a reserved occupation, yet believed it was his duty to join up. His crew at 12 Operational Training Unit at Chipping Walden, Oxfordshire, had been split up after completing training when their pilot was taken ill. Handbury travelled alone to Stradishall in May 1942, having reluctantly been pushed temporarily into the unenviable position of a spare bod. Neither Woods nor his crew welcomed their new navigator with enthusiasm.

'For the first five ops in our Stirling no one spoke to me, unless it was in the course of duty,' Handbury recalls. 'Then, after the last trip Clarrie turned to me and said: "All right, you Pommie bastard, you'll do." From that moment I was one of them and I got on marvellously with Clarrie.'

Handbury equates much of his aircrew career with that of farming.

'It was a job, quite boring for long periods,' he says. 'I drove a tractor up and down fields for maybe twelve hours a day. To fly an aeroplane across the North Sea into Germany and back for five or six hours was no more exciting than that really, unless anything happened. You saw a lot of things happening outside your own aircraft, but if you were lucky, none of it happened to you. There was a great deal of luck involved, but we thought there was also a little bit of skill.'

Luck and skill were needed in full measure when Clarrie Woods and his crew packed six tough sorties into eight hectic days and nights during September 1942. They included, on 14 September, trips to Bremen and Wilhelmshaven, with takeoffs at 12.50am and 6.45pm and precious little time for sleep in between.

All aircrews wanted to survive the war, not all of them planned their survival as meticulously as Woods. They had seen other bombers transfixed by searchlights, fluttering helplessly like massive butterflies with no plan for escape, being hacked to pieces by the German gunners. Woods had not yet been coned, but it could happen, and he wanted to be ready for the worst the enemy could throw at them. The Australian talked to veteran pilots who had approached survival and extinction from all angles and he lay awake at night, considering all the options. They must outwit the searchlights which had already given the kiss of death to many hundreds of aircrews.

'If we're coned, we must dive,' he told his crew decisively in the mess one day. 'We may never be coned, but if we are, we must be ready for the bastards.'

They trained to outsmart German searchlights and guns high above the trilling skylarks, undulating patchwork fields and ancient huddled villages of Suffolk. At 17,000ft Woods put down the nose of his Short Stirling and shrieked earthwards. Many a farmworker flung himself in terror to the ground as he saw a four-engine bomber apparently hurtling to destruction, then rose to shake his fist angrily as the Stirling pulled out of its dive to climb again, believing its sole aim was to fill his trousers. It became a gripping story to recount frequently to the countryman's children and grandchildren.

Sometimes Woods cut three engines and dived to start them again. Handbury's pilot during his second tour, New Zealander Squadron Leader Ken Climie, stopped all four engines, just to see what happened. This was not an irresponsible act for Climie had a wife and family, and a long life appealed to him. It was merely to satisfy his curiosity and make sure he would know how to cope with a similar situation if it occurred over a burning German city. It was sensible to be prepared for anything during an operation. Clarrie Woods also frequently scorched across the countryside at low level to complete his pilot's brief of Preparing for the Unexpected. Outraged folk who rang Stradishall to complain about reckless young pilots bringing down the milk yield of their frightened cows, were patiently told: 'There is a war on. Our aircrews need to train properly if we are going to beat the Germans.'

The crews of 214 Squadron had needed low level flying experience on the moonlit night of 18 September when they were briefed to go gardening (minelaying) in the harbour at Copenhagen.

Clarrie Woods and his crew took off in Stirling W7631 G-George at 8.20pm. There was no problem with navigation and Woods brought G-George down to 600ft as they flew briskly across Denmark. They were met by a sudden frightening blizzard of flak from German ships moored in the harbour.

Handbury again: 'All hell was let loose. We thought the entire German Navy was there because the sky was full of light flak tearing into us. Most of it came from the ships. It was as if they knew we were going to be there. We had to drop the 1,500lb mines at 200mph. We shot across the harbour, dropped the mines, and kept going at maximum speed, turning at Malmö. Sweden was neutral during the war and all the lights were on.'

They landed at Stradishall next morning at 5.55. The crew were exhausted and were on ops again that night.

Clarrie Woods' crew were less likely to be involved in high jinks in the mess than others. That did not mean they were not high spirited, occasionally finding the need to let off steam, but Handbury described them all as 'seriously minded' most of the time.

'We all worked very hard at becoming proficient at our various jobs, that was foremost in our minds,' he says. 'We didn't leave the camp much. We did have the odd pint, but we drank more in the mess rather than trailing about. There were pubs in the village and a liberty coach went to Bury St Edmunds, which was not far away. I occasionally visited friends at Newmarket. Most of the crew – all sergeants – were Dominion types and I used to take them home on leave with me. We were like a Band of Brothers.'

When they stayed at the Handbury farm the crew sometimes visited a local pub, the Tyrwhitt Arms, which stood high on the bank of the river Witham at Short Ferry, near Fiskerton. They were fond of the Sharpes who ran the pub and once shot them up during a training flight, charging low across the fields, startling the landlady who stared down at them from her bedroom window. The incident also demonstrated the pilot's wild streak which usually remained heavily concealed.

One of the Dominion types was Max O'Neil, the handsome wireless operator, who was more typically Australian than his skipper, once setting back Handbury's romance with his future wife, Jean Dracass. He told her untruthfully that her boyfriend had been drinking heavily, was flat on his back and unable to crawl to the phone. Bomb aimer Elmer 'Bunny' Wilson, a Canadian, from Halifax, Nova Scotia, was quiet and straightforward, and later married an English girl, with Doug Handbury as best man. The flight engineer, described by Handbury as 'a nice old boy', Londoner Jack Beaumont was in his thirties, and his baldness made him appear even more elderly to the younger crewmates. A perky Cockney, he found humour in the dourest situation. He was keen and competent, but obviously not in robust health. Later, a medical board found Beaumont was suffering from a serious condition and he was taken off flying. New Zealander Jimmy Callister had already completed a tour in the Middle East, where he was the only survivor in a Wellington crash, before joining Clarrie Woods as his mid-upper gunner.

A self-employed milk deliveryman in Dunedin before and after the war, Callister gave Handbury a piece of advice which the navigator never forgot: 'If you want to survive this lot without going off your head go easy with the booze. If you're sure you're not flying tomorrow you can go out tonight and have a good drink. But if you think you're flying tomorrow, keep away from it.'

The crew's regular rear gunner was Don Beale, from Whiteplains, New York. Before America was dragged into the war Beale travelled eagerly north to join the Royal Canadian Air Force and have a go at the Germans. A quiet and kindly twenty-four-year old, he reported sick after the trip to Copenhagen. His place was taken on the next trip by a young Canadian, on his first operation. It would be Clarrie Woods' last trip, completing his first tour.

They slept in until 8am on 19 September and went out to G-George at dispersal to check everything was okay. The skipper had a word with the ground crew and although they usually did an air test before an op, he decided that day it was not necessary. In the afternoon, at briefing, they were told that night's target was Munich. It was Handbury's twenty-second operation and he was relaxed, quietly confident and busy, for there was a long route to work out.

'By this time we knew a good deal about things and were no more worried than before' he says. 'It would be a long trip but we had great confidence in our pilot and the aircraft. The disadvantage with Stirlings was that they struggled for altitude and Lancasters could get 6,000ft or so higher. We later converted to Lancasters, but the Stirling was roomier, much more comfortable and easier to get out of if necessary. It was quieter and more manoeuvrable. It had a main spar, but this was not the horrendous obstruction it was in the Lanc, which was no faster than the Stirling, which we preferred.

'Earlier in the tour, before we had Gee radar equipment, I had to drop the bombs. It wasn't until we had Gee that Bomber Command thought navigators had sufficient work to do and we got a bomb aimer. In our case I trained our front gunner, Bunny Wilson, with the help of various instructors at Stradishall. It was interesting and spectacular dropping the bombs, and I saw a lot of our bombers being hit and going down. I was glad to get back inside my navigator's cubbyhole and draw the curtains. In the early days of Gee, the equipment was top secret and, when it was working, navigators had to keep their curtains tightly drawn. Even their crewmates weren't supposed to get a glimpse of it. Eventually, the Germans took a Gee set from an aircraft they had shot down.'

They had supper after which Doug Handbury settled into a comfortable armchair in the sergeants' mess and went to sleep.

'Your stomach starts turning over during the afternoon,' Handbury recalls. 'It was not fear, but excitement and apprehension, the sort of feeling you might get before going to an important interview. I just went to sleep. I've always been a great one for sleeping if I've got a bit of time, I still am. Everything just carried on around me.'

Handbury dozed off happily with a *Daily Mirror* resting on his chest. He woke abruptly, smelled burning and jumped up with a yell. The newspaper was in flames. He beat out the fire, carried the mess to the coke stove, thrust it inside and turned to roar: 'Silly buggers!' at a group of chortling aircrew. The incident eased tension for a few minutes and Handbury found himself promising someone his bike if he didn't return from Munich. The navigator's sporty Raleigh bicycle with its three-speed Sturmey Archer gears was much admired in the mess and if he didn't get back it might pass through the hands of several aircrew before the war ended. Handbury's twelve-year-old brother Bruce eventually got it.

They went to the aircraft at least an hour before takeoff to stow their kit inside and prepare for the flight. Nellie, a pleasant good-humoured young WAAF driver, always drove them in a Bedford van to dispersal. She was in her mid-twenties and called them 'my little chickadees'. She also transported the Canadian flight commander, Squadron Leader Elmer Sturdy, and his crew to the aircraft adjacent to G-George and had a good line in cheerful chat to help keep up everyone's spirits. As the crew of G-George got out of the van they gave Nellie their caps. She looked after them until they returned. Nellie was always there waiting for them hours later. They admired her loyalty and would have been alarmed if she did not wave them off at the start of each operation.

They took off at 7.55pm, turning towards the coast. Handbury was wearing his lucky blue silk scarf, a present from his mother. She had also thoughtfully given him a brandy flask to wear in his breast pocket to protect his heart from German bullets. He never took the flask on operations, using it instead for breaking open walnuts. After buckling the inside he showed it to his mother and told her it had worked well.

They crossed the coast near Bradwell Bay, Essex, rumbled over the Channel and flew south over France where it was quieter. They turned east when they were almost in a direct line with Munich. Eighty-nine aircraft set off to bomb Munich: 68 Lancasters and 21 Stirlings. Three Lancasters and three Stirlings failed to return. On the same night another 118 bombers attacked Saarbrücken. Five of these were lost.

'There was flak over the French coast,' Handbury recalls, 'but it didn't give us any trouble. It was fairly quiet until we reached the outskirts of Munich. I was busy checking our route and Bunny told me over the intercom when he saw any landmarks, like a river or a railway line. It was important for a navigator to find the winds and calculate our drift. The prime object of a navigator was to find out the wind effect on his course. You had forecast winds when you left base, of course, but they weren't always right.

I think the forecast winds were wrong on the Nuremburg raid in March 1944 when so many bombers were lost. On long legs I checked our route with a sextant, taking star shots. It was a laborious way of finding our position, but it helped.

'The flak started as we approached Munich. My curtains were open because the Gee was switched off, it had a very limited range. We dropped our bombs from 17,000ft on the Pathfinder markers. That was the easy bit. The bomb doors were closed and we had just turned for home, hopefully avoiding concentrations of flak in Munich, when we were coned.'

German radar had been patiently following G-George, like a starving spider tracking a meandering fly. The blue radar-controlled master searchlight struck like a bolt of lightning, glueing itself on to G-George. Other lights flashed across the sky following their leader. The Stirling was a blob of bright light exposed to every German gunner for miles around. Inside the cockpit it was as bright as day and the pilot cried: 'Hold tight fellers! we're going down!'

As they plunged into a deep stomach-tumbling dive, seeking a dark refuge, the guns opened up in earnest. At Copenhagen the flak had been intense, but shells and bullets had been aimed hopefully at many different aircraft. Here they were all firing at G-George believing it to be a certain kill. Handbury left his office and scrambled into the astrodome as the Stirling's nose pointed towards the ground. He saw no point staying beside the navigator's table. If they were going to crash he had as good a chance of surviving in the astrodome as in his seat. He wasn't scared, and as the bomber dropped through the first mile of sky, all four Bristol Hercules engines roaring, he was even exhilarated as they drove down, down, down. They were followed inextricably by blazing searchlights and flak, almost as if they were all tied neatly together in a big silk bow as a present for Adolf Hitler. There was no time to think that it would take only a single shell smashing into a petrol tank to blast them into eternity. Nor was there time to gather up parachutes, clip them on and wait for the order to bale out.

Handbury clung to a metal grip behind Clarrie Woods, whose face beneath his leather helmet was set in a grim mask and covered by streaming rivulets of perspiration. This was the moment he had trained for, but had it been enough? Woods threw occasional anxious glances at the altimeter but, sitting beside him, engineer Jack Beaumont, for once at a loss for a suitable wisecrack, calmly read out their descending height: 'Fifteen five, fifteen four, fifteen three – '

Seven young men in the prime of life passed swiftly through 15,000ft, 14,000ft, and 13,000ft at well over 350mph, unable to shake off lights and flak, but there was still a long way to go. Still a chance of escape. The juddering Stirling's bellowing engines hid the sound of flak clattering incessantly against it.

'The light was intense,' recalls Handbury. 'It was so bright it appeared to be coming in through all sides of the aircraft. None of us could help Clarrie except Jack whose eyes took in all the instruments, keeping the skipper informed. We could only wait and hope. Bunny, the bomb aimer, was in the front turret. The gunners were hanging on in their turrets. It was a whole new experience for the chap in the tail. The wireless operator stayed at his position. I saw my charts, instruments and pencils fly off the table, but I wasn't bothered. I had plenty of spares in a big pencil case safely stowed in a metal storage bin. The dive went on and on and still the searchlights stayed with us. We'd never dived like this before on an operation. We'd done all these things in practice, but that was without the German lights and guns chasing us.'

This was the first time Clarrie Woods had really felt like a sinewy flesh and blood part of his aeroplane. He believed that together, he and G-George could outwit the bloody Germans. His powerful fingers gripped tightly on the steering column. The pilot's strength was puny compared to the power of the four great Hercules engines and yet it was the guiding force to their survival. Handbury could see the altimeter over the pilot's shoulder – 12,000ft, 11,000ft, 10,000ft. There would be a moment when exhilaration ended and doubt, then fear infiltrated their minds and they would start thinking seriously about baling out, but was that possible in this mad downward plunge? It was unlikely. Besides, fear wiped out clear thinking. Clarrie Woods would not panic, of that nothing could be more certain. That ugly wonderful little man had pulled them through all kinds of impossible situations, including Copenhagen. My God, that was only last night and here they were in all kinds of shit again – 9,000ft, 8,000ft, 7,000ft. The German gunners had not yet blasted them apart but their frustrated guns were still flinging a torrent of death their way.

Other aircraft, having dropped their bombs, were relieved that the unfortunate occupants of G-George had given them a relatively clear exit from Munich. None could see if the diving bomber, swept by light and flak, was on fire, but it was something that happened every night. Thank God it wasn't them. They headed home, thinking only of a job well done, a quiet meal, a comfortable bed and their own survival.

G-George's Canadian rear gunner, tasting fear in his first operation, had believed what everyone said during training about gung ho, over the top and the big adventure, but this was nightmare stuff that seemed to have been a surreal scene ripped from a movie. His turret pointed in the direction from which they had come. He could do nothing except cling on, wait and worry. It probably crossed his mind about the strength of the Stirling, whose engines were screaming at maximum revs. Would the aircraft hang together? Was there a chance a wing might be torn off? He thought forlornly of his parachute, stowed securely behind the turret inside the fuselage. Would the G-force keep him stuck to his seat so he couldn't reach it? On the ground, German observers, licking their lips, watched G-George through binoculars for telltale streaks of flame, ready to lead the cheers.

Clarrie Woods started pulling out of the dive at 4,000ft. Any lower and they would smash a hole in the ground so big it would become a tourist attraction. Searchlight and flak stayed with them, but as they dropped lower, the lights wavered. At 200ft, the lights cut out, the last shell was fired and G-George charged exultantly across Munich, too low for the enemy's light flak; only machine-guns could get it now. There was no sign of hunting fighters. The pilot blinked in the sudden darkness and mopped his sodden face. His throat was dry, he could murder a beer. Church steeples, rearing up like giant stalagmites, passed a few feet below or to the side of them. The empty grey streets of Munich stretched to the horizon. Thousands of people huddled together in air raid shelters and cellars, shifting nervously, like trapped rats. Some were not so lucky. Fires burned in the receding distance, where the searchlights had sprung up again like mad demons, having located another victim.

Now, even G-George's tail gunner began thinking of home. He rotated his turret, with growing confidence, looking for fighters, but saw none. He and the others reported they were okay. No one was hurt, a miracle of sorts. Engineer Jack Beaumont was consulting the fuel gauges when his skipper sent him back down the fuselage to check the damage. Beaumont found plenty of holes, but nothing vital had been hit. Woods shook his head in silent disbelief, as they passed over the city limits and anonymous black countryside at 200ft. He pulled back the stick and started climbing.

Puffs of flak occasionally appeared in the distance like inquisitive fire flies. They were on a course which took them at a safe distance from any gun emplacements, but they could never be sure. The Germans were wily opponents. After such a mauling a crew are always afraid of being caught again. As always, on the way home, they remained vigilant. The return flight was not entirely serene, nor free from further moments of gut-churning dread. One or both gunners sensed they saw a darting shadow. It was no more than the unravelling tendrils of a cloud, a smear on the perspex turret, or a demon in the mind. Having expended so much effort in attempting to smash G-George into the ground the German gunners and searchlight crews had not alerted their fighters about the lone Stirling. Perhaps they believed the bomber had crashed. But as the all-clear sirens howled over Munich and people emerged fearfully from their holes, Clarrie Woods and his crew were a high distant blob, wrapped happily in darkness, heading west.

Safely down at Stradishall, the engines were cut and the silence, as usual, was uncanny. The pilot murmured: 'Christ! that was a bit dodgy,' as he sat looking out at the airfield. He allowed himself a grin. There was Nellie, holding their caps. He eased himself out of the seat and nodded gratefully to his engineer. Woods had finished his tour. The skipper's next stop would be a training unit as an instructor, which he would love, but he wouldn't forget those last two ops; they were absolute bastards.

On the ground six men murmured 'well done' to Woods, who would have been embarrassed by more fulsome praise, even though he had just saved their lives. When they looked at the scores of holes drilled into G-George it was clear his sharp reactions had kept them just ahead of the guns. The holes were all aft of the wings. The gunners had always been chasing them as they dived, yet if G-George had faltered for a second, the flak would have caught up, tearing into the wings and fuel tanks. The rear turret had collected a few pieces of shrapnel, none had touched the awed spare bod rear gunner, who murmured: 'Is it always like that?' Theirs had been a remarkable escape. Clarrie Woods and the others collected their caps from Nellie, got into the van and puffed on cigarettes as she drove them across the airfield for debriefing.

The citation for Clarrie Woods' DFM drew attention to his supreme ability as a pilot which had brought them safely through his first tour. He was commissioned and became a flying officer. Handbury received a DFC on his second tour, going on to complete forty-five operations. Callister received a DFM and flew to the Far East to complete a third tour. Three tours in three separate theatres of war was quite a performance.

Six of G-George's regular aircrew lived through the war. Having survived his first tour, largely through his own intuitive skills, Clarrie Woods' death came as a terrible irony. Based at Waterbeach, near Cambridge, he was on an instruction flight on 31 August 1943 when he felt the need to visit the toilet at the back of the Stirling. While he was away from the controls, the pupil pilot crashed near Ely. All nine aboard were killed.

CHAPTER TWELVE

THREE BRIDGES TO CROSS

When Prime Minister Winston Churchill called for Allied air supply drops to be rushed into Warsaw during the summer of 1944 Royal Air Force chiefs protested, predicting such heavy aircrew casualties that the operations could not be justified. They were right, but Churchill got his way. He said Britain had declared war against Germany on 3 September 1939 because Hitler had invaded Poland. Now, five years later Britain must continue to support the Poles who were convinced the time was right to rise up against their cruel Nazi oppressors. Stalin, they believed, would support them in kicking the Germans out of their country.

Warsaw was out of range of British airfields and Stalin refused Allied bombers permission to land in Russia. Churchill turned quickly to Allied air bases in Italy.

The Polish dream would soon crumble, for the Russians waited at the gates of Warsaw as Germans and Polish Resistance fought savagely to the death. Then, with the Poles defeated and the German forces driven from Poland, Stalin's army marched into the devastated city of Warsaw on 17 January 1945, and installed a government of its own supporters. The Warsaw Uprising was one of the bloodiest episodes of the Second World War, in which the display of courage and fortitude in the air and on the ground was almost unequalled. And yet this remains one of the most scantily documented wartime operations.

Many of the men who flew into the horror of Warsaw came from 178 Squadron which was based at Amendola airfield near the town of Foggia. The Allies had swept through Foggia which had been severely damaged and its airfields were sabotaged by the retreating German forces.

These airfields were strategically important, for bomber and fighter squadrons operating from them could dominate the whole of Italy, the Balkans and southern Germany. As soon as they had been captured, the airfields were repaired. Even so, Amendola had none of the comforts of home. Ground and aircrews lived in tents and were given unappetising food.

Lloyd Lyne had gone straight into the RAF in 1940 after leaving Launceston College, a boarding school, which he disliked intensely. Now,

on 13 August 1944, he was twenty-one and had not been home for two years
to Bugle, north of St Austell, where his father ran a general store. He would
be a farmer, a tenant of the Queen on Duchy of Cornwall land near Truro
after the war, but now, after failing a pilot's course in Bulawayo, Southern
Rhodesia, he was a sergeant bomb aimer. He and his crewmates had shared
twelve operations. These had included laying mines from a height of 200ft
in the river Danube, and bombing marshalling yards and well-defended oil
refineries in the Balkans. None of those raids was a soft touch, but it could
not adequately prepare these young men for the hell of Warsaw.

The crew was skippered by Flying Officer Dougald MacRae, who came
from near Ardbeg, Ontario, where his family ran the Linger Long Lodge at
the remote hunting and fishing resort situated on Wahwashkesh Lake. He
fell in love with a guest at the lodge, British heiress, author and adventurer
Philippa Paddon, who was the first woman to drive a car the length of
Africa. They married and opened an even more remote outpost to the lodge.
MacRae, one of seven children, was 6ft tall, handsome with a Clark Gable
moustache. He had already appeared in the Warner Brothers film *Captains
of the Clouds* with James Cagney, and a postwar future in Hollywood
beckoned.

Lyne recalls his former skipper: 'Being Canadian he mucked in more
with the rest of us than a lot of the English officers would do. I hated that
officer-NCO divide during the war, particularly for aircrews who depended
so much on each other.'

Lieutenant Gordon Coutts, of the South African Air Force, was the crew's
navigator. A well built man, also married, he was less extrovert than
MacRae. Sergeant John Porter, a man of Kent, was the wireless operator. He
did not go out on the occasional crew rave-up, perhaps because he was
engaged to be married and conscientiously saving up for a new home. His
fiancée's wedding dress was hanging in her wardrobe waiting for his first
leave. Sergeant Dick Scott, from Sudbury, Surrey, the flight engineer, an
only child, enjoyed fun and games in the sergeants' mess, where young men
could forget the insanity of war. Mid-upper gunner was Flight Sergeant
'Mac' MacLanachlan, a six-footer from South London. Sergeant Arthur
'Buff' Sharpe, easily the oldest, at thirty-one, was rear gunner. His home
was in Norfolk.

'We were,' says Lyne, 'a good team.'

Not so good were the living conditions at Amendola. Lyne recalls: 'They
were rough. We were only there that summer, the winters were said to be
terrible. We had no beds, only thin mattresses. Amendola was also used by
Americans with Liberators and Flying Fortresses. The Yanks were better off
with decent beds and food. Our food was horrible. I've never eaten corned
beef since. There was a lot of dehydrated stuff, including potatoes, carrots
and powdered eggs. We made fires outside the tent to heat up tins of food.
John Porter once put a tin of baked beans in a billy can over the fire without
puncturing the top. It exploded sending red hot embers and baked beans all

over the tent. The boozing wasn't very good either. You couldn't get much British beer and the Italian wine was like vinegar. The loos were a couple of pieces of wood you sat on over a trench. We had makeshift showers which were buckets holding cold water, with a rope to tip it over you. It was disgusting to think that young men had to fly for seven or eight hours into enemy territory and come back to this. We were frightened off the Italian girls by stories that the Germans had given them all syphilis. The only trips out were by truck for swimming at Manfredonia on the coast, which we enjoyed.'

The bulk of the supply trips to Warsaw during the Uprising were made between 12 and 17 August 1944.

Dougald MacRae's crew were lounging about on the morning of 12 August when an RAF truck puttered between the tents with an erk using a loud hailer calling for all aircrews to assemble quickly for an unexpected briefing. As usual in wartime, anything unusual triggered a flood of rumours. Today the word flashed round that the squadron was being posted to England. It was the most popular rumour and never failed to get even the most cynical aircrews off their backsides. No one was surprised when they learned England was not on that day's itinerary. Instead, they were to fly to Brindisi on the Adriatic coast, no more than an hour away. They were told nothing more except they had to go in full flying gear.

The American-built Consolidated Liberator Mk VI EV961 C-Charlie, with Dougald MacRae at the controls, lifted off the Amendola airfield, its four air-cooled radial supercharged engines roaring. The ball turrets, which weighed almost a ton, and the front turret guns, had been removed some time ago from the RAF Liberators, allowing them to carry heavier bomb loads.

Shortly after takeoff, Lyne walked through the fuselage to the beam gun area and opened up the big shutters where he was joined by Dick Scott and Mac MacLanachlan and the three of them drank in the scene through the apertures. It was a gloriously warm day. The sun hung like a huge pulsating fireball in a flawless azure sky. It was impossible to see where the sky finished and the sea began. They decided it was a day which could be more agreeably spent swimming than waging war.

C-Charlie had a scare on landing at Brindisi when a tyre burst and a stream of smoke erupted behind them. Almost before they had stopped a blood waggon (ambulance) and fire tenders were fussing beside them. No one was hurt and the Liberator only needed its tyre replacing.

Here they learned that instead of dropping bombs or mines they would be delivering arms, ammunition, medical supplies and food to the beleaguered Poles in Warsaw. The aircrews were told by briefing officers that they would meet resistance from the Germans, but received no clue of the determination and ferocity the enemy would employ to defend ground they had held since the beginning of the war.

They were also told to look carefully for the river Vistula, the key to their destination. They must fly along the river, gradually losing altitude, crossing three of its bridges in the city before turning to port at 400ft, flying parallel with Miodowa Street which led to the dropping area at Krasinski Square. The square would be lit by women of the Polish Socialist Party militia using hurricane lanterns. Pilots were told to make a sharp climbing turn to port after the drop to avoid colliding with the tall Prudential building.

After briefing, MacRae said it was a hell of a long way to go. That was an understatement. The round trip was a marathon 1,750 miles mainly over enemy-held territory. Each bomber carried auxiliary fuel tanks and took off with 2,100 gallons, enough to keep them airborne for twelve to fourteen hours. It would be a journey to tax the endurance of the fittest aircrews. C-Charlie also carried twelve 500lb containers of supplies.

Ten Liberators of 178 Squadron left at about three-minute intervals. Because of the great distance they could not travel together and arrived singly over Warsaw, a decision that suited German anti-aircraft gunners who could concentrate their fire power on one aircraft at a time. Not surprisingly, aircraft and aircrew losses were high. Another eighteen bombers joined the long haul to Warsaw. These were from 31 (South African Air Force) Squadron, and the special operations units in 148 Squadron and the Polish 1586 Flight, which were also based in southern Italy.

C-Charlie took off with maximum power around 7pm, wallowing over the airfield, heavy with fuel and supplies. It was still light and Lyne lay in the nose picking out landmarks which he reported over the intercom to navigator Gordon Coutts who was busily plotting their course.

Lyne recalls: 'We had none of what was then sophisticated radar equipment like H2S, ground-scanning radar, which bombers used operating from England. Our navigators mainly used dead reckoning, wireless fixes, astro-navigation and visual aid from the bomb aimer.'

They maintained a height of 10,000ft, passing over enemy territory in Romania and Hungary in daylight which caused a few flutters of apprehension. They took care to keep clear of any built-up areas on the outward flight which was without incident until three quarters of the way to Warsaw when Buff Sharpe, alert in his rear turret, spotted a German Messerschmitt Bf110, keeping pace with them in the dark.

MacRae said: 'Keep quiet, don't open fire, we don't want to draw attention to ourselves.'

Lyne again: 'We watched it. The fighter was just stooging away. We were the only other Allied aircraft in the sky. Gordon wondered why the German didn't press home an attack, but he didn't. Perhaps the pilot was an old stager who didn't want to get mixed up in a fight or maybe he was a youngster who was scared of having a go. The fighter made Doug seek cloud cover pretty quickly and we started to throw out window. We got rid of a lot and this perhaps gave us a false sense of security. We felt a bit safer and imagined the enemy radar would be plunged into confusion.'

Shortly after the navigator said they were getting near Warsaw Lyne reported a large river winding below them. It was the Vistula.

Lyne said: 'Good on you, mate,' to Coutts for an excellent piece of spot-on navigation.

When the Liberator turned to port above the Vistula they saw the burning city. The Germans had set fire to Warsaw, and were intent on razing it to the ground, killing every Pole who had not already been murdered in concentration camps.

Lyne again: 'It was an awesome sight. We couldn't actually see the city which was covered by a massive pall of smoke with orange flames intermittently darting through it. We started coming down quietly to 400ft. The Russians were on our starboard side, the Germans on the port. We didn't see any fighters, although the majority of bombers which were shot down by Messerschmitts were attacked when they had completed the drops and were returning to Italy. The barrage of flak seemed to start all of a sudden. I don't know if they waited until we had come into range before opening up, but that's what it seemed. It was an enormous barrage, a great wall of fire, and we flew straight into it. It didn't look at all promising and I am absolutely certain that this was the moment which saved my life. The skipper said, over the intercom: "Lloyd, this is looking a bit rough. I'll get Gordon to drop the supplies. You go back on the beam guns and help the rear and mid-upper gunners".'

They were down to 400ft. German gun posts were strung out on both sides of the Vistula. Shells and bullets were finding their mark as navigator and bomb aimer passed each other grimly in the fuselage. Lyne left his parachute stowed in the nose, believing he would be back there after leaving Warsaw, not thinking the odds against their survival had lengthened when he had been told to leave the nose.

He recalls: 'I lifted up the heavy metal shutters of both beam 0.5in Browning machine guns, but only operated the port one because that was where most of the anti-aircraft fire was coming from.'

The smoke and stench of the burning city poured into the fuselage and the Liberator's great engines drummed fiercely into his skull like giant drills as he fired into German positions. A steady rattle of fire also came from MacLanachlan and Sharpe in the mid-upper and rear turrets. C-Charlie crossed the three bridges and swung to port. Fifteen women from the Polish militia waited bravely in Krasinski Square ready to light their hurricane lamps and lie down with them to form a cross when they heard the rumble of C-Charlie's engines. It was then the Liberator crew's task was made even more formidable when the port outer engine was hit and erupted in flames. The port inner engine was also struck and fire began consuming the port wing and the bomb bay. The struggling bomber became part of the horrifying tableau of a tortured burning city. They all continued to play their role to keep them going. Anyone letting his mind slip might have been panicked into baling out into the inferno below. Each man was occupied with his own discipline and duties, fear of tragedy barely kept at bay by the overwhelming desire to find the dropping zone and get back to Amendola.

The pilot was doing a remarkable job keeping the Liberator straight and level. Engineer Dick Scott fought with him to keep the Liberator at 400ft. The fire extinguishers had failed to put out the flames. Navigator Gordon Coutts stared down into the nightmare of smoke, fire and death, looking for the lighted cross in Krasinski Square, his thumb on the button which would release the supplies.

Lyne recalls: 'Although it is hardly believable, I saw the German anti-aircraft shells bursting through the bottom of the aircraft and going out through the top. They were like flaming cricket balls, about the same size. I could have put my hand out and caught them. I was incredibly fortunate not to be hit and it's possible one of those shells killed the mid-upper gunner. I was watching the flaming shells and firing at the same time. The future did not look terribly bright although I thought at the time we would be all right because the Jerries had got their timing wrong. The shells should have hit the bottom of the aircraft and exploded. Instead, they were going straight through and exploding at a higher altitude. Then, seconds after I first saw the flaming shells everything became a blank until I woke up on the ground.'

He remembers coming to in a crumpled heap, unable to rise. It was midnight, he could not see anything and believed he had lost his sight. In his mind he should have still been manning the port beam gun. He could not understand where he was, what had happened to the Liberator and how, without a parachute, he had been mysteriously spirited out of it. Slipping in and out of consciousness, he heard the sound of lapping water. Then came the squeaky splish-splash of oars and the sound of guttural voices.

Lyne again: 'I thought I must be dreaming. One moment I was in an aircraft with my crewmates, the next I was in a boat with three or four German soldiers. I thought we might have ditched, but where and what had happened to the others?'

Much of what happened in those few terrible minutes Lyne has pieced together from Polish witnesses whom he met in Warsaw forty-two years later. One of them was General Tadeusz Bor-Komorowski, commander of the Polish resistance in Warsaw, who was at his headquarters in the Old Town when he saw the blazing C-Charlie battle through the German shell fire and drop its supplies.

In 1986 Lyne was told how German searchlights followed the blazing Liberator, illuminating it clearly for the gunners. The aircraft staggered almost to Napoleon Square, an alternative dropping zone, releasing the containers before there was an explosion on board. Lyne believes the blast flung him clear of the aircraft which made a lumbering turn to port towards Paderewski Park. The six men aboard, who had fulfilled their orders, now had no more than a minute or two to save themselves. Their parachutes would be useless 400ft above the blazing city. One of the crew must have seen the glint of the lake in the park. MacRae, desperately fighting the controls, recognised the lake as their last chance, somewhere to ditch, however shallow the water. Lyne fell on a small island in this lake, half in the water, about 70yd from the mainland.

The Liberator, no longer a finely tuned flying machine, its starboard engines bellowing like a great herd of mortally wounded elephants, its controls unresponsive, sank lower over the Vistula, skimming the rooftops, watched by Poles holding their breath. C-Charlie missed the lake and plunged into a wood. There was an earthquaking explosion and the bomber erupted in a sheet of flames. The six men aboard died instantly, torn to pieces among the burning shattered trees.

At this time Eugeinusz Drzewiecki was a sixteen-year-old freedom fighter in Poland's Home Army, organising day and night guards. He said: 'I saw the Liberator in a sky lit up by bright chains of missiles directed towards it. The aircraft became a fiery ball and quickly began to fall. There was a roar, an explosion and a big fire about 800m from my observation post. We went there secretly, looking for weapons.'

It is difficult to imagine the agony of the MacRae family. Two days before Dougald MacRae died in Warsaw, his married brother Jamie, serving in the Argyll and Sutherland Highlanders, was killed in Normandy.

The Germans may have seen the tiny figure of bomb aimer Lloyd Lyne hurtling through the air illuminated by the fires. Certainly, they reached him quickly. Although brutal in their treatment of the Poles they were gentle and courteous to Lyne. Perhaps they were so staggered by the miracle of his survival they regarded him as a lucky talisman, one who might, if treated with respect and compassion, help bring them unscathed through the war.

Lyne again: 'I must have been flung out through the beam aperture, probably catching my head on the gun. I had a gash on the head and think that was how I was knocked unconscious. I had burns to my forehead and nose and my right leg was hurt. Most badly burned were my hands which were kept bandaged for a month or more. Bushes on the island helped cushion my fall on to the ground which was silty and muddy. My escape was unbelievable. The most amazing thing was that no bones were broken. I didn't know all my crewmates were killed until I came home after the war.

'When I came to I assumed I had fallen into the Vistula but now I know I was on a small island in Kamionkowskie Lake. My reaction was to swim away from the area, but I was unable to get up and realised swimming was out of the question. I didn't know how long I remained where I landed but found I had no flying helmet, parachute harness or flying boots. Eventually I heard voices and shortly afterwards several German soldiers were grouped around me. They lifted me very gently and put me into a rowing boat. I remember very little after this although I heard continual explosions with buildings crumbling and the whine of shells overhead as the Germans systematically destroyed Warsaw. I was taken by lorry to a casualty station where a German medical officer gave me an injection. He spoke good English, said he had cleaned me up and I would be taken to hospital in Warsaw.

'I don't remember the drive to Modlin Hospital but I awoke to find myself in bed with white sheets, top and bottom, pillows, and several people standing round me. Next time I woke a doctor told me I had slept well for several days. I don't know how long I had gone without food, but I was very hungry. Pretty Polish girls, cleaners, smuggled in boiled eggs and buns for me.'

Undoubtedly, the girls regarded Lyne as a hero, one of the Allied fliers who had faced death in order to bring them guns and ammunition to fight the Germans. One Polish girl gave Lyne a mirror which he still has. This was a less thoughtful gift. He could see his battered face: the burns and lacerations. His hair had been cut off for bandages to be wound round his head.

Lyne recalls: 'My watch was missing and also a ring which had belonged to my grandmother; part of the spoils of war, I suppose. The biggest worry was that my identity discs were no longer with me and I had no uniform, in fact I had no clothes at all.

'There were two medical officers at the hospital and after I had been there for some time and was beginning to feel a bit better they put me in a window seat and we talked for some time, but never about the war, except the futility of it, and nothing that would implicate me in any way. They twice shared a bottle of wine with me. I'm sure that wasn't brought to make me talk more readily, it was more an act of friendship.

'Eventually the time came for me to be moved. I was given a shirt which came down past my knees, a pair of trousers which would have been suitable for someone about 6ft 6in – I was a little over 5ft 7in – a pair of socks and a very large pair of rubber galoshes. I resembled a Charlie Chaplin caricature. Walking was still difficult because of my injured leg and I was taken by stretcher to a waiting Army ambulance. Things soon changed at the railway station where I was put in a normal compartment with other German soldiers coming from the Eastern Front, some of them badly wounded.

'During the journey the food given me was the same as that given to the Germans, consisting mainly of hot stews with very dark brown bread. Two tots of either vodka or cognac were brought around daily and these had to be purchased, but not once did my German companions fail to buy them for me. There was also a medical orderly who conversed with me using a dictionary. He asked what I thought would happen to Germany when the Allies had won the war. I was offered cigarettes, but said I only smoked a pipe. Sometime later a pipe was produced and cigarettes were broken up to fill it for me. After three days and nights, which included stops because of air raids, we arrived at a town called Gira, I was taken off the train and handed over to a German escort.'

Lyne had to walk through the town which he found very difficult, with an injured leg, flip-flopping galoshes and baggy trousers. He was interviewed at a civilian prison and later transferred to the interrogation centre at

Frankfurt-am-Main where he was threatened with being handed over to the Gestapo as a spy because he lacked identification dog tags and uniform. He became very hungry and licked up soup spilled by a guard on the cell floor. When taken to have his burned hands treated he saw a bedpan, which had not been emptied, but it contained a chunk of bread which he quickly slipped inside his shirt.

Days passed and Lyne's despair and helplessness increased until he was sent to Stalag I, a prisoner of war camp at Barth on the Baltic coast, where it was so cold the sea froze. He stayed here until released by Russian Cossacks on horseback in early May 1945. A female lieutenant was at the head of one column. He was flown home in a Flying Fortress.

Lyne's six crewmates were buried by the Germans near where they were killed in Paderewski Park. Flowers were laid on their grave when the Germans were not around. One of the Liberator's propellers was used as a headstone. Their remains were exhumed after the war and reburied in the British and Commonwealth section of the cemetery in Krakow, where The Cross of Sacrifice is permanently bedecked with flowers and candles glow. Parts of C-Charlie can be seen at Warsaw Military Museum where there is also a painting of the aircraft in flight. Lyne was awarded the Polish Cross of Valour, the Warsaw Uprising Cross and the Home Army Cross.

On 4 November 1988, Lyne watched British Prime Minister Margaret Thatcher, in a moving ceremony, unveil a memorial to the crew of C-Charlie, close to the site of the crash in Paderewski Park, since renamed Skaryszewski Park. The likeness of a Liberator was etched into the memorial, which is a huge boulder dug out of the ground nearby. A brass plaque carries the names of the crew, including that of survivor Lloyd Lyne.

CHAPTER THIRTEEN

ROLLER COASTER OF DESPAIR

The German guns waited patiently in Warsaw for the Allied bombers during the autumn of 1944 as they swooped low over the Polish capital, carrying vital supplies for the hard-pressed Resistance fighters. As the Germans tightened their savage hold on the burning city of Warsaw so they inflicted a terrible toll on the brave young aircrews who were attempting what proved to be the impossible: to help the Poles beat back the Germans before the Russians moved in.

The Germans knew their route, it hardly wavered. The bombers came, one by one, lumbering slowly along the river Vistula, counting off three bridges before turning ponderously to port and attempting to parachute supplies into Krasinski Square. The Resistance occupied only a small area which meant that, inevitably, many supplies fell into German hands. And yet the morale of the Polish people was uplifted as aircraft followed aircraft in a brave attempt to give them guns and ammunition. A lot of crews did not make it, either shot down on the outskirts of Warsaw by prowling night fighters, or stabbed by searchlights and easily picked off like great meaty birds by gunners on the banks of the river, on the roofs of high buildings, or perched in church towers. Those who actually delivered the huge containers of supplies to the dropping zone and survived the flak out of the city, then faced the hazard of German night fighters lurking on the way home.

One of the four-engine American-built Consolidated B-24 Mk VI Liberators which flew into Warsaw on 13 August was A-Apple, piloted by Johnny Morrison, a blue-eyed red-haired high-spirited Yorkshireman from the bleak village of Haworth where, a century before, the Brontë sisters had written their romantic novels. His navigator was Sergeant Des Matthews, known to everyone as Dizzy.

'We were told to drop supplies from 400ft at a speed which was only 20mph above stalling speed,' recalls Matthews. 'We had the usual briefing, and were told what winds to expect and how to get there. It didn't look a good trip. It would be difficult and it was a long way. We were based at Amendola in Italy, but set off on this operation from Brindisi, on the south-east coast. After we left, around 7.30pm, we found the forecasted winds were wrong, everything was wrong. Clouds came over, we were not allowed contact by radio, and navigation was all by dead reckoning. Then the sky cleared enough for me to use astro-navigation. I got a few fixes from the stars. They were quite good fixes, too, though one never has the same faith in astro-navigation as one has with direct bearings from radio.

'We were well on the way when Johnny, the pilot, said: "Dizzy, come and have a look at this." He sounded excited. We looked to port where a big city was in flames. It was identified as Krakow in southern Poland and it stood on the Vistula. I got a running fix from the Krakow bearing which led us to Warsaw.

'When we arrived over Warsaw, which was the biggest city on the road between Moscow and Berlin, we saw ground activity down below in the middle of flames and smoke. Suddenly flak came pouring up at us from both sides. At this stage we were almost at the same height as their small arms fire. You are going very slowly, a terrific target for their machine guns and heavier ack-ack. On the other hand, and I've thought of this since, imagine being at the top of a church or a tower and a bloody big Liberator comes roaring in at no kind of height, bashing away at you with its .5 Browning machine guns.

'We found the dropping zone, Krasinski Square, though it had been poorly marked for us by the Resistance. We dropped the supplies, then turned for home. Fighters were around. We had been hit by flak and there was anxiety among the crew. It was dark, cloudy, no stars to be seen, all dead reckoning now. We went through the Balkans, over mountains. There was still no visibility as we flew over Yugoslavia. At the calculated time we altered course and turned starboard to southern Italy. After forty minutes' flying the cloud cleared and we could see the ground. I had hoped to see the coast, but after hours of blind flying I could not expect to be on track.

'After a further half-hour there was still no coast. The fuel gauge reading became critical. I was worried and Johnny knew I was worried. Suddenly, there it was – the coastline, and we were dead on track. I was the luckiest devil ever because I calculated that winds had blown us some eighty miles to the east. But God was with me and I had turned at the right time. We got down at 9am. It had been a long night but we enjoyed a bacon and eggs breakfast and lounged about afterwards. We were tired, no one was eager to get home. After we touched down at Amendola our intelligence officer said they had written us off. It was then we had the first idea about what a massacre the Warsaw trip had been. Two squadrons had almost been wiped out. We were lucky. We counted over forty holes in our aircraft. They needed patching up, but four of 178 Squadron's twelve aeroplanes sent to Poland had been shot down. Many of those which returned were badly damaged.'

It was difficult to raise the spirits when so many mates had not come back. They spent a gloomy time in the tents, sorting through the belongings of dead or captured men, making sure no embarrassing letters from girlfriends were left around that might be sent home to grieving or anxious wives. There were also letters written but not posted by their missing mates which had to be sent home with sympathetic notes from the commanding officer. The cigarettes of absent friends were shared out and more cheerful memories of their old mates revived, but it was difficult to lift the gloom. Warsaw would be remembered as one of the war's more horrific series of operations. Des Matthews was one of those who went by truck for a swim in the Adriatic, where it was possible to forget the bloody war for a few hours. But sooner or later they had to come back to Amendola and the fighting.

The trip to Warsaw had been Matthews' sixteenth operation. He was the oldest of his crew and they called him Dad as often as Dizzy. Matthews didn't mind. Even at the great age of twenty-four there was plenty to look forward to. His home was in Hull and he had been a trainee sales rep there for a milling and flour company before joining up in March 1940. A whisker under six feet he had been, like so many young men, frustrated in his ambition to be a pilot. He told an aircrew selection board he wanted to be a pilot, but they sent him to train as a wireless operator/air gunner. He finished the training, then returned to the board and asked to be remustered as a pilot. He was sent to initial flying school and flew two solos in Tiger Moths. When it was clear Bomber Command had too many pilots, but not enough navigators, resignedly, he became a navigator. He flew with Morrison on Wellingtons and was more fond of them than the bigger Liberators or any of the four-engine bombers.

Matthews had a high regard for the Wellington, its tough geodetic construction and the aircraft's ability to screw its way out of trouble. On Wellingtons, they usually dropped their own flares. He recalls a raid from Amendola on Milan when, at briefing, they were told to forget about marking the target. It was a sortie which reinforced his preference for two-engine bombers.

'We were told we would arrive over Milan and see green flares, followed by reds, dropping from Halifaxes which had flown from England. We were to bomb on the red flares. Easy. We got there, no sign of the Halifaxes. We flew over the target then came back on a reciprocal course before the Halifaxes appeared. There was a snag, they dropped their flares from 20,000ft. I was in a Wellington, carrying a 4,000lb Cookie, unable to get above 6,000ft. The flares fell among us, we dropped the bombs and got the hell out of there.'

Morrison's crew went out together when they were not flying. The nearby city of Foggia was dull, much of it flattened by fighting, no one wanted to go there. There was swimming in the Adriatic, boozing in the mess and, on leave, Alexandria.

'Every so many trips we had leave and flew to Alexandria in Egypt, where there was an Air Force hotel,' Matthews recalls. 'At night we visited the Wrennery, signed for some Wrens, took them into the city and had a nice dance and a party. We took them home in a bus and signed them in. There were some pretty girls in the Wrens and although we couldn't get home to England we had some good leaves in Egypt.'

Some aircrew cracked, unable to take the continual stress and anxiety linked to bombing operations. If they were taken off flying the incriminating initials 'LMF' (Lack of Moral Fibre) were written boldly on their documents and they were posted to a unit where they were given "general duties".

'I shared a tent with another navigator who failed to return from an operation,' says Matthews. 'Another young chap took his place in my tent. He was a rear gunner and did a couple of operations. One night I returned late from a mess party as drunk as an owl. The tent smelled awful and he was crying and had messed himself. He couldn't stand it any more and he went down as LMF. That affected me. I didn't think it was fair. Some could take it, others couldn't, but I didn't think they should be punished because their nerves had snapped.'

The skipper, Johnny Morrison, was keen as mustard and wanted to do well in the RAF. He was small, slim and had the utmost confidence of his crew. Londoner Sergeant Jimmy Hilton, the wireless operator, was popular, and very much in love with his fiancée. Bomb aimer Sergeant Norman Dorling, from Surrey, was a romantic and innocent young man. Matthews only knew the flight engineer Sergeant George Dixon for a short time. Dixon and the rear gunner joined the former five-man Wellington crew when they were being converted to Liberators. Matthews remembers Dixon's difficulties at high altitudes when his oxygen mask often slipped, leaving him gasping for breath.

The skinny and diminutive figure of Sergeant John Higgs, a cheerful and cocky Cockney, gave him a considerable advantage over many other gunners when it came to scrambling in and out of the mid-upper turret. Rear gunner Flight Sergeant Bob Evans, a Welshman, had more experience than the rest of the crew, having completed several operations in England before being posted to Italy. He was married with a son.

Seven days after the trip to Warsaw only one Liberator was available from 178 Squadron for the 205 Group raid on the Hermann Goering panzer works at St Valentine, near Linz, Austria. This was Johnny Morrison's A-Apple, which had been patched up and serviced.

Matthews again: 'At briefing, we were told it was a toughie. The target was very well defended, about two and a half hours from Amendola. It was a crucial raid. The Russians were advancing and by taking out the tanks at the factory we could make it easier for Stalin's troops.'

All the crew went up for an air test that morning, which was normal before an operation. The test satisfactorily completed, they touched down, left the aircraft in the hands of the ground crew and returned to their tents for a few hours' sleep.

It was a warm cloudless night when they took off from Amendola. The horror of the Warsaw trip was fresh in their minds, although tonight they did

not have the long grinding flight that had worn them out the previous
Sunday. What they did not know was that in Linz, fifty-five years before,
Adolf Hitler had been born. He had great plans for turning Linz into the
most beautiful city in Europe after winning the war. Not surprisingly, the
target was fiercely defended.

Fifty miles before the target, at 11,000ft, they ran into heavy flak.
Matthews was in his little office and did not see the first shells being
pumped up at the bombers. Later, as usual, he went up to the flight deck.

'I always went on the flight deck as soon as we were over the target, not
to see what was going on, but to be ready with the compass when the attack
was over. I would alter the compass and the skipper got on to that course for
home as soon as he could. I was up there that night. I saw fires and a lot of
mess down there. There was a lot of opposition with flak and searchlights.
We had no Pathfinders, we went straight in and bombed. We carried nine
1,000lb bombs. Our ETA was 11pm. We were dead on time. Everything was
going according to schedule, except our intercom went u/s.'

Matthews was about to alter the compass when A-Apple was coned. The
crew had dealt with searchlights before, but these were different. They were
new predicted searchlights with synchronised ack-ack and they stuck to
them like leeches. The aircraft shimmered in a blast of light.

Morrison muttered: 'Shit!' and flung the Liberator into a violent
corkscrew. The others hung on. It was a bit like being on a roller coaster at
a fair, but the screams of fear and excitement were only in the mind. At the
end of the ride they would be safe, injured or dead, with no chance of
getting their money back.

'The rest of us couldn't do a thing,' recalls Matthews. 'It was the
skipper's job to take evasive action. I don't think he could see a damned
thing, I couldn't. The cockpit was filled with a blinding white light, but even
if you can't see, you can throw your aeroplane around. The flak was bad,
shells screaming up at us. You're rarely hit by a shell, you are hit by the flak
as the shell bursts. If you are near the explosion your aircraft is flung about.
We were thrown around even as we corkscrewed. We were hit several times,
then we were on fire amidships and aft, but the flak didn't ease. Johnny
didn't tell us to bale out, it was his job to get us out of it. You don't bale out
in those conditions, particularly when you're not far from the target where
you've been knocking hell out of people on the ground. The intercom was
gone. I heard nothing from the rear gunner. Things were looking bad, but we
were clinging on and Johnny was doing all he could.'

Smoke began pouring into the fuselage. Matthews was standing behind
flight engineer George Dixon. With each passing second the chances of a
safe return to base seemed more remote. Suddenly a piece of flak struck
Dixon. He slumped to the floor. Seconds later the pilot was hit and he
crumpled over the controls. A-Apple fell through the sky in a sideways slip.
There was nowhere to go now except down. The fire had taken a firm hold,
the aircraft might blow up before it hit the deck and Matthews knew he had

to act quickly. There was no time to examine Morrison or Dixon to see if they were still alive and clip them into their parachutes. If he did that, they would all die. He had a slim chance of escape and he had to take it. Behind Matthews Johnny Higgs hung lifeless from his mid-upper turret. The navigator believed only himself and the wireless operator were still alive. Matthews was unusual among aircrews. No less keen than anyone else in staying alive, he was aware more than most that death did not always happen to the other fellow. In the interests of self-preservation he carried his parachute with him at all times on the aircraft.

'It was a habit I had and it saved my life,' he says. 'In the navigator's office, the parachute was always there beside me. It was a clip-on parachute and I carried it around like an attaché case. When I went up to the flight deck that night I had the 'chute with me. I clipped it on and then, for some reason, remembered how I could open the bomb doors manually. I must have taken it aboard during the aircraft familiarisation class because it was never mentioned after that. Going out this way was safer than leaving from the front. I stood just off the flight deck and Jimmy Hilton was crouching on the floor looking up at me, scared stiff. I pulled the handle which operated the bomb doors. It was a slow job, but there was no panic and no time to be afraid. All I could think of was opening the doors and getting out in plenty of time before the Liberator blew up. The bomb doors inched open and I judged there was enough space for us to slip through. I saw fires burning on the ground, but there was no time to think about them or what might be waiting for us. I gestured to Jimmy for him to follow me down. It was a tight squeeze, but I dropped out at 11,000ft. Then I passed out.'

Matthews does not remember pulling the ripcord, but his parachute opened. A-Apple, a mass of streaming flames and black smoke, containing the living and the dead, hurtled earthwards. Jimmy Hilton's corpse was found with the others in the wreckage, which came down near Mitterkirchen. Hilton's parachute may have become entangled with the bomb doors, possibly he ran out of time. A German fighter pilot claimed a Liberator kill over Linz. Only one Liberator was lost that night and Matthews believes a coup de grâce attack might have been made as he left the aircraft.

When Matthews regained consciousness three hours later he was hanging in a tree three feet from the ground. As the navigator had slipped out of the aircraft he passed through flames and was slightly burned around the face not protected by his helmet. At first, he believed he was still floating down from the aircraft.

'When I looked round I didn't know where I was, but I could see lights and I thought: "The bastards are looking for me." I looked up and saw a great white thing hanging above me. It was my parachute. I was so lucky. I could have been killed or broken a leg. As it was I hadn't got off scot-free. I released the parachute, got down from the tree and found that the lights were from thousands of glow-worms. I'd lost one flying boot. I was in a bit of pain. I had a dislocated shoulder and two broken ribs. The parachute drop had taken all the skin off the inside of my legs and my balls. It does that sort of thing. It's a hell of a jerk when your 'chute opens. If you're not well strapped up it's going to mess you about. I collected myself, then got out some maps from my escape kit. They were on rice paper. I had a bit of chocolate then opened out the maps. I worked out that I was only 150 to 200 miles from Switzerland. We had been told to eat these maps if we landed in enemy territory. It seemed silly to eat a map that might serve some useful purpose, but I ate the bloody thing. I preferred the chocolate. I also had fifty American dollars escape money. We'd been told to hide these in a tree or bury them in the ground to prevent them getting into enemy hands and I did, but it seemed a stupid thing to have to do.'

Afterwards Matthews reflected that he might have used the map until capture was inevitable, although he had a good idea where he was. His plan was a simple one, but it had the disadvantage of being impossible. He would walk to Switzerland, outwitting the Germans. He had, after all, been educated at Riley High School, Hull, where they approved of initiative and self-sufficiency. Matthews, disregarding his dislocated left shoulder, broken ribs, and the nagging soreness from his legs, started limping towards Switzerland with fierce determination. He hoped he might meet Jimmy Hilton on the way.

'It was a warm August morning, about five o'clock and light,' Matthews recalls. 'God knows what it would have been like in winter, with snow on the ground. I wasn't in much pain, but I had a useless arm hanging down and I was hobbling along on one boot. I didn't get far. A Wehrmacht motorbike and sidecar came along, and stopped. They got out and a pistol was pointed at me. I put my hands up, the left one raised less sharply and not as high. They ordered me to hand over my pistol. I said: "What pistol? I haven't got a pistol." You were issued with a .38 Smith and Wesson revolver but you only carried them on Balkan operations in case you came face to face with a wolf. It's not much bloody good having a .38 revolver in the middle of the Third Reich. They searched me anyway and it was clear they didn't consider me a great threat.

'I was put into the sidecar and taken to a civvy clink in a village, where I was brought a cup of acorn coffee, bloody awful stuff. I was also given a slice of black bread covered with a cheese curd. I didn't think much of that either, I didn't have much of an appetite. There was a cell but they didn't bother to put me in it, that's what they thought of me. Boys and girls kept coming into the little police station. They brought leaflets and handfuls of window, tin foil strips that we used to drop out of the aircraft to confuse the German radar. One came in with a flying boot. I was amazed to discover it was mine. It was the best thing that had happened to me for a long time. Oooh, it was good to get that boot on.'

At 9am four soldiers arrived, carrying rifles. They put Matthews in the middle of them and marched through the village, which had been bombed.

They went to a big detached old house from which stretched a long queue of people. They went beyond the head of the queue which became noisy and restless when they spotted the British airman. The civilians grabbed at him, spat into his face and aimed punches. Inside the building was a doctor who fixed his shoulder and put a big piece of plaster across his chest. The soldiers took him away. By now the queue had turned into a mob. One old man armed with a stick tried to club Matthews round the head. One of the soldiers had a girlfriend who was doing a lot of the spitting. The airman was wearing a beautiful Irvine jacket. The soldier made him take it off and threw it to the girl. She was delighted and Matthews was returned to the police station where he had a nap.

At 4pm a one-armed Luftwaffe officer, who could speak a little English, told the airman laconically: 'You are coming with me. Do as you're told and you'll be all right. If you don't do as you're told I shall kill you.' It was a fine summer evening. They called into a pub where the officer bought Matthews half a pint of beer. Matthews was surprised and delighted by this chivalrous gesture from one flier to another. The German took Matthews by train to Frankfurt-am-Main to be interrogated for 26 days and kept in solitary confinement.

'From when I was shot down neither my parents nor anybody else heard anything about me apart from knowing I was missing,' says Matthews. 'None of my letters got through. They were afraid I had been killed. Then one night my mother was knocked up late by an excited neighbour who said she'd listened to Lord Haw-Haw's latest propaganda broadcast from Germany. I'd been mentioned as a prisoner-of-war. My father rang the Air Ministry who had heard the broadcast but said he shouldn't take any notice of it. Haw-Haw, the British traitor William Joyce, had been known before to give the names of airmen whom he said were POWs, although they were actually dead. He had done this to cause further misery and doubt for the listeners. Then, in November, three months after I was captured, my parents heard from the British Red Cross that I was in a prisoner-of-war camp, Stalag Luft VII at Bankau, Poland.'

On 16 January 1945, Matthews was one of 1,565 POWs who left Bankau on a forced march through the snow and ice of the Silesian winter, ahead of the advancing Russians. Seven weeks later, 1,493 survivors, suffering from a variety of illnesses and severe malnutrition, crawled into an overcrowded camp at Luckenwalde, near Potsdam. When the hard-bitten Red Army arrived, they refused to allow Allied prisoners to be repatriated. Matthews and two other RAF navigators escaped, but were foiled by Russian soldiers at every turn. In Zerbst, they found high-ranking American and Russian officers celebrating Russian VE-Day. The three men sneaked into an armoured car and kept their heads down. They were driven through the Russian lines by an American colonel and major. A week later Matthews was reunited with his family in Hull.

Matthews visited the families of his crewmates who had died and saw in their eyes the unspoken question: 'Why did you survive?' Years later, having trouble with his conscience, he looked at the medals he had been given by Poland for the part he played during the Warsaw Uprising. The others got nothing. Rear gunner Bob Evans was the only one of his crewmates who was married. Matthews tracked down Evans' son Robert in Yeovil, Somerset, and arranged for him to receive the Warsaw Uprising Cross posthumously for his father. It was presented to him at the Polish Embassy in London in November 1992.

CHAPTER FOURTEEN

NO ENGINES AT 1,000FT

In early October 1943 one hundred newly qualified aircrew reported to 21 OTU at Moreton-in-Marsh, Gloucestershire. They arrived by bus, motorbikes and small beaten-up old cars. They all wore broad relaxed grins, brand new brevets and an earnest air of expectancy. As they piled noisily into their billets, the talk was of the blessed end to interminable training and boring examinations, while the war rushed unsportingly towards its conclusion. They talked of girls too; many pretty WAAFs had already been spotted at the new station and things were looking up. They were sprogs, new boys, eager to please, keen to join the fight against Hitler. They had trained long and hard and wanted to claim part of the war for themselves. Training had not been a picnic. There had been accidents, men had died, friends were lost. Many of these one hundred young men would not survive the war, but at least they were ready for the real thing, where the enemy could be shot at, bombed and killed, without inquiries or recriminations. But first, they had to crew up.

At a reception briefing they were told they were free to form their own crews, then left to get on with it. Some thought this arrangement at best haphazard, at worst, barmy. In a service where, pre-war, everything had to be done by The Book, Bomber Command had found ways to cut out some red tape and bullshit. Crewing up in this way was brilliantly effective. No brasshat with a deskful of files, however inspired, could produce a more suitable and cohesive collection of crews. Like inevitably attracted like. Quiet thoughtful men were drawn together, while the more boisterous teamed up with whoops of delight. They were crewing up for Vickers two-engine Wellingtons, so there were enough men for twenty crews.

The unfortunate few, unwanted or unable to make a choice, were left at the end, a little bewildered and unhappy. It was these men, least comfortable in each other's company, who had to be thrown together as one or two makeshift crews, and would be most vulnerable on bombing sorties.

Twenty-one-year-old navigator Dick Morris hit it off straightaway with pilot Victor Jackson. Born in Wandsworth, south London, Morris, slim and fair haired, a former civil servant clerk, saw in the stocky Jackson two characteristics which he shared. The pilot was calm and cheerful and, Morris and the rest of the crew discovered later, he was also totally unflappable. This was a useful attribute in any desperate situation, and they would find themselves embroiled into plenty of those. Jackson and Morris both stood two inches under six feet. Unusually, in those days, Jackson was a non-smoker. The pilot joined the RAF as a Halton apprentice before the war. Even now he was only one year older than his navigator. Jackson's father was a squadron leader serving in India and the boy had been mad about flying from an early age. He loved being in charge of a bomber and hated the thought that one day he might have to step back into the tedium of civvy street. Nothing could compare with the excitement of dicing with death, while attacking the enemy. Jackson, a flying officer, was known as Jacko by his crew, who were, at this time, all sergeants. All five were bachelors.

Bill 'Monty' Montgomery, from Kendal in the Lake District, a slender six-footer, became the crew's imperturbable bomb aimer. When not occupied with bombing the enemy, he was the second pilot. Montgomery was a charmer with the easy knack of getting settled wherever he was posted. He was going bald and claimed this was caused by the shock of being thrown through the windscreen of his car during a race on a beach in 1939. A year older than Jackson he was, at twenty-three, the oldest of the five. At 5ft 8in, wireless operator Geoff Ward was the shortest. From Lowestoft, Suffolk, he was always perky and positive. A carpenter before volunteering for aircrew in 1941, he was a conscientious wireless operator who always managed to get accurate bearings in tight situations. Ward was a year older than rear gunner Ted Hook, twenty-one, from Upminster, Essex, who was sparely built, cheerful and reliable.

At operational training they blended well as a crew and afterwards were allocated a Wellington to fly to southern Italy. They left Portreath, Cornwall, at 2am on 9 February 1944 arriving at Foggia eight days later, after stops at Rabat, Morocco, and Maison Blanc, Algiers. They joined A Flight of 150 Squadron in 205 Group and though they regretted being posted so far from home, they learned to thank their lucky stars they were not stationed in England, pitted against the more savage opposition of the Germans. They flew all over the Balkans, Austria, and northern Italy, where targets were generally defended with less ferocity than Berlin or cities in the Ruhr. They were living it up on leave in Sorrento the following autumn when Allied bombers were sent on the ill-fated operations to Poland to drop supplies for the freedom fighters during the Warsaw Uprising, but 150 Squadron was not sent to Poland as their Wellingtons did not have the range.

They were based at Amendola, sleeping in tents which was pleasant in the heat of summer, but miserable during howling freezing winters with snow deep on the ground. Amendola was one of several airfields operating in the Foggia area. They were simply large fields with temporary control towers and metalled runways made from perforated interlocking steel sheets.

Dick Morris recalls: 'When we arrived at Amendola we were each issued with three blankets. The tents were up but we had to make our beds as best we could. I shared a bed with Monty. We found two 12ft long planks, rested them on jerry cans, and nailed a blanket across. We slept at either end with greatcoats on top when it was really cold. But we were fit young men and it didn't do us any harm. When we became well established we set up petrol drip stoves. A can which contained a reservoir of petrol stood outside the tent. A pipe led from it into the tent, dripping petrol slowly on to sand at the bottom of a 50-gallon oil drum. This was lit and heated up nicely. It was turned off when we went to bed. It was a bit dodgy, but I didn't hear of any drums exploding or tents catching fire.

'The cookhouse was a series of tents and an outside oven where we queued for meals, hurrying the fifty yards back to our own tent to eat before it got cold. We ran even faster in the rain and snow. Wooden boxes served as chairs and we knocked several together for a table. We didn't expect anything better.

'The only navigational aids we had consisted of a number of D/F (direction finding) radio stations scattered about southern Italy. Their beams were picked up by our loop aerials. In the spring of 1944 no radar had been established in the area and Pathfinders did not start operating until later that year, when Gee was also introduced.'

They had successfully completed four operations when, after their customary delicious porridge and condensed milk breakfast on 1 April 1944, they learned there was a bombing trip that night. It was All Fools' Day, but no one considered this was significant. Days were now either one thing or the other. They were either flying or not flying. A truck took them the three miles to the airfield where they talked to the groundcrew and carefully checked the equipment in their Wellington X, LN908 A-Apple.

Aircrews were briefed at the only building on camp, an old farmhouse. The target was the Macchi aircraft factory at Varese, north of Milan, some 450 miles away in the foothills of the Alps. They were told that Varese was well defended. Squadron commander Squadron Leader Boxall advised them to attack the target as low as conditions allowed to make sure they hit the factory, thus avoiding the need for a return trip.

'We did everything ourselves,' says Morris. 'Although we had been given a recommended route we just took off and navigated to the target by dead reckoning. Rivers were useful landmarks. We were completely on our own and always identified the targets ourselves.'

They took off at 8pm on a clear night. The outward flight was uneventful, droning northwards at 8,000ft along the east coast up the Adriatic, then cutting north-west across the mainland.

'We identified the target area without difficulty,' Morris recalls. 'Although there was some light flak coming up there appeared to be no serious opposition. We were a relatively novice crew on only our fifth operation and we followed our briefing instructions to go down to about

5,000ft for our bomb run. We were confident of hitting the target from that
height. Monty, the bomb aimer, got a good line on the target and released
his bombs, a mixed load of high explosives and incendiaries, on the first run
and kept going for the photoflash to operate. There wasn't time. Within
seconds the aircraft was hit by what we thought was flak. The bomber
juddered and veered to starboard. The port engine immediately cut, the oil
pressure dropped and the skipper, feathering the propeller, briefly reported
what had happened.'

The Wellington began losing height as Jackson put the starboard Bristol
Hercules engine on full boost and turned south, away from the mountains.
The engine had not been hit by flak. They could not know in the dark that
they had been 'bombed' by one of their own aircraft flying at a much higher
altitude. The culprits were probably a more experienced crew who had not
taken the briefing instructions seriously, realising that safety lay at a much
higher altitude. Three incendiaries had hit the Wellington. One plunged
through either wing, leaving holes a foot wide. The third smashed into the
port engine, and part of it struck the oil sump. Amazingly, the engine did not
catch fire. The pilot checked over the intercom that everyone was all right
and sent Montgomery through the fuselage to have a quick look round. He
returned to report everything okay except the dead port engine, which
worried them all, they were a long way from base.

Jackson continued to lose height until managing to stabilise the aircraft at
around 1,500ft, the expected ceiling for a Wellington flying on one engine.
As the starboard engine fought to turn the aircraft to port, Jackson, equally
determinedly, with his foot pressed hard on the right side of the rudder bar,
tried to keep a straight course. It was fiendishly difficult and exhausting for
the pilot.

Dick Morris remembers their unease: 'We were a bit scared. At that low
level our immediate problems were to avoid defended areas where a slow-
moving Wellington would easily be picked off by the ack-ack, to keep away
from hilly areas and get out to sea. Coming back with two engines we would
have crossed some of the mountains on a south-east course. Luckily for us
the Po valley runs from near Milan eastwards to the Adriatic, so we
followed this rough line, with Monty and myself map reading at the front of
the aircraft and adjusting course regularly to avoid approaching towns such
as Milan, Lodi, Cremona, Verona and Padua, most of which were well
defended. The Po valley is fairly wide and once we got into the middle of it
there was plenty of room for manoeuvre on either side. German fighters
were stationed along here but we didn't see any of them. This was a
distance, overland, of about 175 miles. Jacko had to steer with hard right
rudder to compensate for the loss of the port engine and after about 100
miles his right leg began to give out. As I continued to navigate Monty
helped hold the rudder bar and see what he could do to relieve the pressure
on the skipper's leg. Then, with real originality, he disconnected two or
three rubber hoses from our oxygen masks which were only needed at

10,000ft and above and used them to tie back the rudder bar. This took most of the strain, but still left sufficient play to allow Jacko to make course changes.

'Having successfully avoided all defended areas a relieved cheer went up when we reached the coast and turned south along the coast back to base. At the mouth of the river Po our wireless operator Geoff Ward sent the first Mayday back to base, telling control about our difficulties. With only about 300 miles left to go we thought we'd just about manage to get home. Our speed was down to about 112mph. Normal cruising speed for a Wellington was around 130mph. Stalling speed was about 90mph.

'Ted Hook, our rear gunner, helped with map reading and occasionally, when we got over the Adriatic, he took drift bearings. This involved dropping a smoke float into the sea to check for wind direction. He took a bearing with the barrels of his guns as the aircraft drifted with the wind. He measured that by pointing his guns at the float. It would always be off-centre, possibly only one or two degrees but with a scale he had in his turret he could measure the direction of the wind, but not the speed. The only object of navigation is to find out the wind speed and direction. The maps showed true bearings of any place you wanted to get to. The difficulty in getting to that place is compensating for the wind speed and direction.'

The reliable starboard engine continued to roar at full boost as they limped down the Adriatic towards Foggia. Geoff Ward, the wireless operator, fed Morris with regular D/F bearings. The efforts of Hook and Ward helped the navigator to give the skipper the shortest route home. Jackson and Montgomery began casting anxious glances at the fuel gauge. The fuel from the port tank had been transferred to starboard, but the single engine was gulping petrol at an alarming rate to maintain their modest height. One engine at full boost used more than two on normal cruise setting.

The pilot's anxiety spread through the struggling bomber. Would they make it? No one had considered ditching in the sea or turning inland to bale out, but these were all possibilities. No one had clipped on their parachute, but these were all within easy reach in an emergency. Thirty-five miles from Amendola the fuel gauge was flickering a fraction above zero. Fingers were crossed, and some checked that parachutes were still close at hand. Geoff Ward continued sending Mayday distress signals and Amendola control made encouraging noises as A-Apple clawed its way over the sleeping countryside of southern Italy.

Time dribbled away as the dregs of the fuel tank were fed into the bellowing thirsty engine and the Wellington lumbered through the wide valley separating two small ranges of hills of up to 3,000ft, which towered above them. Any mistake now and they would be smashed to pieces like a crate of eggs on the slopes of some miserable crag. They crossed the Foggia Plain and nosed on to the airfield circuit, which was lit up like a welcoming Christmas tree in the cold darkness. At that moment the fuel ran out and

A-Apple's starboard engine stopped. They were at 1,000ft. For a moment the roar of the hot parched engine hung in the air like a brutal booming echo, then it was gone, replaced by an uncanny quiet that seemed to soft pedal the crew's potentially catastrophic situation. The pilot could only say, brusquely: 'The engine's cut, we've got to land. Hold on!'

They held on desperately, tensely, as Jackson banked steeply and dived to maintain air speed. A stall at 1,000ft would lead very swiftly to a perfectly good Wellington with a u/s engine being turned into a heap of scrap and five telegrams having to be sent by the squadron commander to the families of young men who would be almost unidentifiable. They had been at the wrong end of the runway for landing and Jackson headed for the other side of the airfield, but he did not have enough air speed and had to turn before reaching it. He was attempting a wheels-up landing on the grass beside the runway, which had been cleared for this emergency landing.

The hissing sound of the wind reached Dick Morris who remained sitting in his little navigator's compartment, clinging with white knuckles to a metal stanchion, unable to see what was happening. Perhaps that was no bad thing. Vickers-Armstrong's engineer Barnes Wallis had not designed the Wellington for gliding. And although Morris and the others had great faith in their pilot, this was only their fifth operation. They had never run out of fuel before and the skipper would certainly have been on the carpet had he used a training flight to practise a landing without engines. Their lives were in his hands and the most critical moment would be pulling out of the dive beside the lighted runway. The pilot knew what he was doing even if he had never trained for this unnerving manoeuvre. He had to get everything absolutely perfect. There wouldn't be a second chance. To his right, Bill Montgomery waited tensely, ready to leap to his assistance.

'It took about thirty seconds to get down after the engine cut,' recalls Morris. 'We could have stalled at any time and that would have been curtains for us all. But Jacko maintained control. We flattened out at the last second, no more than ten feet off the ground. We struck and slid. There was a terrible ripping sound as the bottom of the fuselage was torn off and a torrent of earth came pouring in at the front. Jacko and Monty's boots were filled with dirt. Dirt was no problem. If we'd landed on the metalled runway the guts of the Wellington would have been gouged out and we might easily have been badly injured or killed.'

Then someone said in a mixture of relief and disbelief, echoing everybody's feelings: 'Christ! We're down and all right!'

Morris again: 'Although we had run out of fuel there was still a danger of fire, there was plenty of petrol vapour and stuff. The four of us at the front of the aircraft got out as quickly as we could. We thought we'd made a pretty speedy exit until we saw our rear gunner, Ted Hook, galloping 100 yards away. He hadn't had time to get out of his turret through the fuselage. He had sensibly turned his turret sideways in good time so the doors at the back could open on to the ground. He got out and ran like hell. It was brilliant piloting, but afterwards we agreed we were bloody lucky. Our zig-zagging course had forced us to take an extra fifty miles to get back to Amendola. The starboard prop was smashed. The port prop was at an angle when we landed, missed the ground and wasn't damaged. I believe the 500 miles from Varese was the longest ever flown by a Wellington on one engine. Jacko was given an immediate DFC for his determination and skill. The aircraft was repaired and used for training flights.'

They did four more operations on Wellingtons before being converted to Liberators. The last of these was on 17 April 1944 to Plovdiv, Bulgaria's second major city, where they were to bomb railway marshalling yards. They took off in Wellington LN919 at 8.20pm, carrying six high explosive bombs of 500lb and two of 250lb. They headed east across the Adriatic, towards the Albanian coast and onwards across mountains to Bulgaria. They came down to 7,000ft as they approached Plovdiv, which lies in the valley of the river Maritsa.

It was a clear night, Montgomery easily identified the target and released the bombs at around midnight. Sporadic flak was flying as they turned away from the city and, without warning, the port engine failed. There was no fire and they believed it to be engine failure. The bomber began losing height. This time there was no way back to Amendola. Reduced to a single engine the Wellington could not climb the long range of mountains ahead, whose peaks touched 6,000ft. There was not enough fuel to go round them. Since the trip to Varese they had planned what should be done if they lost an engine while bombing in the Balkans and beyond. The crew agreed that, if possible, they should head for Turkey, the one neutral country in the area.

'As we continued to lose height Jacko called for a course to the Turkish border,' Morris recalls. 'Luckily, my maps showed in one corner about one inch of the border. I was quickly able to work out a new course along the valley of the river Maritsa, away from the mountains and towards the piece of Turkey which showed on my map. Our height stabilised at 1,500ft and we settled down for the hundred-mile trip to Turkey. Having no maps of Turkey and not knowing what kind of mountainous terrain might be beyond the border Jacko decided we should all bale out as soon as we crossed the Turkish border.'

With the exception of Morris the crew agreed that having got them into Turkey, their navigator should bale out first. They had received no training for this, their first parachute jump and Morris pulled the ripcord as soon as he had cleared the escape hatch. To his horror the ripcord and handle all came away in his hand. This was normal, but no one had told him and two seconds later the canopy opened, pulling him up with a jerk. Ward and Hook followed him down as Montgomery finished clipping on his skipper's parachute. The bomb aimer then created problems for himself by trying to go out backwards instead of the recommended headfirst. The six-footer got himself into a muddle with his backside stuck in the hatch being whipped by the slipstream. He untangled himself, dived out, quickly followed by his skipper. The Wellington flew on at 1,200ft and probably crashed into the Black Sea.

Morris hit the ground heavily, but he was uninjured. He had landed beside a stream in open countryside and could see no signs of life. He hid the parachute and harness under bushes and began walking away from the border. It was 2am. The sky was starlit but there was no moon. The ground was rough but flat and sometime later he found a lane which led into a small village. He was greeted by the barking of dogs, but no people. It was 4am and he was tired. A pole, with a flag fluttering from it, stood outside a small building and suggested officials of some sort might be inside. He struck several matches in an attempt to identify the flag, which he thought was Turkish. He began knocking on the door and the sound echoed eerily through the sleeping village of Gillobilu, but nothing happened until a light went on, a curtain was tweaked half open and he saw a dim figure waving angrily at him to go away. Morris continued to knock, shouting he was English. The door was eventually opened by the sleepy village policeman.

Morris again: 'When he knew I was with the RAF he became very friendly, produced thick Turkish coffee and cigarettes and invited me to rest. Not surprisingly, my arrival had awakened Gillobilu and for the next couple of hours there was a steady stream of grinning villagers with their children, peeping round the door to inspect me. By 6am it was getting light and I had become worried about the rest of the crew. An hour later I saw a group of men approaching with Geoff in the middle. He was in animated conversation with everyone. No one knew what he was saying and he couldn't understand them, but they were having a fine time. At midday Monty and Ted arrived on donkeys, with a friendly escort, but there was no news about the skipper. In the afternoon we were taken by a military truck under guard to the nearest garrison border town of Kesan. Here we were delighted to be reunited with Jacko, who was our only casualty. He had a sore foot from walking after losing a boot when he baled out. We were given comfortable accommodation in the barracks and that evening met the governor of the area and other dignitaries at a formal reception dinner: seven courses with drinks and cigarettes between each course and lasting about three hours.'

Two days later they were in Istanbul, billeted at a military barracks where they met a German tank commander who had deserted from the Russian front. On 22 April the crew were moved to Ankara to be interned. The tented base at Amendola was a fading memory as they moved into the Yeni Hotel. Security was lax and although they had to observe a curfew from 10pm to 10am, life became comfortable, even pampered. They were given pocket money by the British Embassy and breakfast in bed by the hotel.

'We quickly settled into the routine of internment and began to enjoy ourselves,' Morris recalls. 'There was a sizeable group of British nationals working in Ankara and as soon as they learned of our arrival we received a flood of invitations. The first, a formal lunch, came from the British ambassador, Sir Knatchbull-Huggesen and his wife, at which we managed the gaffe of drinking from finger bowls. Life continued very pleasantly with good food and new friends, but it could not last. The Allies were supplying arms to Turkey and in return the Turkish government periodically repatriated Allied internees. On 18 May we left on the first leg of our return journey to Amendola. We arrived on 4 June and rejoined our squadron.

'While in Turkey we all agreed we'd had enough of flying in a bomber with one engine and decided to apply on our return for a transfer to four-engine aircraft. This we did as soon as we got back and three days later we flew to Lydda, Palestine, to start an immediate conversion course to four-engine B24 Liberator bombers. Postings were delayed but eventually we were sent back to Foggia on 16 September to complete our tour of operations with 178 Squadron.'

Dick Morris and Bill Montgomery were both commissioned in November 1944 and each received a DFC at the end of their tour early in 1945.

CHAPTER FIFTEEN

THE LONG DROP

Most aircrew were familiar with terror during the bomber war. Few admitted their fears and those who did and could not carry on were branded cowards and had stamped on their RAF records the dreaded LMF (Lacking Moral Fibre). They were stripped of their ranks and given the dirtiest jobs, cleaning toilets and sweeping roads. Their noses were rubbed daily into the bitter ignominy of failure, for while the RAF refused to accept cowardice, it did not understand that men's levels of endurance were all different.

Pilot Neil Scott, a married man of twenty-two, fair-haired, tall and slim, knew fear when flying into battle but, like most aircrew, he was able to conceal it within his mind. The important thing was to concentrate on the job in hand, so one's apprehension became a stimulus to effective action rather than a disabling panic.

'Chaps handled fear in different ways but nobody would ever admit it,' he says. 'Some people seemed to take it calmly, but you never knew what went on beneath the surface. I was, I suppose, a nervous type, and found flying exhilarating but fearful. Flying in the war was a perilous business, but I did what needed to be done. I was surprised I got so far. I was not a natural born aviator.'

Despite the strain Scott, the eldest of five children, from Newcastle-upon-Tyne, was reluctant to go on his regular seven days' leave every six weeks.

He says: 'It's not true to say I didn't want leave. Yet when I was away I felt that life was going on in the squadron and I wanted to be there and had no business being away. I might lose my touch and need to relearn how to fly. It may seem a curious thing to say but I always wanted desperately to get back to Oulton to keep the squadron effort going.'

The most exciting time at RAF Oulton, despite numerous hairy moments on the airfield, was when the film *The Wicked Lady* was being made on location there, at Blickling Hall, the squadron headquarters. Scott recalls the embarrassment of sitting next to glamorous actress Margaret Lockwood in the officers' mess, nursing a drink, trying to think of something to say.

Prewar, Scott had been a clerk – and secretary of his local banch of the Young Communist League. An angry young man, who wanted a more just society, and saw the Nazis as the barbarous enemies of freedom, he flew Boeing's four-engine B-17 Flying Fortresses, but did not carry bombs. These Fortresses were based at RAF Oulton, Norfolk, with 214 (Federated Malay States) Squadron. It was a radar countermeasures squadron. Its job was to jam enemy radar and night fighter communications, creating maximum confusion among the Germans while giving the main bombing force opportunity to arrive more safely at their appointed target. Its aim was also to reduce the heavy losses which threatened to cripple the whole bomber offensive.

'The Fortress was given this job rather than the Lancaster because the B-17's bomb bay, which carried the equipment, was inside the fuselage,' says Scott. 'Our apparatus included a big pressure tank, which needed height inside the aircraft. The total weight of the equipment was around three tons. About one-third of our trips was with the main force on a specific target. The others were spoofs of various kinds. You threw out window, operated your jamming devices and weaved about the sky trying to look like several hundred aircraft. The Germans were deceived by this and sent up their night fighters to defend what they thought you were aiming for, while the Main Force went elsewhere. At the appropriate time we switched everything off and turned back to base. The Mosquito night fighters from our group then went after the Germans who were looking for a non-existent Main Force. It was a nice bit of timing.

'Although we didn't carry bombs we all felt intense keenness, seldom expressed, about backing up the chaps who actually did the bombing by doing our diversionary and jamming work at all costs to help keep down bomber losses. The evidence was that we were succeeding. Our own losses were less than the squadron had previously suffered while on Main Force duties with Stirlings in 3 Group. There was a brief rumour that window sorties might only count as a half operation. The loss of two of our crews in succession was enough to see off that threat. Besides, our jamming equipment weighed the same as a heavy bomb load. Not only did we take it to the target we had to bring it back too.'

Although the Fortresses of 214 Squadron in 100 Group did not bomb, they were still shot at, subjected to intense scrutiny by searchlights and preyed on by German night fighters. The great clutter of jamming equipment included an apparatus codenamed Jostle, which had a large tall high pressure tank and was carried amidships in the bomb bay. Jostle jammed radio telephone communications between German ground controllers and their night fighters. Piperack, the other device, blurred the image of the night fighters' radar predictors when they were trying to home in on the Allied bomber force. They returned with it to base at an invariable 155mph, unable to gleefully kick up their heels like the Main Force who had been liberated from their bomb loads. The night-flying Fortresses were armed with six .5in Browning machine guns and carried a crew of ten men.

Although Flying Officer Neil Scott had already completed thirty-one operations, most of his crew were still one sortie away from completing their first tour of thirty ops when they returned from an attack on Leuna, near Merseburg, early on the morning of 16 January 1945. It had been an exhausting eight-hour trip and they had been diverted to Tangmere, near Chichester, because fog had closed in at Oulton.

Scott again: 'We slept at Tangmere for an hour or two, got up very early, returned to base and had a few more hours' sleep there. We went to the crewroom later and learned we were on the battle order again that night. It surprised us a bit, we thought we might have had a night off. I joked about it but our flight commander gave us the usual flannel about us being an experienced crew and said it was a hard life. What really made my heart sink was finding out which aircraft we had been allocated. You did not have your own aircraft on 214 Squadron, you were given whatever was available. I'd flown all sorts of aircraft, none like KJ103 M-Mike, a Fortress III. We'd been in this aircraft ten days before for a window throwing mission on the Dutch-German border. It somehow lacked guts. The engines delivered full power, but it wouldn't climb. It seemed as if it didn't want to go. I couldn't really say what it was, so I reported it and presumed it would be looked at and put right, but I wasn't happy to see it again, especially for this long trip. Our squadron letters were BU. We regarded M-Mike as the BUM kite.'

Before Scott embarked on his first operation, the thirty trips needed to complete a normal first tour seemed such a long way into the future, almost belonging to science fantasy. No one knew how long the war would last, but Scott equated it to old age, which he did not expect to reach. They had agreed as a crew to go on to do forty-five ops in one tour after being promised a choice of any subsequent posting.

'None of us in the crew talked about our pasts,' says Scott. 'None of us had much of a past. We talked about the present, about survival. I feel ashamed that we knew so little about each other. We just knew what we could do with the aircraft. The important thing was: "Are we on the battle order tonight? If we are, where will it be? Will we survive and is anybody going to the pub tonight?" We lived in our own little bubble of a very circumscribed existence. Your life was devoted to the next operation, you couldn't see very much farther than that.'

On this occasion the squadron was to support 231 Lancasters and six Mosquitoes which were attacking a synthetic oil plant at Brüx in western Czechoslovakia. One Lancaster would be lost, but the raid was a success, causing a serious setback to the plant's oil production.

Scott's Fortress was to switch on its jamming equipment at H-minus 5 – five minutes before the bombing was due to start. It would have to circle the target for ten minutes, taking their chance with the flak and fighters in the same way as their comrades in the Main Force. RCM Fortresses were to join the circuit every five minutes, overlapping each other's presence over Brüx to cover the whole raid, before switching off their apparatus and heading home.

They took off about 4pm into a mist which enveloped the end of the runway. Heavily laden with jamming equipment and 2,316 gallons of fuel, with auxiliary Tokio tanks, Scott soon realised this was the old M-Mike, nothing had been done to sort out its problems. The Fortress dragged itself down the runway and he had to haul it off at the last minute. Normally, a Fortress III floated off the ground, even with extra fuel, not M-Mike, which had really proved itself to be the squadron bum.

Fences, trees and a railway line flashed by below as M-Mike staggered reluctantly into the sky and the flight engineer, Flight Sergeant Dick Willing, sitting beside Scott, murmured: 'You did well there, skipper.'

Willing, was, at thirty-one, the oldest of the crew. He was also, at 6ft 3in, the tallest man on the squadron and it was difficult for him to pull his long legs into the Fortress. A former guardsman and Metropolitan policeman, he was married with several children. He had joined the RAF to learn everything he could about engines. Flying Officer Bob Houston, a married man, from London, Ontario, was the navigator. Tall, slim, quiet and unassuming, he was a restraining foil to his ebullient cousin Terry McKee, who was also in Scott's crew. Both were in their mid-twenties. They had debated whether cousins should serve in the same aircraft. Bomber Command frowned on two brothers flying together, but Houston and McKee were keen to do so. Flying Officer McKee originated from the same city as his cousin. He was one of the Fortress's special operators who worked the jamming equipment. He was always cheerful, even in the most alarming situation, which he would find some way of lightening with a smile and a joke. He and the other special operator, Tasmanian Flying Officer Rick Hardman, had both trained as bomb aimers.

In Scott's words: 'Rick was a good example of an Australian. He was a tough wiry compact sort of bloke who didn't care a bugger about anybody.'

McKee and Hardman operated their apparatus from the cramped office they shared with wireless operator Flight Sergeant David 'Taffy' Lewis. Lewis, a former apprentice electrician, from Pontardulais, South Wales, presented a small, neat and tidy figure, whose work was meticulous. His training had been exceptional for he was a ground staff wireless operator before volunteering for aircrew. Mid-upper gunner was Yorkshireman Sergeant John Smith, always known as Little Smithy because of his diminutive appearance. Smith was nineteen. He was due to be rear gunner that night, but Scott allowed him to switch positions with Sergeant John 'Chalkie' Chalk. It was a decision which would return to haunt Scott. Chalk, a Londoner, thick set of medium height, was calm and self-possessed.

The Fortress also carried two waist gunners. Sergeant Bob Knickle, from Halifax, Nova Scotia, was a small jolly man with dark hair and dark eyes, whose chief concerns were the maintenance of his .5in Browning machine gun and whether there would be beer in the sergeants' mess that night and girls in the nearby town of Aylsham. His partner was Sergeant Bernard Lunn, eighteen, who had briefly been a van driver's assistant after leaving school in Wednesbury, Staffordshire. He was inclined to portliness which caused problems during ditching drills. Lunn was so slow he was forced to the back of the queue where the affable Chalk was waiting to give him a heave out. The waist gunners operated swivel-mounted .5in Browning machine guns. They were exposed to the cold after removing perspex panels through which they were also employed to heave out hundreds of packets of window, an exhausting job while wearing oxygen masks. But that night, M-Mike was not carrying window.

As they crossed the English coast, M-Mike's four Wright R-1820-97 air-cooled radial engines were making heavy weather of Neil Scott's attempt to gain altitude. Each of 214 Squadron's four Fortresses had different ETAs over the target and left Oulton at regular intervals. M-Mike was ahead of the main force, slightly astern of the Pathfinders.

Scott was pleased that other aircraft no longer nosed up inquisitively to inspect his Fortress. On earlier trips the black Fortresses had been regarded as very rare birds and more than one startled pilot believed them to be German aircraft infiltrating the Allied flotilla.

As M-Mike struggled to gain height in a fair imitation of an ailing pensioner attempting to climb impossibly steep and rickety stairs, Scott worried that the Fortress might be piling up problems for them. The pilot knew he must remain calm, but this was not always easy when a chap's imagination was trying to persuade him that the next thing to go wrong might be an engine cutting or a vital piece of the aircraft falling off. Scott had a lively imagination which was often invaded by a number of mischief-making elements. He held long sometimes hair-raising conversations with himself in the privacy of his mind to relieve the boredom on a long run. M-Mike's engines crawled towards the stars, but at least they didn't falter. The tail wind en route to Brüx was stronger than had been forecast and despite M-Mike's slothful attitude they were, surprisingly, ahead of time.

They were drifting over Germany when navigator Bob Houston reported: 'We're well ahead of time, skipper, we'd better lose five minutes.'

'We waited until we reached a spot where there were no fighter bases and no potential problems and turned to port to do a short dog leg,' recalls Scott. 'We came back on course and on time. M-Mike needed more engine, it seemed to be all right straight and level, it just wouldn't climb.'

The Fortress had taken an age to claw its way up to 21,000ft. It had to operate 1,000ft above the main force, otherwise its circling of the target might have led to some interesting confrontations. The Pathfinders' flares were just floating down, illuminating the oil plant as the jamming equipment was switched on aboard M-Mike, which was the first Fortress to arrive over the target. As they began the perilous circling over Brüx, the Main Force roared in below them, bombs started falling and fires erupted on the ground. Flak began streaking up from the German gunners who had held their fire until the first bombs began falling.

A voice, expressing apprehension and astonishment, spluttered over the intercom. It was one of the special operators. 'I'm sorry, skipper, but neither Jostle nor Piperack is working.'

The news jolted Scott who replied brusquely: 'For God's sake, that's the only reason we came all this way. Do you think you can do something about it?'

Terry McKee and Rick Hardman enlisted the expertise of wireless operator supremo Taffy Lewis to help them search for the fault in the vast array of equipment as Scott continued to fly in the five mile circle, grinding his teeth. It soon became clear that the three men's task was the equivalent of searching for one particular grain of sand on Blackpool beach at dead of night with a candle.

They had been circling uselessly for about eight minutes when back came the report: 'Sorry skipper, there's nothing we can do with it. The bloody gear is u/s.'

Bombs were still falling as they turned away from Brüx with heavy hearts. The grindingly miserable journey aboard M-Mike had all been wasted effort.

Scott recalls: 'The apparatus was supposed to have been checked, but because we had arrived back late that morning after being diverted to Tangmere there had been no chance for us to do an air test which would have revealed any problems. We went to the aircraft before takeoff and assumed everything was in working order, including the kite. We could not test the jamming equipment on the way to Czechoslovakia because it was not supposed to be switched on until we were over the target. It was extremely frustrating. We left Brüx with our tails between our legs.'

As they cleared the bombing area M-Mike was shaken viciously by a ferocious whooomph!

The engineer said anxiously: 'We've been hit, skipper.'

Scott replied in a tone, not brimming with confidence: 'I think it was a near miss or another aircraft's slipstream.'

He recalls: 'I asked the lads to check the aircraft and they all reported back saying there was no sign of anything. We never did know if we had been hit and, if we had, whether the fuel tanks had been holed. What we did know was that on the way back we were faced by this powerful headwind and the wretched aeroplane needed more power to keep its speed up. It was speed we didn't have. We made slow progress. We had 155mph on the clock, but when you have a 60mph wind against you you're doing less than 100mph ground speed with several hundred miles to go. Luckily, we didn't meet any opposition over Germany although we did spot areas of flak where there might have been another raid or a bomber which had strayed off track on the way back. We were concerned about being a lone straggler. I tried to maintain our height at 21,000ft, but we were using a lot of fuel and came down gradually on the way home. The engineer was constantly doing calculations about fuel consumption. The navigator gave me a course to the emergency airfield at Woodbridge in case of problems. We decided to review the situation there. In emergency we'd put down at the Suffolk airfield. By the time we had crossed the North Sea, losing height, the engineer said we would just make it back to base.'

After crossing the Norfolk coast at 2,000ft, it was decided a few miles from Woodbridge that they could press on to Oulton. Dick Willing, the engineer, was confident they would get there, although there wouldn't be much fuel splashing around in the tanks when they landed.

'The fatal bit came into operation as we drew near to Oulton,' Scott recalls. 'A few weeks previously one of the Fortresses had landed here, quite safely it was thought, with three green lights showing its undercarriage was down and locked. On touching down the undercarriage collapsed. It was discovered that although the green lights showed, the undercart was not fully locked down. So the instructions were now that the mid-upper gunner, normally Chalkie Chalk, was to take the undercarriage emergency handle and wind it down another few turns. He just had to nip out of his turret and the handle was on the side of the fuselage. But tonight, Chalkie was in the rear turret.'

Scott called up John Smith on the intercom: 'Skipper to mid-upper, put the last few turns for the undercart, according to the instructions.'

As Smith climbed down from his turret they were delighted to see the airfield runway lights at Oulton ahead. This had been a miserable trip, they would be pleased to see the end of it.

Approaching the runway, Scott called up the control tower. 'I haven't got much fuel. Please give me an early turn.'

They replied: 'All right, turn number one.'

Scott turned tidily on to the cross-wind leg as Smith reported: 'I can't manage the handle, skipper, I'm not sure it's fully down.'

Scott, running out of time, exclaimed: 'No! no! you've got to wind it down.' He heard the anguished panting of the gunner striving in vain to move the handle.

In the rear turret, John Chalk, sensing trouble, said: 'I'll come and do it, skipper. I know the knack for turning it.'

As Chalk left his turret and stumbled forward through the fuselage in the dark, the Fortress was turning in to the approach and Dick Willing, the engineer, was calmly calling out air speeds: '135, 130 —' while the pilot looked out for runway lights and glide path indicators.

'I intended to cross the aerodrome boundary at 120mph,' Scott recalls. 'Everything seemed to be all right except we hadn't wound down this last bit of the undercarriage. I didn't intend collapsing on the runway and Chalkie was still scrambling forward. In order to give him time to wind it down I called up control and said: "I haven't enough fuel to go round again, but I'm going to make a rate one turn to starboard on the approach to give my gunner time to wind down the undercarriage." Control said that was okay.

'In retrospect, that was fatal. I would have done better, in view of the shortage of fuel after eight and a half hours' flying, to have said "Bugger it, we'll go straight in" and it would probably have been all right. We were turning in towards the final approach and committed, and this was an unusual manoeuvre. I commenced a rate one turn with the flaps down and Chalkie had made the last turns of the undercarriage handle. The engineer was still calling out our speed. Everyone else had gone to their crash positions for landing behind the main spar, except the navigator and his cousin who were in the nose. Somehow they didn't manage to get themselves out in time.'

At about 500ft M-Mike fell like a lump of concrete out of the sky. The fateful extra turn to make sure the undercarriage was locked in position had consumed the last spoonfuls of petrol. The aircraft disintegrated with a shattering kerumph as it hit the ground just short of the runway and burst into flames which began spreading rapidly through the debris. An ambulance and fire engine sped across the airfield. They found the body of Terry McKee who had been killed instantly. Bob Houston, his cousin, who had been carefully putting the finishing touches to his log, was seriously injured. Neil Scott was unconscious in his crumpled seat with severe concussion, head injuries and numerous cuts and bruises. He would remember nothing of that terrible plunge.

The other seven men staggered out of the wreckage in fearful shock which totally concentrated their minds on leaving the burning Fortress before they were incinerated. They crawled away from the aircraft until forced to press themselves against the ground to avoid being hit by flying ammunition which had been set off by the fire. No one else was injured except Dick Willing, whose face had been badly gashed. The Fortress lacked the full British-type safety harness, having only a lap strap which allowed the upper body to swing forward and strike the instrument panel.

Later, the engineer told his skipper that, just before the crash, he was conscious of a diminution in sound as one engine, then another cut. It was possible that all engines had stopped before they struck the ground. Willing found there were no sides to the Fortress and walked out, feeling lucky to be alive. The three men left aboard, hidden by the wreckage, were carefully removed by the crash crew as firemen put out the flames which were threatening to consume them. Both wings had broken off, only the starboard tailplane stood up at a defiantly jaunty angle from the mangled wreckage. No one would ever know what the problem had been in the jamming equipment or why M-Mike had been such a pig to fly.

Scott believes his life was saved by his parachute. He says: 'I was wearing a long American back parachute. Normally chaps had a harness to which you clipped your 'chute. I always thought if anything happened and I was last out I probably wouldn't find the damned parachute in the dark. I managed to get an American one which I had on my back throughout each trip. I felt reassured, knowing that if we were blown up or badly shot up I should be all right. That night my parachute had burned. All that was left when I regained consciousness in Norwich Hospital two days later was the ripcord attached to some charred fragments, which were given to me. If I hadn't been wearing the parachute it would have been me on fire.'

Bob Houston never recovered from serious head and face injuries and received a 100 per cent disablement pension from the Canadian Government. Dick Willing's face was stitched up and he returned to the Metropolitan police. The Australian, Rick Hardman, joined another crew to complete his tour and was awarded a DFC. Taffy Lewis became a successful insurance broker in Swansea. After a long period in hospital Neil Scott returned to 214 Squadron cleared to fly non-operational, UK only at a maximum 10,000ft. These restrictions did not prevent him from applying to join Tiger Force in the Far East, but before the force was assembled, two atom bombs were dropped on Japan, who surrendered. Scott was not disappointed, there had been enough killing.

He says of the bombing campaign: 'Anyone who has seen Auschwitz, as I have, can have no doubt that any means, however imperfect, were justified in bringing an end to such an inhuman terrorist regime as the Nazis imposed on Europe, and had in store for us. It was a sin, yes, as all war is a sin – "Thou shalt not kill" – but not a crime. I feel privileged to have played my small part in it.'

Neil Scott went to Newcastle University where he obtained a BA degree in politics and economics, flying occasionally in the University Air Squadron. He eventually became head of the Careers Advisory Service at Nottingham University, and was later awarded an OBE.

CHAPTER SIXTEEN

THE WRECKAGE THAT 'FLEW' TO EARTH

Halifax LK628 Judy Garland climbed into the patchy cloud above Leeming in north Yorkshire at 7.24pm on 6 September 1943, joining 403 other heavy bombers to attack Munich. There was no happy stage-managed performance for Judy that night. The crew had an uneventful trip to the target, then Judy was shot down seconds before they could bomb the German city. The aircraft's destruction and the remarkable escape of the survivors is one of the more amazing stories of the Second World War.

They had been to Mannheim the night before, flying EB241. There was nothing untoward about this operation except their replacement gunner, Sergeant Henry Jackson, a Canadian, fell asleep in his rear turret. The exhausted crew slept in at Leeming until around 12.30pm and went to the sergeants' mess for lunch. They were joined by their skipper, 22-year-old Pilot Officer Billy Biggs, who said he had been told they must fly to Munich in a different aircraft, LK-628. Another less experienced pilot had returned from Mannheim with the fairly new Halifax because he couldn't get airspeed.

Biggs told them: 'We've been asked to see what's wrong with it.' This was not good news, but there was nothing they could do about it. Biggs, newly commissioned, had moved into the officers' mess earlier that day. The men belonged to 427 Squadron, known as Lion Squadron after being adopted by MGM Studios in Hollywood. Several of its aircraft were named after American film stars. The squadron was in 6 Group which was equipped and had its running costs paid for by the Canadian Government.

Biggs had been awarded the DFM for a trip to Mannheim the previous month when his bomber had been attacked by a German fighter. Stocky, 5ft 8in, he had a good sense of humour, but there was a more serious and dark side to his character. As he was leaving home in Burton, South Wirral, at the end of his last leave, Biggs sombrely told his sister she would never see him again.

A trainee pilot flew as 'second dickey' on his first operational flight beside Biggs. He was a Canadian, Sergeant Bob Dresser. The navigator was Flight Sergeant Joe Read, who spent every spare moment with his girlfriend in Durham. Wireless operator Flight Sergeant Les Moyler, of St Albans, sustained a slight wound from shrapnel in his shoulder on the first Mannheim trip. Sergeant Jack Elliott's family owned a fish and chip shop in Leeds. At spare weekends several of the crew often piled into Biggs's old car to spend carefree weekends in Leeds, accompanying the flight engineer's sisters and female cousins to dances. Elliott, who was always smiling, and Moyler were both awarded DFMs after the trip when their skipper was similarly decorated.

Fair-haired Flight Sergeant Alf Richards, the bomb aimer, came from Truro, Cornwall. He was nineteen, the same age as mid-upper gunner Flight Sergeant Harry McLean, a powerfully-built blue-eyed youngster from Portchester, Hampshire, who had a quick temper and did not suffer fools gladly. He had been an apprentice shipbuilder before volunteering for aircrew. His father was a Royal Navy chief petty officer who was on leave when war was declared. McLean recalls meeting a friend at the end of his street after Neville Chamberlain's 'This country is at war with Germany' speech on 3 September 1939 and gazing into the sky, awaiting the arrival of the Luftwaffe. They were disappointed when nothing happened. Rear gunner was a spare bod, Canadian Sergeant Henry Jackson, who looked older than his twenty-two years. Their regular gunner, Flight Sergeant Bobby Fisher, of the Royal Canadian Air Force, from San Diego, was in London joining the United States Army Air Force (USAAF) before returning to the squadron.

They found out what was wrong with LK628 as soon as they went to the aircraft before takeoff. The pitot head, which was part of the speedometer system, had been bent downwards, consequently registering the wrong airspeed in the cockpit. This was a common problem and one of them bent it back. The pitot head was fixed under the bomber's nose, high off the ground. It was covered by a canvas hood at dispersal to stop dust and grit being blown into it. Removing it was difficult. One man was usually hoisted on another's shoulders and snatched off the cover, sometimes bending it.

At takeoff LK628's port outer engine failed to give maximum boost and the aircraft swung about, but Biggs managed to get them away safely. The Handley Page Halifax, with its four Rolls-Royce Merlin engines, was popular among Leeming aircrews, who admired its robustness.

Harry McLean said: 'We weren't waiting for the Lancaster on our squadron. We were looking forward to the Mark III Halifax which had Bristol radial engines. There was nothing wrong with the Merlins, but an air-cooled Bristol engine would get you home if half the cylinders were shot off. The Halifax could withstand far more of a hammering than a Lancaster. We loved them.'

This was McLean's twenty-fourth sortie. He recalls: 'I always claim we were worked too hard. You needed time to unwind between operations. We were tired setting off for Munich, not in peak condition after the previous night's op. You didn't sleep well after a sortie, kept awake for quite a while by nervous reaction. It was very tense on the morning of an operation. The word came out around lunchtime whether or not you were flying, then you'd go out and check over the kite. The tenseness didn't relax until you took off, but that could be a bit hairy. The main runway at Leeming ended at the Great North Road and there were a number of gaps in the hedge where wheels had gone through. That night we were carrying one 2,000lb bomb, and a load of incendiaries, 56 of 30lb and 540 four-pounders. We were briefed to bomb the BMW works and told the engines for Hitler's V-weapons were being made there. The month before we had bombed Peenemünde on the Baltic coast, where the V2 rocket was being developed.

'Our route to Munich had been plotted to fly directly over the capital for the first time to enable the Londoners to hear what their own bombers sounded like. We had also been briefed that it was possible a unit of the USAAF would be flying their Fortresses in our stream as "aerial gunships" and to keep a careful watch for them. This information did not please us, but we didn't see any. Our trip nearly ended over the capital when we almost collided head on with a Lancaster. It was about fifty feet above us. I didn't see it coming, just heard the loud "schow!" as it passed over us. I saw the dark mass going away. It was probably someone in a bit of trouble who, without thinking, had simply turned round, instead of dropping his height gradually and turning when he was well under the stream.'

The cloud thickened to eight to 9/10ths over Germany and LK628 was flying along the top of it at 14,000ft. It was tiring as they passed in and out of thick cloud. Heavy cloud over Munich prevented the Pathfinders' ground- and sky-markers being very effective. Many frustrated crews could only bomb on a timed run from the Ammersee, a lake twenty-one miles south-west of the Bavarian capital.

McLean again: 'We had been routed past Munich and were to do a reciprocal course, bombing as we passed over the city on the way home. We commenced the bombing run, always a tense time as we had to fly straight and level for four or five minutes. At this time we were at our most vulnerable. About two minutes into the run a stream of heavy tracer passed astern, diagonally from the starboard quarter, away across to the port bow. Although this was roughly at our height, it was directed in a completely different direction. I reported to Billy: "There's a stream of tracer just gone by, across our stern. I don't think it was meant for us, but I can't see the Jerry. Will you weave?" This manoeuvre would have destroyed our bombing run, meaning we would have to make a complete circuit of Munich and try again, never a popular move among aircrew.

'Billy replied: "We're on the bombing run", to which I replied sharply: "But I can't see the bugger, for Christ's sake do something."'

The pilot replied: 'All right, Mac,' in a tone that suggested he would abandon the bombing run, but it was too late. The German fighter fired again from astern, hitting the Halifax in the overload fuel tank. This was situated in the rear of the bomb bay, immediately under McLean's mid-upper turret. Massive flames roared up around the side of the bomber.

McLean was surrounded by flames and there was an overpowering stench of 100 octane aviation fuel. He bellowed: 'Billy, we've been hit in the overload tank. We'll never put this one out.'

'OK, Mac.' The pilot's reply was unruffled. 'Bale out, chaps. Good luck.'

'I believe the ammunition tanks, located in the front of my turret, had the same effect as armour plate and saved me from injury,' recalls McLean. 'I dropped out of the turret and saw flames pouring up through the fuselage floor, where my parachute was surrounded by flames. It was in a container and hadn't caught fire. I clipped it on and went to the rear door. I bent down to open it, but it seemed jammed.'

The gunner's next memory is of slithering out of unconsciousness and realising the bomber had been torn in half by a massive explosion. There was no sound except the eerie wail of a wind rushing through the rear section in which he was sprawled. Les Moyler lay heavily across McLean's legs and the pair of them were covered by ammunition belts which hung from the rear turret track. Moyler had been stationed in the back throwing out window, the strips of metal foil used as a radar jamming device. The Elsan toilet, which they rarely used, had emptied itself over them. The two men were trapped in a great useless steel coffin which was hurtling earthwards. They seemed either resigned or unaware of death which was rushing to meet them. Moyler was not wearing his parachute. There had been no time to collect it from near his seat at the front of the Halifax before the explosion.

McLean croaked: 'Les!' and Moyler replied: 'I'm here.' McLean said, more sharply: 'Lay off me, Les, for fuck's sake.' The wireless operator said, shortly: 'I can't.'

McLean could not avoid inhaling the petrol fumes and kept passing out for short periods. Although there was, lurking at the back of his mind, a small voice urging him to bale out he had neither the energy nor the inclination to move. He was comfortable just lying there. When he next came to he realised the aircraft was still falling and he wondered vaguely how far he was from the ground. He prayed for his death to be swift then went out again. Awake once more, McLean's thoughts were confused and he believed it might be possible to survive the crash if he braced himself. He hung grimly, briefly, on to the ammunition tracks, until losing his grip. There was only three feet of cold metal between him and the torn edge of the fuselage, which led into the black sky. Out there was the chance of life. In this unreal tumbling coffin there could only be death. The fuselage suddenly rolled and Moyler was flung off McLean's legs. McLean crawled weakly towards the sky and the advantages it offered to a man wearing a parachute.

'Whether I scrambled out or was thrown out I will never know but I found myself out in the air, falling,' McLean recalls. 'I pulled the ripcord without any bother and must have passed out again for I have no memory of the 'chute opening.'

As his head began to clear, the front half of the Halifax passed 400ft in front of him, pointing straight down like a rocket, with flames streaming from the wings. He couldn't understand why the front of the bomber, which contained five men, four engines, the full bomb load and fuel was following the lighter section down. There was an extensive dark patch on the ground, no more than 1,000ft below, which he recognised as woodland. A few heartbeats later his parachute caught in the branch of a tree. He dangled there wondering if he was alive or dead.

'I must have hung there for a few minutes while my head cleared,' says McLean. 'I looked around and saw a tree trunk about five feet in front of me. Some way off dogs were barking. I started swinging myself towards the trunk which I gripped with my feet, discovering that one of my flying boots had come off. There was a loud crack and I fell a few feet, but remained hanging. I tried swinging again. There was another crack and I fell to the ground. I lay there in absolute bloody agony. I'd fallen on my back across an exposed tree root. I got up to a sitting position and looked around. It was dark but I could see I had landed in fir trees on a slope leading down to a valley. I was about ten yards from the bottom where I saw the edge of a flat field. I took off my remaining flying boot, freed my electrically-heated inner canvas shoe and used this to support the foot which had lost the boot. I hauled myself up the tree trunk and released the parachute harness, but didn't try to roll it up and conceal it as most of the canopy was still hanging in the tree. I heard dogs again and, by the sound of them, much bigger dogs. After hurting my back I was afraid if the animals found me they might knock me to the ground. I needed to hide. It was obvious I needed medical attention. I decided to walk until I was apprehended, without actually seeking to give myself up.'

McLean moved with difficulty, for the pain in his back was excruciating. He hugged himself in a not entirely successful effort to ease the torment and shuffled slowly out of the wood, rolled agonizingly under a barbed wire fence and on to a rough footpath through marshy ground over which a mist was forming. The path turned into a track which led to a field where he hoped to find a thick hedge to creep into. Then two dogs began barking from inside a nearby building, hidden by mist.

'I stood still,' says McLean. 'A door opened a few yards away and I could see a man silhouetted by the inside light. He called something and I replied: '*Ich bin Englische flieger.*' It was only later I thought he might have been shouting at his dogs. He came across to me and spoke. I didn't understand. My German was self-taught and very limited. He took me inside the house where I met his daughter, a woman of about thirty. Her father went to get help and she rubbed my back. I found out later it was probably the worst thing she could have done but, at the time, I was grateful. I remembered my escape kit which contained money, chocolate and other things and gave it to her. The farmer returned with a policeman to whom I gave my identity discs. My lucky charm, a tiny brass Lincoln imp, was attached to them and caused some curiosity.'

Two soldiers loaded McLean into an ambulance which stopped after a short distance to pick up Jack Elliott, the flight engineer, who had miraculously escaped from the crashed Halifax. He told the gunner his staggering story.

'He had been unable to bale out,' McLean relates, 'and came down in the front portion of the bomber which I had seen diving earthwards. He thought he was for the chop when it somehow flattened out before hitting the ground, almost like a crash landing. Jack had banged the back of his head sustaining a half inch cut. Slightly stunned, he got out through the back and started to walk away from the burning wreck, which still contained the bomb and incendiaries. It was an amazing escape. He didn't get far. Some time later he was picked up quite close to the wreck, still confused. He thought he had covered a fair distance from the Halifax, but he had been circling it in a daze. We spent the night in separate cells at Tutzing police station. I was in such pain I could not lie down, never mind sleep.'

Next morning the two airmen were taken by four Army officers in a Volkswagen open command car to the crash site at Monatshausen near Starberg, twelve miles south-west of Munich. During the journey they were not allowed to talk to each other. Nor did the Germans speak to them.

The two sections of the Halifax were about 250yd apart. The tail section was just off the road. The forward part, hidden among young trees, had escaped being torn to pieces. McLean was left alone in the car while Elliott went off with the Germans to identify the bodies of their comrades. There was no fear of McLean escaping. Still in terrible pain, he could hardly walk.

'After a while they all returned and we set off,' says McLean. 'The countryside was beautiful, very rural and it was a lovely day. At one point we passed a road sign to Dachau, but I knew nothing about the terrible concentration camp there. None of the German road signs appeared to have been dismantled as they were in Britain. I was unable to find out what they had seen at the crash site as Jack and I were still not allowed to talk. Eventually we arrived at a Luftwaffe training aerodrome. At first sight I thought they were flying Tiger Moths, but later noticed their biplanes had a pronounced swept back wing. They were Bücker Jungmeisters. We entered the guardroom where I immediately saw alongside a wall that the Germans had recovered our Gee radar box, the dinghy radio, which sent out an automatic SOS call when a handle was wound, and one of the bomber's two homing pigeons in its container. I imagine they wrung its neck for dinner.

'I was asked here if I would like to go to hospital, but thought I would be unwelcome among the victims of our bombing. I said I was prepared to wait for treatment until I got to a prison camp. A very large piece of sticking plaster was put around my upper body, just like a waistcoat. This was the only treatment I was ever to receive for my injury, apart from a tube of anti-neuralgia pills to deaden the pain, but these were taken away from me in the morning. The plaster dropped off after six weeks and the pain gradually eased. When I got back to England in May 1945, a medical officer told me I had fractured my fourth lumbar vertebra and should have been in plaster for several months.

'Jack and I were kept separate at the aerodrome until next day when we were taken to a railway station by two Luftwaffe airmen. They allowed Jack and me to talk. It was only then I learned what he had seen at the crash site.

'The body of the rear gunner, Henry Jackson, was still in his rear turret. He would have known nothing about us being shot up, he slept through the action. This was not because he was idle. I learned in the prison camp, when I met another Canadian from our squadron, that Henry needed more oxygen than normal and should have had his supply turned up. He hadn't told us. Les, who had been with me in the tail, was lying about thirty yards from the open end of the rear fuselage. He had one arm raised as if he had been crawling. Jack said Les might have been thrown out at the same time as me and fallen to the ground. Alf Richards, the bomb aimer, was at that time unaccounted for. Alf told me later he put on his 'chute just before being blown out of the perspex nose by the explosion. He parachuted down safely. His only problem had been a torn seam in his trouser leg. He sat on the ground, took a needle and cotton from his escape kit, sewed up the seam then walked for three days before being picked up by the Germans.

'Billy and the trainee pilot, Dresser, were lying side by side in front of the aircraft as though they had been thrown out through the canopy. There was no sign of Joe, the navigator. He had presumably also been thrown out and his body concealed by the trees. The two pieces of the Halifax were almost completely whole. Later they were torn apart by the Germans when they recovered the unexploded bomb, which had not been primed, and incendiaries. The starboard outer engine had taken off, leaping over a road and landing in woods which belonged to a convent.'

McLean was interrogated at the Dulag Luft, Frankfurt, by a young German officer who had worked for Whitbread brewery in London before the war. McLean and Elliott then spent three days travelling in a railway goods waggon to Burxdorf.

'The journey was horrific,' McLean recalls. 'I was almost crippled and eventually got stuck up on a bale of hay where I crouched, rather like a chicken on a dungheap for the whole journey. My companions were good to me, for none moaned about me hogging the bale. I was pulled with other wounded in an ox cart to Stalag IVb at Muhlberg an Elbe. I was kept separate and put in a French barrack, which was empty at the time. A Serbian came each day to massage my back.

'After we had been there three weeks some names, including mine, were called out at roll call. We were ordered to report to the German guardroom. About twenty of us, including Jack and Alf, milled around, wondering what was happening when, in the usual German manner, we were told to go back to our billets. As we dispersed, one of the party said we had all been shot down at the same time at Munich. Our apprehension grew. A few days later we were ordered to report to the guardroom "with all our possessions". We had nothing except what we were wearing. We were put in a separate barrack and next day Luftwaffe guards escorted us to the railway station. We were taken back to Munich.

'On arrival we were put in two rooms in a barrack block at Neu Biburg aerodrome. Unteroffizier Richard Dassburger, an Austrian, was our interpreter. He spoke excellent English and asked us to call him Dick. We learned we were to be shown round Munich to see the damage we had caused. We were joined by another eight Allied airmen, all shot down over Munich and paraded by the main gate, surrounded by fifty German airmen brandishing Schmeisser machine guns. We were scared. An officer arrived and addressed us in English.

'He said: "Terror bombers, murderers of the air, after the devastating bombing attacks on the beautiful open city of Munich Reichsmarschall Hermann Goering decreed that the perpetrators of this destruction should be taken back to the scene of their crime and shown the devastation they had caused. Unlike Mr Churchill, Adolf Hitler does not often quote the Bible, but one quotation he has used on occasions is 'an eye for an eye and a tooth for a tooth' and when the time comes, as come it will, you will be made to pay in full for your crimes".'

The young Allied airmen believed they were to be given a tour of Munich's smouldering ruins before being shot. They were taken in sober mood by bus and trailer and shown a maternity hospital, the front of which had been ripped out by a bomb blast. They saw many other wrecked buildings – including a blown-up football stadium and brewery, and the opera house where a bomb had torn through the roof. The Germans asked the airmen why had they bombed Munich and then, to their relief, they were returned safely to Stalag IVb.

'A German historian has told me there is no other record of Allied POWs being taken to see where they had bombed,' says McLean. 'In our case I believe the Germans were pumping us to find out how much we knew about their rocket development in Munich.'

McLean, Elliott and Richards were returned to Stalag IVb. Elliott was later moved to a POW camp for officers when his commission came through.

Years after the war, when McLean was still puzzling over the wreckage that seemed to have flown to earth, he wrote to Professor Reginald Jones, who was assistant director of intelligence on the Air Staff during the war, to see if he had an explanation.

Professor Jones, who was also the wartime head of scientific intelligence to MI6, told McLean in May 1995:

'I am impressed by the detail that you are able to remember of your experiences while being shot down on one of the Munich raids. Even so, it's not easy to find a full explanation of what happened. Although you could see the front end of your aircraft falling to earth in a diving position, it must have somehow flattened out as you observed. I am reminded of the crash of the prototype BAC-111 in 1963 and of a Trident crash shortly after takeoff from Heathrow, when both aircraft were found spreadeagled as a result of stalling. Perhaps the front end of your aircraft somehow got into a stalled attitude as it twisted out of its original dive. If so it might then have fallen more slowly than the rear end which, as you observed, was tumbling. I doubt whether the flattening out was due to the same cause as that which you observed with your paper aeroplanes, which I myself also found. The latter, I think, was not so much due to any increase of air pressure at ground level, but to what came to be known as "ground effect" involving a modification of the air flow around the wings which somehow improved the lift. I myself am not quite sure of the aerodynamics but the effect could sometimes be remarkable. I'm afraid that this is all I can offer, but I doubt whether anyone could give you a fuller explanation of the experience without many tests in a wind tunnel.'

CHAPTER SEVENTEEN

BLOWN UP - AND LIVES

As a schoolboy Bob Burns' main interests, apart from cricket and football, were jazz and flying model aeroplanes, activities which, some years later, formed a major part of his life. Burns persuaded his father, who had been a professional violinist, to buy him a secondhand saxophone on hire purchase, which he would pay for by working a paper round. By the time the war started in 1939 Burns was playing two nights a week in semi-professional bands. Flying real aeroplanes had remained an impossible dream until the great day in 1935 when Sir Alan Cobham and his Flying Circus came to the Coal Aston landing field four miles from the centre of Sheffield. Burns, then fifteen, won a competition for a twenty-minute joy ride aboard a Handley Page HP33 Clive I over Yorkshire. His interest, now further stimulated, had to wait until January 1942 when working as a professional musician, he was told to report to Lord's cricket ground, then functioning as the Aircrew Receiving Centre. Here aircrew were drilled, inocculated, kitted out and tested for Morse code.

He was posted to Brighton for a concentrated course of Morse, mathematics, PT and drill twelve hours a day, but still found time to play his saxophone at the local palais to supplement his 2s (10p) a day RAF pay, becoming quite well off compared to his service contemporaries. Although he trained as a pilot, his ambition was thwarted when big four-engine bombers were being produced and Bomber Command radically restructured aircrew training. The heavy bombers needed only one pilot and used the more swiftly trained flight engineer to carry out most of the duties normally performed by the second pilot. Existing second pilots were given their own commands. Fewer pilots were needed and many of those under training, including Bob Burns, were remustered to navigator or bomb aimer. Burns was trained mainly at Canada's Central Navigation School in Rivers, Manitoba, and Llandwrog, an airfield in the shadow of Snowdonia, where many training aircraft crashed among the mountains.

Burns, a tall man at nearly 6ft 2in, was crewed up at 29 OTU at Bruntingthorpe, Leicestershire. It was here he met a small, voluble and extrovert wireless operator, Percy Daw, who, like generations of his family before him, had been been a gardener on the royal estate at Sandringham. Burns joined forces with pilot Cyril Bishop, a quiet journalist from Bristol, whom he later found to be an exceptional pilot. Daw found a Canadian gunner, Bill Stevens, from Winnipeg which Burns knew well from off duty weekends spent there while at Rivers. Stevens had been a printer and could read type equally well upside-down, a useful talent he employed when scanning important gen on the desk of a superior's office. They chose a bomb aimer whose results had been the most accurate, but who later proved to be unreliable, and often inexplicably missing, although he never skived off flying. He became a constant headache to the rest of the crew. They were all sergeants although later the skipper was commissioned to pilot officer and Burns promoted to flight sergeant.

In their last night training exercise, while on Wellingtons, they encountered dense fog and, almost running out of fuel, made for Gravely, near Cambridge, a Pathfinder station which had the first and, at that time, the only FIDO installation. FIDO involved pipes containing petrol laid along both sides of the runway. When the petrol was set alight the heat from the flames dispersed the fog. Bishop put down at his second attempt, an outstanding effort by a rookie pilot. It was the first time a training aircraft had used FIDO, which was later used at other bomber stations, including Metheringham where they were to be based on operations.

The crew became complete at the heavy conversion unit on Stirlings at Swinderby, Lincolnshire. Harold 'Joe' Brad, a happy-go-lucky Canadian mid-upper gunner, who lived near Rivers, Manitoba, had joined the Royal Canadian Air Force straight from college. Ted Healey, a quiet and unassuming man in his thirties, became their flight engineer. He had been a pre-war RAF fitter and had also served in the Merchant Navy. Percy Daw called him the Old Seadog, and the nickname stuck.

Cyril Bishop, fed up with covering for his unreliable bomb aimer, got rid of him while training on Lancasters at Syerston and they were a man short when reporting to 106 Squadron at Metheringham in mid-March 1944. They had a spare bod for their first op before Jack Pickstone, from Manchester, and recently married, became the crew's regular bomb aimer.

Their most immediate impressions of Metheringham were deep mud and, unusually for an operational squadron, bullshit. The squadron had been led by Wing Commander Guy Gibson before he left to form 617 Squadron to attack the great German dams. Gibson took 106 Squadron's best crews with him to Scampton, having stamped his mark on those who were left behind.

Bob Burns recalls: 'The flight commander, obsessed with the Gibson persona, told us not to expect an easy time and that everything would be done "in shades of Gibson". And so it was. During our first forty-eight hours on the squadron we spent thirty actually in the air, performing exercises. Every day, when not flying, crews carried out dinghy, parachute, and other exercises. It was this kind of training in automatic response to situations which later saved my life.

'Luck, as so often happened in wartime, played a part in our lives. 5 Group, of which 106 Squadron was part, was commanded by Air Vice-Marshal the Hon Ralph Cochrane, a long time subordinate of Bomber Command chief Sir Arthur Harris. Now, in the wake of the Dambusters raid, Cochrane prevailed upon Harris to allow 5 Group to carry out their own specialised operations. We joined 106 Squadron just as these tactics were being formulated. On the whole they were successful, but proved to be expensive both in aircraft and crews.'

In the spring of 1944, with the Allied invasion of Europe imminent, Bomber Command switched its tactics to destroying German transportation, mainly railway installations in France. At this time 5 Group began marking targets using a new low-level technique with Mosquitoes, before turning its attention to deeper penetration of Germany. Bishop and his crew endured a tough trip to Munich on 24 April. They were among Lancasters who flew a leg over the Alps towards Milan to fool the Germans before retracing their steps and joining up with the rest of the force to bomb Munich. Master Bomber Wing Commander Leonard Cheshire and his 617 Squadron Mosquitoes dived through intense flak and searchlight dazzle to rooftop level to place their markers and this was considered the most accurate raid of the war on Munich. Cheshire and his squadron were then sent off on a well earned leave.

After bombing Munich, Bishop was low on fuel and, now flying in daylight, had no option but to drop his aircraft to rooftop level over France, in an attempt to dodge flak and fighters. They put down at Thorney Island, near Portsmouth, for refuelling after a flight of nearly ten hours.

During main briefing at Metheringham next day Bishop and his crew learned that night's operation was to be to Schweinfurt.

'Where the hell is that?' demanded Bill Stevens.

Burns, who had attended the earlier pilots' and navigators' briefing, had already checked out the target with the intelligence room. He told the rear gunner that Schweinfurt was a small town in Bavaria which made sixty per cent of Germany's requirements for ball bearings. Intelligence said the town was well defended and not easy to find. It stood among valleys and hills and had an irritating reputation for covering itself with smoke whenever enemy aircraft appeared.

Sixteen Lancasters of 106 Squadron, including Bishop's crew in ND853 XN J-Jig, together with 199 other Lancasters and 11 Mosquitoes, were detailed to bomb Schweinfurt, while the Main Force of 493 aircraft attacked Essen. Another 217 bombers hit French railway yards at Villeneuve-St-Georges. Metheringham crews going to Schweinfurt were subdued at briefing, no one was looking forward to the trip and Burns, chatting to the ground crew later, felt distinctly uneasy about this, his seventh trip.

The route was said to have been carefully chosen to avoid flak and searchlights. It had been last flown a month previously on an attack against Stuttgart on which casualties were low. After passing over Deauville and to the north of Châteaudun there was a long leg due east of over 300 miles, which stopped short of Stuttgart to swing abruptly north-east towards Schweinfurt. Problems began almost as soon as they entered enemy airspace. The route may have been chosen to avoid ground defences, but it went almost directly over two night fighters' airfields. To make matters worse the forecast winds changed both in direction and velocity with the result that many aircraft were blown well south of track and were easy prey to the fighters. J-Jig's gunners, Brad and Stevens, reported several combats on this long leg which claimed twelve of the twenty-one Lancasters that did not return, including five from 106 Squadron.

Fifty miles from Schweinfurt the bomber stream split, with half going on to the target and the rest, including J-Jig, flying a 100-mile detour to the north in an area patrolled extensively by fighters. This second wave was to bomb twenty minutes after those who were heading straight for Schweinfurt.

Problems, starting with a 45mph head wind, now began to pile up. The Master Bomber, Wing Commander Jimmy Carter, of 97 Squadron, realising he would be late, cut through the defended area of Karlsruhe, instead of the direct route and arrived just before H-hour. Unfortunately, the Mosquito marking force, 627 Squadron, in taking a different route, arrived at Schweinfurt early, giving away the target. This allowed the town to belch out a thick black smokescreen. The Lancaster flare force, already late by up to ten minutes, were further hindered when many of their H2S sets were found to be unserviceable. Flares were dropped, but with the town obscured by a pall of smoke, these were unsatisfactory. The first red spot fire markers were dropped south of the river, well away from the aiming point. Time was lost while the Master Bomber assessed the situation before calling for more flares and spot fire markers. Although flares and markers were dropped accurately they were barely visible because of the effective smokescreen. A green target indicator and green spot fire were dropped and found to be 1,500 yards short. By the time Carter had assessed these, calculated a 1,000-yard over-shoot, and called in the bombers, they bombed in an area full of night fighters and twenty minutes later than scheduled.

'Furthermore, this coincided with the second wave coming in from the north,' Burns recalls, 'and when we arrived at 17,000ft, about 2.30am, amid fires, smoke, searchlights and flak, the course into the target was lit by an avenue of flares dropped by Luftwaffe aircraft. The inferno below must have been hell on earth.'

The Luftwaffe flares were designed to light up the invading bombers to make them more vulnerable to night fighters.

Jack Pickstone, the bomb aimer, gave his skipper instructions for bombing and the Lancaster jumped skittishly as their bombs fell to earth.

Almost immediately the bomber was attacked by a night fighter. Bishop threw the Lancaster into two swift corkscrews and rear gunner Bill Stevens yelled: 'I've got the bastard! He's going down!'

An alarming crunching noise was heard ripping into the bomber's belly. Burns does not know if it was last gasp cannon fire from the crippled German or from another fighter fitted with the *Schräge Musik*, a pair of upward firing cannons, which was unknown to Bomber Command until after the war. These cannons were ideally suited for firing into the unprotected bellies of the Lancasters. It was common for German fighters to hunt in pairs, one to engage the bomber and the other to sneak up unnoticed.

The Lancaster was on fire and diving. The skipper snapped: 'Bale out!' Everyone sprang into action.

Burns again: 'I made my way to the back after clamping on my chest-type parachute. All the emergency drill we had been made to practise ensured that escape procedure was now being carried out automatically and instinctively. I had the hated main spar to negotiate, a feat said to require the agility of a trained gymnast, especially with all our heavy gear on. Every step to the door required an immense effort as the G-force tried to press me to the floor. I saw the rear door had been opened, probably by Joe Brad, the mid-upper gunner. He and Percy Daw, the wireless operator were pinned helplessly to the floor. I managed to drive myself to the door, but the G-force won and, like a cork in a rough sea, I was tossed to the floor to join my crewmates. Few escaped from the back door in a diving aircraft. If you got out there were the added obstacles of the rudders, wing and even the propellers as later research discovered.

'It's commonly believed that when facing death one's life flashes before you. I have no such memory. Everything happened so quickly. We were no higher than 3,000ft when there was a sudden explosion and I was thrown headfirst upwards towards the roof of the Lancaster. I then blacked out. In later years I've wondered many times how I escaped having a piece of the aircraft embedded in my skull.'

A microsecond later he was in the sky, revived by the icy air, and what remained of the dying Lancaster was describing a fiery loop below and to his right. Instinctively, while thanking God for his good fortune to be blown safely out of it, and for all the emergency drills they had been forced to practise, he pulled the parachute ripcord and floated downwards with no sense of movement. As he slipped through the cold night he ran his hands over his body and happily discovered everything was there, although the battledress trouser, covering his right thigh, was torn to shreds. Burns felt inside and found his thigh was covered in blood, although he was not in pain. Suddenly, up came the ground, a ploughed field near the town of Arnstein, 20km south of Schweinfurt.

He examined the wound by the light of the moon and heard the steady drone of late aircraft far above returning to England. He was suddenly overcome with terrible impotence and rage at being stuck in a German field hundreds of miles from England, while those lucky buggers were homeward bound. Without a crew, he was forced to act alone. His leg, which did not hurt, appeared to have stopped bleeding. He bandaged the wound with a field dressing and remembered those drills which seemed to have taken place in another life. Burns rolled up the parachute and buried it in a hole he dug with his hands in soft soil beneath a hedge.

Considering which way he should go his mind was made up by the far off rattle and clank of a railway train. Intelligence had always told them the best way to escape was by quickly leaving the area into which you had parachuted by using the railways. This proved to be the worst thing he could do. Burns did not know that, unlike England, German railway installations were heavily guarded. He took three hours to find the sidings where trains were being shunted. It was still not light and his leg had stiffened up, making progress slow and difficult. He was a few yards away from one of the waggons when the goods yard became flooded with light. Burns froze in fear as he saw at least twenty soldiers aiming rifles at him from all sides. Someone yelled at him in German and, dispiritedly, he lifted his hands. He was taken to a small building where his bandaged leg was cursorily examined. A few minutes later he was put in a car and driven away.

'I had been so very lucky,' says Burns. 'I had been blown up and survived. When I returned to England fourteen months later I found out that all but one of my crewmates aboard J-Jig had been killed.'

Jack Pickstone, the bomb aimer, is believed to have jumped to safety before the aircraft exploded. He was uninjured, but Burns has not heard of him since.

The sky was lightening when he was delivered to a small cottage hospital, which was run by nuns. No one here could speak English, and Burns knew no German. The nuns removed the bandage, now sodden with blood, tended the wound, re-dressed it, gave him food and a strange drink which he came to recognise as the bitter erzatz coffee, made from acorns. Then, given pyjamas, he was put to bed. He awoke about midday to find he was being closely scrutinised by six other patients. Five young Germans, probably soldiers, were friendly. Another, much older man, did not try to disguise his contempt for the British airman. When he left the room, one of the others mouthed the word 'Gestapo!' and pulled a face, showing that he and his companions preferred the company of the enemy to that of their morose fellow-countryman.

That night a doctor removed several fragments of metal and paint from Burns' leg, including an envelope-sized piece of J-Jig's fuselage, one side painted black. His leg was stitched up. Fifty years later, when examined by an RAF pensions doctor, Burns was told his wound was no more than a hairsbreadth from the main artery. He was lucky not to have bled to death.

Two days later Burns was collected by two Luftwaffe corporals and they walked to Arnstein railway station, where he had been captured, and then by train to Schweinfurt.

'All I could see in any direction was flattened rubble. Nearby some kind of parade was taking place with a Messerschmitt Bf109 flying overhead no more than 100ft from the ground. I asked one of the corporals, who could speak a little English, what was happening, and he said it was the funeral of a night fighter pilot killed a few days earlier over Schweinfurt. He must have been the victim of our rear gunner Bill Stevens.'

They caught a train to Frankfurt and from there walked several miles to the Dulag Luft interrogation centre at Oberursel. The walking tore open the stitches in Burns' now painful leg and the flesh resembled a lump of red meat. He endured over two weeks being kept in a small, deliberately hot cell, with no washing permitted, while enduring long sessions of harsh questioning, thinly veiled threats, and inadequate and tasteless food. He repeatedly demanded that his wound should be treated by a doctor and eventually, when this was done, he was allowed a shave and a bath. He was moved to the military hospital at Obermassfeld near Meiningen which, although German supervised, was staffed by prisoners, mainly New Zealand doctors. Here Burns received regular treatment, but the leg would always trouble him.

Shortly after arriving at Obermassfeld Burns found that British troops who worked at the hospital had a fine selection of musical instruments, but no band. Burns began eagerly recruiting bandsmen from staff and patients. There was no sheet music available so he wrote parts for the ten piece band he put together.

'The hospital staff were mainly Glaswegians,' he recalls. 'They had been captured at Dunkirk with the 51 Highland Division and as old hands were experts at making POW life as comfortable and bearable as possible, while continuing to hinder the Germans. Like most other POW camps they had assembled a radio and the BBC news was spread around the wards only minutes after being broadcast in London. One morning, we learned the D-Day invasion had started and I was asked to organise a band concert in the main ward in celebration. The Germans, unaware of the real purpose of the concert, allowed it to be given that night, while insisting that national tunes, such as "Land of Hope and Glory", should not be played. Instead we played such tunes as "White Cliffs of Dover", and "Hang out the Washing on the Siegfried Line". The concert boosted the patients' morale. The Germans, who attended the concert, were not familiar with any of the music.'

After nearly three months Burns' leg had healed sufficiently for him to be transferred to a permanent POW camp. He set off with four other ex-patients and two Luftwaffe guards for a newly opened camp for airmen, Stalag Luft VII at Bankau in Silesia. Trains were changed at Erfurt, which meant a long wait on a platform. None of the prisoners were aware that the Americans had bombed Erfurt that morning. News that English airmen were at the railway station travelled fast. An angry crowd of civilians, shouting abuse, gathered on the platform which formed part of a viaduct and stood fifty feet or more off the road. The little party of airmen was being steadily shoved nearer to the edge. The situation was becoming explosive when one of the guards, a little English-speaking corporal, tried desperately to reason with the mob, but they ignored him. The other guard stood by impassively as the snarling crowd pushed them closer to the long drop. Suddenly, in an extraordinary gesture, the corporal handed his submachine gun to Burns, who was the tallest man among them. The airman, taken by surprise, did not know what to do with it, but the reaction of the crowd was immediate. They melted away, the corporal retrieved his gun and they moved to a safer position on the platform.

Burns offers explanations for the incident: 'The guards' duty was to deliver their prisoners and the only punishment in the German military for failure was to be sent to the Russian Front. German propaganda branded British airmen as "Terror Fliers", with horrifying reputations as people who would not hesitate to kill their own mothers if they believed it was necessary. The little corporal must have gambled on this, but his bravery and presence of mind undoubtedly saved our lives and we were eternally grateful.'

The POWs at Bankau organised several events during the warm weather, including boxing matches, athletics and two band concerts, which were performed with two broken-down violins, provided by the Germans, and a piano that took a pianist several days to repair, using cotton and string. On 21 November 1944, Burns' twenty-fourth birthday, the Red Cross delivered sports gear and musical instruments, which included a superb saxophone. There were enough instruments to form an orchestra but, again, no sheet music. Burns wrote parts for the fourteen piece Bob Burns Orchestra, which was soon being rehearsed. A band show was put on in December, but by now the German Army was in full retreat from the Russians.

At 3.30am on 19 January 1945, around 1,500 airmen were given two and a half days' rations and evacuated from Bankau into a raging blizzard. They were told that for every man who fell out of the march, five would be shot. Among the marchers was Bob Burns, carrying a case which contained the precious saxophone and a clarinet. Both were beautiful instruments, much better than his own at home and he was determined to hang on to them, although often, as his energy was drained, the case slipped out of his frozen fingers. That first night they covered 28km. In three weeks they marched 240kms through deep snow, sleeping in cowsheds, surviving on starvation rations. On 5 February they were crammed into cattle trucks without water at Goldberg and taken to Luckenwalde. They disembarked as tottering skeletons, suffering from frostbite, dysentery and malnutrition. The new camp was grossly overcrowded and food was sparse.

On 21 April the Germans disappeared and the Russians arrived. The former POWs were taken to Elbe, transferred to American trucks and driven to an airfield near Halle. Here they were deloused, given new uniforms and fed like kings before being flown back to RAF Cosford to be interrogated, kitted out and sent home for two weeks' leave.

Burns stayed in the RAF until the end of 1946 when, for a year, he resumed his career as a professional musician, using his Bankau instruments. He later became a civil engineer.

He says: 'In 1986 I met Vic Cooper, who played the cello in the Bankau orchestra. Until then neither of us had known we were both in 106 Squadron and for twenty years we lived only eight miles from each other in Devon without realising. Vic, a retired clergyman, is the Air Crew Association padre and each Christmas we play carols in the local church, with me using my Bankau instruments.'

After extensive research Bob Burns has concluded that a curious conspiracy of silence hangs over the Schweinfurt raid. Little corroboration is available in Britain, where the attack was said to be a failure. In fact a map drawn up shortly after the operation by the Munich State Survey Office, shows the locations of all bombs, including duds and incendiaries and confirms that considerable damage was done to the town, an Army barracks and the ball bearing works. German archives have no record of the raid, nor of another attack on the town on 30/31 March 1944 when 120 RAF aircraft bombed it by mistake, instead of Nuremburg. Could it be that strenuous efforts have been made since the war to save the embarrassment of Sweden, a supposedly neutral country during the conflict, and whose involvement in Schweinfurt is less well known in the wider world?

Burns says: 'Two of the five ball bearing works in Schweinfurt were, and still are, owned by Sweden. Throughout the war the Swedes were paid premium prices for supplying Germany with significant deliveries of ball bearings. Britain and her allies paid Sweden huge sums of money not to make these deliveries. The Germans then negotiated a further increase in the price to ensure deliveries. All this time Sweden assured both sides they were honouring the respective agreements, although the Allies and Germany were aware of the situation. Sir Arthur Harris said at the time that he hoped this double-dealing would be exposed after the war. He repeated these charges at the end of hostilities but no record can be found of these events which appear to have been an embarrassment to all sides who have conveniently hushed it up.'

CHAPTER EIGHTEEN

THE HORROR OF NUREMBURG

There were clear signs which could identify someone in a bomber crew who was cracking up. Terror became rooted in the eyes and sent trembles rippling through the hands. It was difficult, even impossible to make decisions and as the time for takeoff drew near, such a man could conjure up the terrible vision of his own death. Most aircrew could control the fear which might easily have overwhelmed them. Others could not, although some successfully concealed their terror until they could take no more. One of these was Ron Munday's flight engineer, whose apparently equable demeanour was shattered during his fourth bombing operation when he hid crouching fearfully behind the pilot's seat as flak and fighters joined forces to kill him. The catalyst for this young man's misery was almost certainly the crew's very first operation, the distant target of Nuremburg.

Their names were on the battle order pinned up in the flight office at lunchtime on 27 August 1943. They were based at Scampton with 57 Squadron and apprehension was running high. They had completed all their training and been told what to expect, but being told was not the same as actually flying over Germany with a full bomb load. Flying Officer Ron Munday, a thoughtful and sensitive skipper, knew that hundreds of men had not survived their first trip for a variety of reasons: carelessness being one and rotten luck another. Munday had only one operation behind him, as second dickey at the right hand of an experienced pilot, but he knew that a vital factor for survival was for a crew to work together as a team. This was the first stage in creating their own luck. He got them together in the crewroom after lunch before briefing and said they must remember everything they had been told. That night's operation was the culmination of all their training. The pilot then shook hands with everyone and they went off and learned they would be flying to Nuremburg that night.

Munday's mid-upper gunner, Sergeant Stan Bradford, says: 'He didn't whip us into a frenzy, he was a calming influence. We were all scared but he brought it out and made us feel easier. He spoke to us as our fathers might have done, although he was only twenty-five himself. We were less scared than we might have been when we got into our Lancaster later on.'

The flight engineer was twenty-three, a slim six-footer from Derbyshire, and was, according to Bradford, a good man and friend who was first class at his job. They were all scared, especially over the target, but there was no time to analyse fear. Perhaps that was what unhinged the engineer's self-control: he forever dwelled on what could happen and, given time and the grim mounting statistics of war, probably would.

Munday, from Buckinghamshire, was short and slim, a strong disciplinarian, but not dogmatic. He was always prepared to talk through anybody's problems and ideas. They had a close relationship with the ground crew and if any of them were going on leave, Munday tried to arrange an NFT (night flying test) so he could take them up and land them at the base which was nearest to their home. They sat on the main spar or the sick bed, rather pleased they were not going to Germany. They drank together at the local pub, taking their own jamjars to hold the beer because there was a shortage of glasses.

The navigator was Pilot Officer Tony West, twenty-three, from Goole, Yorkshire. He was good at his job and prepared to help other navigators who were less able. He was over six feet, slim and pigeon-toed. Before the war Pilot Officer Dennis Bracher, twenty-two, a placid man had worked for a brewery in Stafford. Now he was a wireless operator.

The crew later discovered they had another misfit among them when their bomb aimer failed to return from leave. He was a tall, thin and pimply-faced twenty-four-year old from Essex, whose reluctance to have regular baths made his crewmates' nostrils twitch. They heard he had become involved with a religious sect which briefly diverted him from the job of bombing Germany. Later this young man came to his senses, extricated himself from the sect, returned to the RAF, became an outstanding bomb aimer with another crew, was commissioned and decorated with the DFC.

Stan Bradford, the mid-upper gunner, at nineteen the baby of the crew, was brought up strictly at his Lancashire home in Astley, a small coal mining village. His father was an austere figure, a sergeant-major from the First World War, and the young Bradford had to attend church three times on Sundays. Tall and broad in his late teens, Bradford was taken advantage of as an apprentice sheet metal worker and panel beater for a company which repaired coaches used to transport troops. Disenchanted, he spotted an RAF recruiting centre in Wigan while delivering a repaired Leyland Tiger coach to Blackpool in the summer of 1942. He hopped eagerly off the coach and signed on for aircrew. Six weeks later he was in the RAF and loving it. Bradford learned a good deal from Canadian rear gunner Sergeant Douglas 'Chick' Lightfoot. Lightfoot came from Saskatchewan where he worked hard on his father's farm and built up solid muscles on a short stocky frame. Lightfoot became the squadron clay pigeon champion and, after some steady tuition, Bradford was runner-up.

'I learned such a lot about gunnery from him,' says Bradford. 'He was a wonderful gunner. He used to say watch the clay pigeon coming up to the top of its trajectory then, a split second before it starts to drop, bang! Another thing I learned from Chick was that you don't trust anybody when your lives are at stake. Never mind that we probably had the best armourers in the world. Check your own guns thoroughly, our lives depended on it.'

The two gunners competed with two armourers to see who was quickest in the dark at taking a Browning machine-gun to bits and reassembling it, wearing heavy gloves. The gunners always won, but nothing was as important for building up Bradford's confidence and honing his skills in the mid-upper turret as shooting those clay pigeons with Lightfoot.

A total 674 aircraft, 349 Lancasters, 221 Halifaxes and 104 Stirlings took off on the night of 27 August 1943 to attack Nuremburg. Thirty-three bombers would be lost.

Ron Munday was at the controls of Lancaster ED308 D-Donald when they lifted off from Scampton at 9.10pm on a clear mild night. D-Donald's young crew settled down to routine tasks. It had been a good takeoff, enough to raise their confidence a notch or two as they pointed towards the North Sea. They had only been airborne a few minutes when that confidence became a little threadbare after a loud thump sent a curious shiver through the aircraft and one of the engines faltered. The engine picked up again as the engineer checked all his instruments. None of them could tell him that a disorientated seagull had been sucked into an engine intake. Its grisly remains would be found later by engine fitters. The engineer watched for signs of overheating, but the engine had settled, he told the pilot, who passed the good news on to the crew.

Bradford recalls: 'Normally we had complete intercom silence, unless there was something important to report. There was no time for small talk. Ron spoke to each of us every few minutes to make sure we were all right and to keep us on our toes.'

This contact was particularly important for the gunners who were isolated from the rest of the crew stuck on the outside of the fuselage in their vulnerable perspex blisters, hearing nothing except the steady pounding of the four engines. They would soon start to feel the cold, despite their multi-layers of clothing. Although it was August and everyone was basking in shirtsleeves back at Scampton, the temperature plummeted at higher altitude, where a gunner's life became uncomfortable.

Bradford, at his position set in the roof of the Lancaster, wore the lucky white check silk scarf, a present from his mum. He had a grandstand view of everything around him. He derived some comfort from being part of a huge armada of bombers, but he watched carefully to make sure none drifted too close. Many bombers were lost through collisions. Lightfoot in the rear turret, bolted on to the Lancaster's broad backside, had an unequalled view of anything approaching from behind or beneath. There would be little warning of a fighter's approach, usually they arrived like a winged devil out of hell. The earlier they were spotted the more time the gunner could give his skipper to corkscrew out of danger.

They were over France when Bradford saw a flash of bright light to starboard. It was an exploding Lancaster, and the awesome sight made his stomach turn over. He spotted something else travelling fast in front of the white glare.

He cried: 'Bandits! bandits! astern to starboard. Prepare to corkscrew.'

The pilot would not react until he heard the word 'Go!', which was part of their training. Bradford didn't tell his skipper to go, there was no time. The Bf109 fighter peeled away from the disintegrating bomber in swaggering triumph, searching for a second kill. The German pilot turned straight towards D-Donald. Normally a bomber didn't draw attention to itself by firing first. German fighters had superior fire power and RAF gunners had been instructed to wait until the enemy knew they were there. Clearly the fighter was closing with them fast. Bradford was not consciously thinking of clay pigeons, but those hours spent with Chick Lightfoot had attuned his mind to know exactly when to pull the trigger.

Bradford again: 'He was coming our way, this was an ideal opportunity, the bugger was after us. It was all in the brain, I knew what I had to do. I opened fire with a good burst when he was within range, about 300 yards away. I pulled the trigger probably a fraction of a second before he fired at us. I believe I hit him in the engine. A lot of flames streamed out. It took seconds. We didn't even take evasive action, that's how quick it was.'

As Bradford watched the mortally wounded fighter disappear towards the ground he reported laconically, but in a voice exuding delight and satisfaction. 'Gottim! Gottim!'

One by one the whole crew came on the intercom to congratulate Bradford. 'Well done, Stan!' The beers would be on him next time they met in the mess or pub. Bradford, brimming with confidence, remembered how swiftly the Bf109 had appeared and continued to scan the skies, his heart still banging away excitedly beneath several layers of warm clothing. The bomber stream droned on over Germany. They were met by heavy flak and more fighters. Bradford saw more bombers in trouble, some sinking to earth trailing a torrent of fire. A knot in their stomachs tightened a little every time another bomber was attacked.

Bradford again: 'Seeing other lads going down was one of the things that really got to you. Sometimes you saw them at the end of a parachute and you thought: "Oh God!" and hoped they would make it. Fighters were coming in and picking the bombers off. The fighters seemed to drop away over the target which was when the flak took over. When you took off you knew in your heart that somebody from somewhere wasn't going to get home. It could have been us, but we never discussed that, it couldn't happen to us, could it?'

They were closing on Nuremburg when Chick Lightfoot picked a Ju88 fighter out of a dark sky. The rear gunner growled: 'Goddam bastard!' his normal guttural reaction to the approach of a hated enemy fighter. He yelled: 'Bandits! bandits! on the port side. Prepare to dive to starboard.'

Again there was no need for Ron Munday to corkscrew. Stan Bradford takes up the story. 'As the German came in Chick opened fire and I'm pretty certain he hit him. When the fighter was going underneath I let him have it. The German shot at us too, but his cannon shells went wide. The fighter flipped over and fell out of the sky. I looked over the side of the aeroplane and watched him going down.'

It is possible that other bombers saw D-Donald engaging and despatching two German fighters and believed they were watching the chillingly accurate marksmanship of veteran gunners, instead of raw sprogs on their first operation who had not even reached the target. This was an astounding start, for some gunners spent an entire tour without firing their guns in anger. Stan Bradford and Chick Lightfoot were feeling pretty chuffed and continued to quarter the sky, looking for more fighters, wondering if they might get the chance to bag a third. They were excited because they had destroyed two German fighters, and scared because the Germans might have destroyed them. Neither gunner was a fool. They were realistic. Their training had shown them there was no place for the fainthearted in a bomber, nor for anyone simply seeking glory. Vigilance was their watchword at all times. Bradford was scared to blink for he now knew how much damage could be caused in a fraction of a second.

Forty-seven Pathfinder aircraft carrying H2S had been briefed to check their equipment by each releasing a 1,000lb bomb on Heilbronn en route to Nuremburg and twenty-eight did so, soon after midnight. Most bombs fell in the north of the town, not touching any industrial buildings. One house was destroyed.

They flew through a storm of flak on their approach to the target. D-Donald shuddered in the heavy shower of red hot shrapnel, which they had been warned about, but still found terrifying. The wings and fuselage were damaged and the navigational equipment went haywire. One engine was causing problems, spluttering a bit, it was a difficult time and, gradually, D-Donald began losing altitude. They went in to bomb at 20,000ft, a little later than their ETA. There was no cloud, but it was a black cheerless night.

This was the most nerve-wracking time of all. Everyone except pilot and bomb aimer sat waiting for what seemed an eternity. Straight and level, buffeted by constant flak, they heard the bomb aimer's measured tones: 'Left, left, steady, steady – ' as he gazed into the flickering glow from the fires which had already been started far below. Ahead of them bombers maintaining their straight and level bombing run were hit, some crippled, losing height, staggering away from Nuremburg, the screams of the wounded and dying being swallowed by this endless bloody night. Other aircraft exploded into fragments of hot metal and soft flesh. There were parachutes, flimsy as thistledown. Men dangled from them, tiny figures as vulnerable as new-born babies. They had escaped from their aircraft, but would they survive the terrible wrath of the civilians in the city below?

Those who could see out of D-Donald felt the horror and misery of war enveloping them in a great crushing tarpaulin of loathing and dread. They bombed on the Pathfinders' markers and the pilot said: 'Well done, lads.' There was a vast sigh of relief as the bomb doors closed and, naively, they thought their first operation into Germany was over.

The massed ranks of searchlights swept the sky, scurrying among the bombers before resting on their chosen prey with a silvered kiss of death which summoned other swooping lights, an official invitation to the flak, which arrived rapidly and the end was sudden, flames engulfing the aircraft. It fell, a great shapeless burning wreckage, men trapped inside, men who had left their base that night cheerfully enough with egg and bacon inside them, and now with seconds to live. Many brave bomber crews died that night and at least sixty-five Germans were killed on the ground. Early Pathfinder marking was accurate, but creepback developed and could not be halted because of problems with H2S equipment. Bomber Command believed most bombs fell outside the city, but German sources claim they were scattered across the eastern and south-eastern suburbs.

D-Donald escaped the horror of Nuremburg when the Lancaster shot high across the city and turned south on a leg which would take them near the Ruhr, but away from the Happy Valley's ferocious defences, before heading north.

Tony West, the navigator, began taking star shots in the astrodome. His radar equipment had become unreliable. West had told his skipper of the problem and was surprised when Munday insisted on informing the rest of the crew that he was uncertain of their position. The navigator believed if the others didn't know about the malfunctioning equipment they would have nothing to worry about. Munday preferred not to keep secrets when men's lives were at stake.

'We had a trouble-free run from Nuremburg to the coast,' recalls Bradford. 'We were buffeted by a head wind which added to our problems. Flak was around, but nowhere near us and we didn't see any German fighters, or any more of our bombers going down. We had lost the main stream and were on our own. Ron told us he was uncertain of our position, then Tony said the fixes he was getting indicated they were within striking distance of the English coast. The engineer chipped in with the news that fuel was running low and Ron started sending out Mayday calls.'

Until now they had maintained R/T silence. As the pilot repeated 'Mayday! Mayday!' the crew were shocked by the 'boomp! boomp!' of flak soaring up from the ground. A bellowing 'Jesus Christ!' rang out from Chick Lightfoot's rear turret and it was a while before they realised they were not over England being hammered by their own gunners. They had strayed over the Channel Islands, the only part of Britain occupied by the Germans during the war. It was not often that a juicy Lancaster wandered within reach of these gunners and this unexpected arrival gave them the chance to show off. The flak was heavy from several batteries on Jersey, but the Germans were not on target. The navigator gave Munday a new course, they scampered out of danger and contact was made soon with the fighter station at Exeter.

'Ron told the control tower we were short of fuel,' recalls Bradford. 'They gave us a course which took us straight on to the runway with only two engines still working. We put down at 5.50am after being in the air 8hr 40min. We were given mugs of tea or coffee and rum. After we'd been debriefed Ron talked to us like a Dutch uncle. He said: "Well, we're not going to get anything worse than that, are we?"

'The officers went off to their mess, the rest of us went to the sergeants' mess where fellows were drifting in for their breakfasts. We were treated like lords. The sergeant in charge shook our hands, gave us bacon and eggs and anything we wanted. He said his son, an air gunner in Bomber Command, had been lost a few nights before. He didn't even know which raid he'd been on. We hadn't had a wash, we had no money and no fags. The sergeant fixed us up with fags, soap, towels and razors, as well as somewhere comfortable to sleep.'

D-Donald was badly shot up. A ground crew were soon swarming over it but they needed a day to get the bomber ready for the return flight to Scampton. They slept for the rest of the day and in the evening the catering sergeant fixed the two gunners up with transport for a trip into Exeter.

Their sightseeing was doomed from the start. Bradford recalls: 'Obviously we had no shoes and no tie. We were wearing flying boots and bulky blue and yellow one-piece Taylor suits, which were designed to keep gunners afloat if they came down in the sea. You needed a hand from a mate to put them on and we stood out a bit in Exeter. The RAF Snowdrops (RAF service police) soon picked us up. The bastards said we were improperly dressed. We didn't want to discuss what had happened and they drove us back to the camp. We went in the mess for a couple of beers, then back to bed. The catering sergeant made it quite clear in front of us to the flight sergeant chiefie of police what he thought, doubting the parentage of the chaps who picked us up.'

The SPs had never been up in an aeroplane. Their blinkered world consisted of orderly behaviour and neatness at all times. They were known for their loud penetrating voices, lack of humour or imagination, and devotion to upholding King's Regulations at all costs, especially now there was a war on. Aircrews might be allowed to be sloppily dressed while bombing the Germans, but by God if they are not smart and clean with creases in their trousers on the ground, they'll be in trouble.

The repaired D-Donald took off from Exeter at 3pm next day, landing at Scampton 1hr 45min later. The following day the squadron was moved to East Kirkby a few miles to the east so concrete runways could be laid at Scampton.

Ron Munday and his crew were never given a soft target. They were briefed thirteen times to attack Berlin, none of them easy rides. They set off for the German capital on their second operation on 31 August 1943, but were forced to abort the sortie after being attacked by an FW190 which raked them underneath, hitting one engine and severing a pipe which fed hydraulic fluid to the rear turret. They bombed Berlin on 3 September, returning via Sweden and landing at Topcliffe, Yorkshire. The next night, on their fourth sortie, they were holed by flak over Mannheim. Back at East Kirkby, the pilot called them together, with the exception of the flight engineer. He told them over a cup of tea that a problem had to be resolved before they went into debriefing. He had called for the engineer to provide him with full power after releasing the bombs, but there was no response. The engineer was crouching petrified behind his seat.

'We had no option,' recalls Bradford. 'The engineer had to be reported. It had been a rough trip, but we all depended on each other. We didn't see him again, poor bugger. What he didn't know about an engine wasn't worth knowing, he was brilliant, but he'd gone LMF and that was that. Losing him in this way destroyed us for a little while as a crew. We'd had no idea he couldn't handle the ops, he seemed a normal outgoing bloke. I always felt more gutted when I got back and had time to reflect than when I was flying. The time everything came home to you was when you were in bed in the billet after a tough raid and somebody came in quietly to take away the kit of chaps who didn't make it back. That was disturbing. The loss of a mate was no more completely pressed home than seeing an empty bed and his personal effects being dropped into a bag.'

Their ops did not get any easier. With a new flight engineer, Sergeant Fred Simmonds and a replacement bomb aimer, Flying Officer Taffy Evans, they were turned upside-down during a plunging corkscrew on another trip to Berlin; in another, their penultimate trip, also to the German capital, they were twice coned for what seemed an eternity, being passed between searchlights like a bulky parcel in a ghastly game in which the continuous flak repeatedly changed the rules.

They were flabbergasted six nights later when they knew the target which had to be attacked on the operation which would mark the end of their first tour. It was 30 March 1944 and the target was Nuremburg. It was the raid in which Bomber Command sustained its greatest loss of the war; ninety-five heavy bombers did not return. This represented an 11.9 per cent loss of the 795 aircraft despatched or, more starkly, 665 men. The met wind forecast had been inaccurate and a strong force of German fighters was waiting after their controller decided to ignore all the RAF's diversion raids.

Stan Bradford admitted to them being 'thoughtful' before setting out from East Kirkby. By now, of course, they were an experienced crew and it was this which probably saved them from any grief.

The former gunner recalls: 'It was one of the easiest of our bombing operations. We were confident, despite that first op to Nuremburg back in August. We hadn't been there since, but we'd come through all those trips to Berlin. We were in the first wave, weren't shot at and didn't see any fighters. We even had to do a short dog leg on the way because we were early. By the time we were back on course the target indicators had gone down. We bombed, went through Nuremburg and were away. Behind us we saw the fires of many bombers going down, but we made it safely home. We knew it was our last op and when we got back to East Kirkby I kissed the ground and we all had a fag.'

They went straight home on leave. Bradford got a lift from the airfield in a lorry delivering blankets to Ringway Airport in Manchester, a few miles from his home. Exhausted, he slept all the way and arrived home to catch his parents in a tableau of sheer horror, his mother frozen in the act of putting his father's dinner on the table. A sombre BBC radio newsreader was saying that the previous night in the raid on Nuremburg, ninety-five bombers had been lost. They turned to their son, greatly relieved, and said: 'Thank God you weren't on that one, Stan.'

'Yes I was,' he said quietly, 'but it was my last operation.'

Ron Munday's crew was the only one to finish a tour between 1 October 1943 and 31 March 1944 on 57 Squadron. DFCs were awarded to Munday, navigator Tony West and wireless operator Dennis Bracher. DFMs went to flight engineer Fred Simmonds and mid-upper gunner Stan Bradford, who was credited by 5 Group at the end of the war with shooting down six German fighters.

CHAPTER NINETEEN

WINGHAM'S SECRET WAR

The small room stood at the top of the house. Tom Wingham was familiar with every blemish on the wallpaper and ceiling, and each rasping creak in the bare floorboards. Awareness of the source of these creaks was important, for after seven weeks, he had still not met the owner of the little cottage who slept each night in the next room. Nor did he want to meet him in case he was thrown out and captured by the Germans.

Wingham had baled out of a Halifax bomber which was shot down on 23 April 1944 between Aachen and Maastricht in Holland. Two of the crew were killed and Wingham was on the run for three days before making contact with the Resistance. He was taken to the Belgian town of Wandre and sheltered in a small house which stood on the main street. He had a lot of time to think: to marvel at his own survival and the generosity of the remarkable woman who had given him shelter, while reflecting on the incongruous twists and turns of a chap's fortunes in war. He also ran through some of his operations, including one they were lucky to survive. Understandably they were feeling pretty pleased with themselves until confronted by an RAF engineering officer in England whose life was ruled by Air Ministry Regulations. This officer figured in a curious incident which Wingham would never forget. His mind slipped easily back to 23 May 1943.

Sergeant Wingham was a bomb aimer with 102 (Ceylon) Squadron, based at Pocklington in Yorkshire's East Riding. His skipper was Dave Hewlett, whose father was a publican in Woodmansterne, Surrey. He was a fine pilot and the following month, at the end of their first tour, he and his crew would be sent to Boscombe Down to carry out development flying of the Halifax III prototype. Hewlett's navigator was Harry Blackallar, known as Blackie, from Littlehampton, Hampshire, a small bubbly man. Jim Nightingale had lost his crew one night when he was unable to fly with them. This was his first trip with Hewlett since replacing the regular wireless operator Flight Sergeant Norman Beale, who had been taken off flying to become an instructor, with a DFM, after completing fifty sorties. Fair-haired Wingham, twenty, born in east London's Mile End, was an electrical and mechanical engineering apprentice before joining up in the summer of 1941. Eric 'Joe' Holliday, from Middlesbrough, was flight engineer. Both gunners were from Ireland, Willie Hall, the mid-upper, from Belfast, and Andy Reilley, who shivered in the rear turret, from Dublin. Their friendly bantering about divided Ireland amused their crewmates. The seven men were all sergeants and they went out as a crew together.

Wingham said: 'This was the mark of a crew most likely to survive. There were times when you saw a new crew join the squadron and they had the stench of death about them. You knew they wouldn't survive more than two or three trips. Invariably they didn't have the togetherness that was the hallmark of our crew. We had our own crew song adapted from that well known ditty "Sweet Violets", which had been sung to distraction in pub after pub since we joined the squadron at the beginning of the year.'

There were groans in the briefing room when aircrews learned the target for the night of 23 May was to be Dortmund in the Ruhr Valley. It was to be the biggest single operation of the war since the 1,000-bomber raids of 1942. Hewlett's Halifax Mk I JB894 X-X-ray was one of 826 aircraft sent on Bomber Command's first large-scale raid for nine days in the period which was known as the Battle of the Ruhr. The bombing force included 343 Lancasters, 199 Halifaxes, 151 Wellingtons, 120 Stirlings and 13 Mosquitoes. A total of thirty-eight aircraft would be lost.

The weather forecast was good with no cloud cover over the target when X-X-ray took off at 11.25pm and headed towards Holland.

Wingham recalls: 'I was in the cockpit during takeoff, acting as second pilot. Halifax bomb aimers always assisted pilots on takeoff and landing. In the event of any injury to the pilot we were detailed to take over. It was usual for fighters to meet us some thirty miles off the enemy coast and continue to make life difficult with the help of various flak and searchlight batteries dotted all over the place until we began to close in on the Ruhr. At that time all German night fighters operated in boxes and were directed in on individual bombers. This was the reason for bomber streaming, for with so many aircraft flying through a box it was difficult for ground control to pick out individual aircraft. It was the stragglers and those outside the stream who were guaranteed most attention. As the bombers approached the Ruhr the game changed. Masses of searchlights and guns took over. It was estimated at the time that the Ruhr was protected by some 10,000 anti-aircraft guns and to meet them on your own was never a pleasant prospect. Once a raid got into its stride the flak became more of a barrage. The Oboe Mosquitoes were controlled by two ground stations in England which transmitted pulses, calculated an aircraft's position and sent a brief signal when the bombs should be released. On a good night Oboe offered a maximum bombing error of about 300 yards. It had proved to be the only reliable and extremely accurate marking system to overcome the notorious mist and smoke cover which had for so long prevented Bomber Command hitting its targets in the Ruhr. It was the job of the Pathfinder Force's heavy bombers to maintain continuity of the markers by aiming theirs, of a different colour, at the Oboe ones.

'We crossed the North Sea and Holland without any problems having, as usual, observed aircraft falling on either side of us. We continued across Germany before turning south for our final leg. As we started to run down to the Ruhr the flak began to warm up and turned into the usual flashes and thumps. I checked the latest wind with Blackie and, after switching on, fed this into the bomb sight before making certain all the switches were on to ensure the bombs were live and the distributor would function. Taking the bomb tit release button in my hand I settled down in the prone position over the bomb sight. It was a clear starry night with very good visibility. As we neared our target at 17,000ft the flak intensified. Thirty miles from the Ruhr the barrage of flak was massive. In the nose I was looking down into it. There was a continual flashing, thudding, phwarh! phwarh! phwarh! and the aircraft juddered as shells exploded nearby and we hit the slipstreams of other bombers. In the first wave we were only two minutes from our ETA and no markers were yet visible. Suddenly, a vivid splash of colour appeared ahead and below and relief set in that this was the primary Oboe marker and we would not have to go round again. Now I took over and guided the skipper through my bombsight. For the first time I had a virgin target to aim at with no other bombs exploding, just the Oboe marker. But we were way out in front, an ideal target for the German gunners.

'"Bomb doors open. Bomb doors open," from the pilot as he operated the controls. Then from me: "Left, left...steady...steady...ri...ight, steady...steady. Bombs gone!" as I pressed the tit and the aircraft jumped with the release of the two 1,000lb high explosive bombs. At the same time the photoflash left its 'chute at the rear of the aircraft and we flew straight and level while I counted out ten seconds. We carried a mixed load of HE and incendiary bombs which had different terminal velocities. This meant the HE bombs had a better forward travel than the smaller incendiaries which fell almost vertically. We still, therefore, had six small bomb containers of 30lb incendiaries and seven SBCs of 4lb to be dropped. These were released in sequence so the hundreds of incendiaries would cover an area over 100 yards long. The idea was that the HEs should open up the buildings with the incendiaries following to set fire to the debris. In order for this to happen there had to be a time lag between dropping the two types of bombs. Hence the ten-second run. The bomb release had also set up the camera ready to record the impact of our bombs. With the bomb doors closed we continued to cross the target, going south. We had just got our photograph and were free to jinx about a bit to confuse the guns when there was an almighty bang. The aircraft almost shuddered to a stop and we seemed to be dropping out of the sky. There was confusion on the intercom which had gone fuzzy with the loss of the generator and, in a brief babble of voices, the crew inquired what had happened. The pilot replied urgently: "Prepare to bale out".'

Only one of the Halifax's four engines was working, the others were windmilling uselessly. No one knew what had happened. The aircraft swung to starboard, heading west along the Ruhr Valley, descending rapidly, all the German gunners had it in their sights and the searchlights closed in. In the nose Wingham and Blackallar clipped on their parachutes, started moving the navigator's chair and table away from the forward escape hatch and waited for orders. Wingham was torn by indecision. He had decided months before not to bale out over a target, afraid he would be torn apart by wrathful civilians. Holliday, the flight engineer, believed the petrol tanks had been holed and hurriedly turned the cocks to switch the fuel to alternative tanks.

Hewlett wrestled with the controls, trying to reduce their rate of descent. At 7,000ft, one by one, the three windmilling engines spluttered into life and they managed to gain height, although they were now in the middle of the Ruhr with flak pouring up at them. The entire incident had taken less than five minutes. Some of the crew murmured: 'Well done, Dave,' but there was no cheer, no shaking of hands, nor slaps on the back as the engines gathered power and the navigator's chair was pushed back into position. Just 'okay chaps, give me a course, Blackie,' from the pilot as they started climbing.

Wingham recalls: 'The first thing to do was get out of the searchlights and this we did by going mad across the sky, weaving and corkscrewing until we left the Ruhr behind. We followed the briefed route home with the main stream and it was nice and peaceful, with the engines running perfectly. We didn't know what had happened until we landed. It was then, at dispersal, using a torch, we found some twenty holes in the aircraft. One large piece of shrapnel had sliced through the fire extinguisher buttons in the cockpit, setting them off in three engines, feeding them foam to digest rather than fuel. If the shrapnel had not smashed into the extinguishers it would have gone into the skipper's stomach.

'Next morning it was arranged for us to meet an engineering officer for a routine inspection of our aircraft. When we got to dispersal we found him already wandering around, poking into holes as engineers are wont to do. He was a flight lieutenant in his early forties, who had been an NCO during the years between the two world wars when everything was governed by books of rules. We all drifted round surveying the damage before we assembled in front of the Halifax and the conversation, which I will remember until I die, began between him and the skipper. Dave told him what had happened the previous night, answering questions. There was a pause before the officer inquired: "How far can a Halifax fly on one engine?"

'Hewlett replied: "Not very far."

'"Could you have flown back from the Ruhr on one?"

'"That would be impossible."

'"You would agree that three fire extinguishers have been operated?"

'"Yes."

'"What are the regulations about using an engine after the fire extinguisher has been used?"

'"Normally, shut down the engine, feather the propeller and don't use again, but this was different. The engines had not been on fire."

'The officer said, authoritatively: "The Book says an engine must not be used again after the fire extinguisher has been used. Three of your fire extinguishers have been used, therefore you could not have used those engines again. A Halifax could not have flown back from the Ruhr on one engine. It just couldn't have happened, otherwise you wouldn't be here."'

The officer walked briskly away to arrange with the ground crew to take the Halifax into the hangar to change the engines and patch up the holes. The crew watched him go then stared at each other in stunned silence.

Wingham recalls: 'There was no sign of a smile on his face. He had seen no humour in the situation. He was brought up doing things according to The Book. But there was nothing in King's Regulations about things being accidentally set off and you dealing with them in the best way you can. Fortunately, there was a lot of sky between us and the ground when those three engines cut. I visited the photographic section later that morning and found, with great satisfaction, my developed photo showing a very clear picture of Dortmund with the aiming point right bang in the centre.'

Large areas of Dortmund were devastated in the raid. Some 2,000 buildings, including factories, were demolished. Official figures say 599 people were killed, 1,275 injured, while twenty-five bodies were never found.

Hewlett was awarded a DFC at the end of his tour.

Wingham, now a flying officer, had been commissioned in June 1943 and by the following March he was a bombing instructor with the heavy conversion unit at Rufforth, Yorkshire. It was here he met Squadron Leader Stan Somerscales DFC, and his navigator from 10 Squadron, Flying Officer Jim Lewis DFM, both instructing after their first tour. When Wingham was invited to join them on 76 Squadron at Holme-on-Spalding-Moors, he jumped at the chance, for he was bored and itching to get back into the war. Somerscales found two more of his old crew, wireless operator Flying Officer John Reavill DFM, the oldest of them at thirty-one, and engineer Pilot Officer Sid Stephen. They were joined by two air gunners, Warrant Officer Jack Rowe and Flight Sergeant Harry Poole, who had also completed their first tour. Somerscales was to be the new commanding officer of A Flight.

The night before a raid on Düsseldorf the crew had been on a memorable binge in York and they telephoned their families in great excitement. Their photograph had been taken and they were featured in the daily newspapers as the most experienced crew on the squadron.

They took off on 22 April for Germany in a brand new Halifax, MZ578 I-Ink. With them were another 253 Halifaxes, 323 Lancasters and 19 Mosquitoes.

Wingham says: 'We were part of a twenty-two-strong force of Halifaxes from the squadron. A fairly quiet trip ensued, if one ignored the thumping drone of the engines. We flew across England, over northern France, turning north towards the Ruhr as we passed south of Liège. About forty miles from the target, there was a muffled crack and several startled voices came on to the intercom, demanding: "What was that?" There was a pause until mid-upper gunner Harry Poole reported: "The port wing's on fire." Within seconds the skipper came on with an urgent "Bale out!"'

Many years later it became known that the muffled crack heard by the crew was the sound of a 20mm cannon shell striking the aircraft. It had been fired by a *Schräge Musik* night fighter Bf110, piloted by Oberfeldwebel Rudolf Frank. The Halifax was his forty-third victim. Four nights later, after claiming two more kills, Frank was himself shot down and killed.

In the nose Tom Wingham opened the bomb doors and jettisoned the bomb load, hoping to give Somerscales a better chance to get out. He turned round to find Jim Lewis having trouble opening the escape hatch. They pulled it open together and dropped the hatch into the night. Lewis was a big Herefordshire farmer and with his mae west and harness over broad shoulders he had a problem getting out, but this was solved by Wingham giving him a push. Up to this point Wingham had acted automatically, but now he lay by the hatch and thought back to when, nearly a year ago, his bomber had dropped out of the sky, with three u/s engines. Last year, of course, there hadn't been a fire in the wing. He looked back towards the cockpit. On the order to bale out John Reavill had keyed a message back to base and then, putting on his own parachute, hurried into the cockpit to collect the skipper's parachute. He was reaching over trying to clip it on to Somerscales' harness, silhouetted against the red glow of the burning wing behind him, with smoke drifting in from the fuselage, when Wingham decided it was time to go. He dropped through the hatch. When his parachute opened he was knocked out by the harness clips and woke up lying in a field.

As Wingham drifted down, an horrific situation was developing in the blazing aircraft. When the order came to bale out, Jack Rowe, in the rear turret, had his guns fully depressed and, with fire at the wing root, found his controls had been affected and he was unable to bring the Brownings back to the normal position. This meant his legs were trapped and he could not get out of the turret. He rotated the turret manually until it was in the fore and aft position and opened the doors. He opened the bulkhead door to get his parachute which had been stowed in the fuselage. He reached over his head in the dark to free the 'chute, frightened that he might catch the rip handle and spill it open in the aircraft. He carefully brought it into the turret over his head and clipped it to his harness before again manually turning the turret sideways so he could drop free. He then flung himself backwards, hoping to jerk his legs free, but was left hanging over the turret ring by his knees, enveloped by flames and smoke. By this time the burning wing had broken off and the aircraft was spinning down out of control with Rowe, being whipped around at the tail end of the spin. Eventually, a few hundred feet from the ground, he got one leg free then wriggled his foot out of the other boot and fell away. His parachute opened in time to check the fall but he suffered from two damaged knees for the rest of his life.

Sid Stephen, a very competent flight engineer, was in his position behind the pilot when the aircraft was hit. The shell had ignited the incendiary bombs in one of the wing bomb bays and he went back to see whether he could deal with the fire which was rapidly spreading into the fuselage. Nothing could be done so he came forward to drop out of the forward escape hatch. His way was blocked by John Reavill and the pilot told him to leave by the rear escape hatch. Stephen turned round and in the smoke met the mid-upper gunner, Harry Poole, coming forward. With no intercom, he grasped Poole and led him back through the fuselage. Poole had probably already found this hatch difficult to open for when Stephen tried it was too stiff to move.

They pushed together in vain. Then, with Poole pushing, Stephen put his feet against the hatch and levered his body against the fuselage. At that moment the wing fell away and the resulting Gee forces threw Stephen out through the hatch and clear of the bomber. He landed near a farm with bad gashes in his leg and scalp. Poole remained trapped in the fuselage and was killed when it hit the ground, just south of Gulpen.

Reavill was still trying to help the pilot get into his parachute when the wing broke off and he was trapped, unable to move, as the aircraft spun down. A further explosion blew him out of the cockpit and he woke to find himself in midair. He reached for the parachute handle on his chest, but there was no parachute. He found it attached to one of the straps trailing above his head, pulled it back towards him and released the 'chute. It had barely cracked open when he hit the trees. With multiple injuries he was to lay there for eight hours before he was found by a Dutch farmer. About fifty yards away from Reavill, the fuselage and one wing lay upside-down in Wageler Wood. Inside it was the body of Harry Poole. Stan Somerscales, the pilot, with his parachute streamed out, lay dead 150 yards away.

Tom Wingham, after making his way into Belgium, made contact with the Resistance and was taken to Wandre, a small mining town north of Liège. He arrived a day later than planned, missing what proved to be the last escape run to the south by l'Armée Secrète, a resistance organisation, under the aegis of SOE in London. This turned out to be a lucky break, for two weeks later, the group of a dozen aircrew in that party were picked up by the Germans south of Paris. Early in May orders were issued from London for a standstill on all aircrew as movement had become too dangerous because of the bombing of the Belgian and French railway systems.

Wingham was escorted to the curé's house in Wandre and after a meal, was taken at about 9.30pm by Madame Coomans and her daughter Madeleine to their home, which had all its windows shuttered. They drank coffee in the living room, which was the only downstairs room apart from the scullery and an outside toilet. The Coomans spoke only French and Flemish and they communicated with the aid of a dictionary. The daughter was about Wingham's age.

It was not long before it was made clear to Wingham it was time for him to go to bed. A living room door opened directly on to the stairs which led to a bedroom. Another door opened from this room into the second bedroom which was over the scullery. Wingham was taken here by Madame Coomans. She used a watch and mime to make it clear he was to sleep here without a sound and must not make any noise until she brought him breakfast at 10.15 next morning. Before he had time to undress the sound of her husband's clogs could be heard coming towards the house. With a last warning for him to remain quiet she left to go downstairs, turning a key in the lock and taking it with her.

Wingham became used to a routine which revolved around the husband's work on a 2 to 10pm shift at the local coal mine. He rose at 8.30am and after breakfast left the house to play cards with his friends at an estaminet. At 10.15 his wife brought breakfast to Wingham in bed after which he could shave and dress, but remain in his room. Shortly after 12.30pm the husband returned for lunch. He left the house again at 1.25. Wingham was now free to go downstairs, having the run of the house until the footsteps were heard again at 10.25pm when he returned to be locked into the bedroom.

Several times he asked Madame Coomans, the curé and people from l'Armée Secrète who visited him what would happen if the husband found him there. Always the conversation was the same. 'He would probably tell you to go.'

'Would he call the Germans?'

'No, I do not think so.'

'Why then would he not let me stay?'

'Well, he is neither for the Germans nor against the Germans. He is neither for the English nor against the English. He is a miner.' With that Wingham had to be content.

One of the Resistance workers who visited Wingham had two mistresses, one of them German. After he dumped her she betrayed him to the Gestapo who arrested him and found the names of all his contacts.

On 19 June, Wingham was downstairs, alone in the house, tuning in to the BBC programme *Sunday Night at Seven* when there was a squeal of tyres, car doors slamming and heavy footsteps running towards the house, followed by crashes on the front and side doors and loud German voices. He switched off the radio, turned the dial away from the BBC, and raced upstairs to escape from his bedroom window. He was too late. One of six Gestapo officers was on the outhouse roof battering at the shuttered window. He ran downstairs to the cellar, which was reached through another door in the living room. Doors burst open and windows smashed as he looked round the cellar which was dark, without lights and empty, except for several empty beer crates. There was a recess at the foot of the concrete steps and he quickly piled six crates three high, crawled into the gap and pulled them tight behind him against the stairway. He watched two Gestapo officers through the crates as they struck matches and looked around without seeing him. They turned the house over before deciding the bird must have flown and went on their way. They picked up Monsieur Coomans as he came off shift and took him to Gestapo headquarters in Liège. They must have been satisfied that 'he was a miner' for they released him after five hours' interrogation.

Wingham reached the curé's house and was looked after by the Resistance before reaching Paris. He flew back to London in September with Jim Lewis, who had also evaded capture. Wingham rejoined Bomber Command, flying Oboe Mosquitoes, and took part in the last raid of the war on Kiel on 2 May 1945. He was awarded the American DFC.

Madame and Madeleine Coomans went into hiding until after their country was liberated.

Stan Somerscales and Harry Poole were buried in the municipal cemetery at Maastricht. Sid Stephen and Jack Rowe were prisoners-of-war. After a barbaric lack of treatment, John Reavill was confined in a slave labour camp near Bonn where a foot was unnecessarily amputated.

CHAPTER TWENTY

THE WRATH OF PFORZHEIM

Towards the end of February 1945 the war with Germany did not have long to run, but the relentless bombing of the enemy continued. Adolf Hitler, skulking like a trapped dog in the Führerbunker deep beneath the Reich Chancellery in Berlin, waited for his diminished and demoralised forces to perform miracles against the advancing Allied forces. Even so, the German defences still functioned, continuing to shoot down intruding bombers. There were battles still to be won in the air as well as on the ground.

Navigator Leo Horrax was convinced that his fifteenth operation, to Pforzheim, on 23 February 1945, would be a piece of cake. His crew had been briefed to attack the town in south-west Germany a few days previously, but the sortie was called off, after he and the other navigators of 150 Squadron and their sister squadron at Hemswell, 170, had prepared their flight plans. Horrax and his crewmates had already rattled through seven sorties that month, and had the satisfaction at briefing that day of seeing their names picked out in red on the battle orders as one of the more experienced crews.

Horrax recalls: 'That month we had been to Mannheim, Wiesbaden, Kleve, Pölitz, Chemnitz, Dortmund and Duisberg, none of them doddles, and we were more relaxed for this one than any other. This was to be the first major raid on Pforzheim of the war and the flight plan was easy. Our confidence was skyhigh.'

The crew's skipper was the extraordinarily charismatic and popular son of a doctor from Port Louis in the Indian Ocean island of Mauritius. Pilot Officer Pierre Aimée Gérard Ythier was known to his crew as Gerry. Horrax believes he was the only Mauritian pilot flying in Bomber Command. He was a man who loved life and was, wholeheartedly, one of the boys.

'He was,' recalls Horrax, 'the most magnificent man you could ever wish to meet. He was quite small, about 5ft 7in, slim, good looking with long elegant fingers. He was full of laughter and joi de vivre. His first language was French and he spoke English with a beautiful accent. He was brave, cool, fearless and determined, and lived for flying. We trusted him implicitly. Popular with the ladies, he didn't knock about with anyone on the squadron, but nipped off to London when we had a free weekend. He, the bomb aimer and I were good friends. I learned my drinking habits with Gerry at 18 OTU, Worksop. It was the first time I had experienced going into a pub with a crowd of bods and talking, it was wonderful. Gerry only drank whisky, they didn't drink beer on Mauritius.'

Sheffield-born Flight Sergeant Horrax was twenty-one, the same age as his skipper. He was slim, a little taller than Ythier although he needed to sit on his parachute pack otherwise he was too low for the navigator's table. His position in the Lancaster was well heated, unlike those of the gunners who shivered with cold, despite thick layers of clothing and electrically heated flying suits. Horrax's only mild complaint was that the sandwiches which he ate on the homeward flight were usually toasted dry. Formerly a clerk, he became a bank manager after the war. He enjoyed all sports and played the piano, and the organ at his local Catholic church. He was one of three brothers who all survived war service. When his crew were stood down for a night he hitched a lift to Sheffield to meet his girlfriend, English Steel secretary Pat Hackett, whom he married in 1946.

The wireless operator was Sergeant Ron Lewis who, no more than twenty three, was considered an old lag because he had already served a spell on ground staff in the Middle East before remustering as aircrew. Divorced, he lived with his mother at Long Eaton, near Nottingham. Jovial Londoner Flying Officer Bert Delieu was the bomb aimer. Tall and thin, with a gaunt face, he amazed Ythier and Horrax one night when he took over the drums at The Nelson pub in the centre of Sheffield with a sparkling impromptu display of virtuosity. Delieu was married two weeks before the trip to Pforzheim.

Flight engineer Sergeant Inis 'Nobby' Clarke, a burly weatherbeaten Shetlander, who had been a whaler before joining up, had a fondness for the bagpipes. Although he did not have any pipes on the station he could provide an uncanny imitation of them, which the others found especially irritating first thing in the morning. Sergeant Bob Conning, was a nineteen-year-old from Toxteth, Liverpool, where his wife waited patiently for the mid-upper gunner's next leave. He was small, tough and sincere, a real Scouse. Sergeant Ted 'Buck' Buckley, from Alfreton, Derbyshire, was the rear gunner. He was tall, powerfully built, forthright and boisterous.

Everything was a piece of cake at the start. Even the met man's forecast of clear weather was spot on for once. It was nearly 5pm and still light when they took off in Lancaster PB780T-Tare. Horrax, lifted by the crew's buoyant mood, even left his curtained position for the first time on an operation to join the pilot and flight engineer waving exuberantly at the ground staff as they left Hemswell. They gained height slowly over Sheffield and Horrax imagined his parents below, exchanging anxious glances as they heard the steady drone of the Lancasters in the wintry sky. They were almost at 7,000ft and still climbing when they lumbered back to Hemswell before turning to the rendezvous point over Reading at 15,000ft.

T-Tare was among 367 Lancasters and 13 Mosquitoes which had been briefed to attack Pforzheim. Horrax recalls:

'Small precision parts for aircraft and tanks were made there. We were briefed to bomb from 12,000ft. The weather was perfect and it was like a pleasure cruise crossing France, south of Strasbourg at 20,000ft. There were kites above, below and on either side, all streaming along like a shoal of fish. Darkness fell as we crossed the Rhine, identified over the intercom by the bomb aimer, and nerves become more tense as we drew nearer the target.'

Although their spirits were high they could not relax. They knew death could strike suddenly out of the darkness. Germany was a beaten nation, but you wouldn't think so from the continued fierce aggression from the German gunners and fighter pilots.

The crew's exhilaration was dampened as they approached the target. Five minutes before they were due to start their bombing run, Lewis, the wireless operator, was standing in the astrodome scanning the sky for enemy activity. He reported, in shocked tones, one Lancaster, engulfed in flames, falling to earth, and then, seconds later, another, both on the starboard side. Lewis watched intently for parachutes, but none appeared. Both aircraft were victims of German night fighters.

The pilot said, sharply: 'Keep your eyes open, it's not going to be as easy as we thought.'

In Pforzheim, residents huddled fearfully in shelters as the bombers rumbled overhead. There had been other raids on their town, but none of them could have been prepared for what was to follow.

'We got to the target, the markers went down ahead bang on time and it really looked like being a wizard prang,' Horrax recalls. 'Our bombing run was perfect and we dropped the 4,000lb Cookie bomb and incendiaries without any problem. The bomb aimer yelled out that he saw our bomb actually exploding. The aircraft shuddered, like a boat running over rocks, from the blast of the exploding bombs below. We remained on the nerve-twitching straight and level for the photo flash to explode so the photograph could be taken and I called out the new course, south-westerly on a short leg before turning west for England. The worst was over with another trip in the bag.

'Then it happened. A couple of minutes out of the target area I heard the rattle of machine-gun bullets too close to be ignored, and the aircraft was juddering. I was uncertain at first whether we were being fired at or if the rear gunner was firing at someone else. Our squadron's .303 machine-guns had been replaced with .5s. The difference was remarkable. When they fired, the whole aircraft reverberated. I heard the rear gunner cry out that somebody was coming across us and telling the skipper to corkscrew to port. There was great confusion. The bomb aimer, who was at the front guns, hardly ever used at night, muttered in angry frustration: "Yeh, and I can't get my bloody guns on him".'

A twin-engine Ju88 fitted with upward-firing guns had streaked beneath and to the side of them, pumping cannon shells into the Lancaster's undefended belly. As Ythier plunged the bomber into an evasive corkscrew, Buckley, the rear gunner, turned his guns on to the swiftly departing fighter, which nose dived out of control with flames bursting out of it. T-Tare's port outer engine was on fire. The flames did not waver when the engineer activated the extinguisher. The rear gunner reported a Messerschmitt 262 jet fighter had sped past without firing at them. He believed the pilot was attracted by the fire, deduced the Lancaster was in its death throes and decided not to waste his ammunition.

Lewis stood in the astrodome, clipping on his parachute, gaping at the fire which had spread rapidly across the wing and was roaring out of control in both port engines. He bellowed at Horrax: 'Bleeding hell! Look at that bloody great fire! I'm getting out!' With one last look at the navigator, Lewis disappeared towards the exit at the back of the fuselage.

Horrax recalls: 'It was Ron who alerted me to the seriousness of the situation as I was "hiding" in my little compartment pretending this was not happening to me. Ron retreated to the rear exit, according to the drill we had been taught. He was never seen again alive.

'As the port wing became a mass of flames the skipper cried: "Emergency! Jump! Jump!" Those three words really shake you. I had already clipped on my 'chute when I thought something was up. Now I lined up to take my turn out of the front escape hatch which the bomb aimer and flight engineer were struggling to open. It seemed an age, but was probably only seconds. Then it was open and Bert Delieu, the bomb aimer, went out, followed quickly by Nobby Clarke, the engineer.'

When the hatch was opened a ferocious draught surged through the aircraft. Horrax's maps and charts leaped from his table and flapped like dying birds along the fuselage.

Horrax was standing near the pilot and yelled at him: 'Come, on, quick!' Gerry didn't hear him, the noise level was too high, but he understood what his navigator was saying from the look on his face.

Ythier's face, half hidden by his flying helmet, was taut and anxious, as he strove desperately to hold altitude. The young pilot nodded at his friend, then Horrax hesitated, clumsily, when his oxygen mask and helmet became entangled with the parachute harness. He quickly sorted it out and dived headfirst into the cold black night, pretending he was back in the swimming baths at Sheffield, jumping off the high board. Here over Germany, the 'board' was close to 6,000ft.

As the navigator disappeared, Ythier switched on his intercom and said urgently: 'Are you still there, Ted?'

Facing backwards, Ted Buckley, the rear gunner, could not see the flames pouring from the port wing, but he had just been startled by two parachutes flashing past his turret and assumed the situation was much worse than he had feared and put his helmet back on. He replied, brusquely: 'Yeah.'

Ythier said: 'For God's sake get out, I can't hold it much longer.'

Buckley muttered to himself: 'Christ! I'd better get a move on.'

He moved quickly, elevating the guns and clipping on his parachute. The rear turret's hydraulics had gone, forcing him to escape over his guns. Luckily for him, at this point in the war, rear gunners sat on specially designed parachutes. Previously, many rear gunners, trapped in their turrets, were killed because they could not reach their parachutes which, during an operation, were stowed in the fuselage. Even so, Buckley was a big man, hugely bulky in his flying gear, and he may not have squeezed through the aperture in the perspex which had been sufficient for the .303 guns. The bigger .5 guns needed a larger gap, and he drove himself through it with the determined ferocity of a man who knew he would die if he couldn't get out. His neck was badly scraped by the guns, which left two terrible weals, but the tension evaporated as he leaped out headfirst and found himself floating free, away from the death trap that was T-Tare. His parachute opened and he wondered vaguely if that was the end of his war.

As Horrax dropped through the escape hatch, both loose-fitting boots were plucked from his feet before the parachute opened. He recalls:

'We were supposed to count to ten before pulling the ripcord. I didn't count to anything. I was afraid I might not find the D-ring so I pulled it as soon as I could and hoped the 'chute would open. Everyone worried about whether their parachute would open if they needed to use it. None of us had baled out before. The only practice we had was at OTU, jumping off a five-foot wall and learning to have our legs together and rolling over correctly. This was somewhat different to jumping off a wall. I was immensely relieved that I was not going to get burned to death as I tumbled, tumbled, tumbled, arse over tit, before the parachute opened. Fortunately I must have been almost parallel to the earth and on my back when the 'chute opened and there was no jerk.

'There was a strange sensation of complete silence and peace, after the roar of the engines and excitement aboard the aircraft. I saw a layer of cloud coming up to meet me and was expecting to go through it, but it was a ploughed field, covered by snow. It was a bit dodgy and hard on my feet, but I kept my legs together, so they would act as splints to each other and rolled over, trying to do all the things we had been taught. I disentangled myself from the parachute then hauled it in, there seemed to be miles of it. I noticed a fire out of the corner of my eye and hoped it was the German fighter burning up, not the Lancaster. Then I saw in the distance the burning town of Pforzheim. I could hear the flames crackling as they ripped through the buildings.'

The marking and bombing of Pforzheim was extremely accurate and 1,825 tons of bombs fell on the town in twenty-two minutes. Over 17,000 people died in a hurricane of fire and explosions which ripped rapidly through the town. More people are believed to have died in this one raid than any other during the war except those on Dresden and Hamburg. The

British Bombing Survey Unit later estimated that 83 per cent of the town's built up area had been wiped out, probably the highest proportion in a single wartime raid. Ten Lancasters were lost during the operation and another two crashed in France.

A South African pilot, Captain Edwin Swales, DFC, from 582 Squadron, the Pforzheim raid's Master Bomber, was posthumously awarded the Victoria Cross, Bomber Command's last of the war. With two engines and the rear turret out of action, he continued issuing instructions over the target. Limping home, he ordered his crew to bale out, but the crippled Lancaster crashed and the pilot was found dead at his controls. He was twenty-nine.

Leo Horrax heard shots some distance away on the ground as he ran with his parachute in the opposite direction from the devastated town. He felt lucky to have escaped a burning bomber and had baled out without injury. He knew he must now avoid the wrath of the civilians. He had heard how ruthless they could be to Allied airmen after a raid.

Civilians outside Pforzheim had heard the great fleet of bombers rumble high over the countryside and could only watch in horror as the bombs started falling and the town they knew so well was systematically destroyed. As the bombing continued and the awesome fires leaped across the town, a group of angry farmworkers to the south, spontaneously agreed that while they could do nothing to save the suffering people of Pforzheim, they might have a slim chance of exacting some revenge on the 'terror bombers'. It was of no concern to them that their beloved leader had started the war, they had seen Pforzheim burning and regarded the Allied bombers as assassins from hell.

The Germans armed themselves with pitchforks and waited hopefully in a field, their eyes turned balefully to the sky. They did not have long to wait before the crippled Lancaster T-Tare, lit up like an expensive firework, headed towards them, gradually losing height. They watched the burning bomber with hate in their hearts, and loud shouts rang out as two tiny specks fell away and parachutes opened. They were united by a terrible force which drove them to run across the fields, a blood-lusting mob, hell bent on revenge. The parachutes grew larger and they saw the men hanging from them, men with the blood of their countrymen on their hands. They had no idea how many bombers had attacked Pforzheim, but at that moment all their loathing and contempt was focused on the two manikins above. Their hands tightened on the pitchforks, as the airmen, about 100yd apart, drew nearer until it seemed they could almost be plucked from the sky and dashed to the ground.

Bert Delieu was first to land. While he was gathering up his parachute he heard a cry and turned to see Nobby Clarke in trouble. The engineer had experienced problems with his parachute. At first it had failed to open and he was falling at around 150mph, expecting to be killed, when it unexpectedly opened with a tremendous jerk, 500ft from the ground. He landed heavily, breaking an ankle, but he was alive. He tried to get up but fell back in pain.

Delieu, his parachute under one arm, began walking towards his crewmate when, alarmingly, he suddenly found himself swiftly surrounded by a silent throng of Germans in rough labourers' clothes. They seemed to have materialised from the darkness like malevolent ghosts. Delieu became afraid when he saw the manic gleam in their eyes as they slowly drew nearer, the long sharp metal tines of the pitchforks pointed unwaveringly towards him. The chance to flee had gone. In any case he could not abandon the injured engineer to a bunch of crazy Germans. He dropped the parachute, raised his arms and began to plead earnestly for their lives. It is unlikely that any of the Germans understood English. Even if they had, the men had already agreed a course of action and nothing would dissuade them. There was a moment for unleashing a guttural stream of withering insults before the first snarling German thrust his pitchfork savagely into Delieu's body. The Lancaster bomb aimer staggered, screaming with pain, then fell.

Delieu's screams pierced Nobby Clarke, who was clutching his damaged ankle a few yards away. Clarke watched in stunned horror as his crewmate was brutally killed. The silence then became more horrifying to Clarke than the screams. The Germans stared in satisfaction at Delieu's corpse then, their rage only partly sated, they turned to Clarke, who had tried in vain to drag himself away. The awful scenario was repeated as they surrounded and taunted the terrified engineer jabbing at him with the blood-stained pitchforks without actually touching him. Suddenly, gunshots rang out. These were the shots which had been heard by Leo Horrax as he ran to safety across a ploughed field not far away. The engineer's tormenters turned to see German soldiers, armed with rifles, advancing upon them. The soldiers had fired in the air to keep the civilians away from Clarke. Another minute and he too would have been dead.

'Nobby was lucky, poor Bert would have been saved too if the soldiers had arrived a little earlier,' says Horrax. 'Nobby was taken into Pforzheim which was a smouldering ruin. He was incarcerated in a police cell, contemplating his fate. He was eventually taken to hospital and was the first of us to get home as the Allies liberated his area. There was no excuse for the Germans killing Bert, but these people knew Pforzheim well and they could see it on fire. Perhaps they had friends and relations living there. They wouldn't have been in a very friendly state of mind.'

Horrax tore off his RAF brevets and hid his parachute and mae west in bushes in a wood beside a ditch surrounding the field in which he had landed. This was on the edge of the Black Forest, near the village of Neuhausen.

'I bet the parachute is there today,' he says. 'After hiding it I ran. It was very cold and the ground was hard on my feet. I picked up handfuls of snow to suck to alleviate the dryness in my throat. Within fifteen minutes of being shot down I can remember a Ju88 coming down very low, at not much more than 500ft. I crouched down, thinking "That bugger's still looking for me". It might have been the one that shot us down. Of course it wasn't, but when you've had a shock like that you are vulnerable and frightened.

'The worst thing for me at that time was not knowing what had happened to the others. You don't know what happened in the last seconds to those who died in the wreck. I know what happened to Ted and Nobby. When I was in prison camp I kept hoping that Gerry would turn up somewhere.'

As he hurried away, the shock of baling out and being attacked by the fighter eased and he was able to think more clearly.

'There was no doubt the Jerries were waiting for us in strength when we got to Pforzheim,' he says. 'They could not have guessed we were going to attack the town that night. We had only carried out minor raids on it before. My theory is that somebody must have carried in their navigator's holdall the original flight plan for the operation to Pforzheim which was cancelled earlier that month. They were probably shot down over Dortmund or Duisberg and the Jerries picked up the holdall, examined the flight plan and assumed we would turn up over Pforzheim sooner or later.

'I ran like hell from the burning town and being a navigator I knew which direction I should be heading. The north star was clouded over so I went where I thought was south and at the rate I was going I believed I should get to the Swiss border in half an hour. It was fifty miles, and I didn't make it.'

Horrax wandered into a church that night, then found a barn with a haystack inside. He dug himself into it to keep warm.

Horrax again: 'It was a big temptation to keep going during the day. The escape people used to say lie up during the day and move at night. These were the only instructions we'd been given about what to do if we were shot down and they were easier said than done, especially without any shoes. You could see where you were going during the day, but that night every dog in the Black Forest was barking after me.

'I started walking at first light next morning and was picked up by a middle-aged railwayman going to work. It was about 7am, I had been on the run for eleven hours. He took me to the police station in the village of Neuhausen. I was searched, my rosary beads were found and returned to me by someone who said: "God has been kind to you." A Canadian bomb aimer was brought in and they threatened to shoot us. We were moved to a Luftwaffe station near Stuttgart and spent a miserable night after being given a chunk of black bread. At dawn we each received a bowl of lukewarm watery soup. From down the corridor, to my delight, I heard a disdainful voice bellow: "Is this all we're fucking well getting?" and knew our rear gunner Ted Buckley was alive.

'That day we were given two guards in their fifties. They protected us from the civilians who wanted to pull us to pieces. They shouted, women mainly: "Pforzheim! Pforzheim!" We were taken to the Dulag Luft at Frankfurt-am-Main and interrogated. We were in POW camps at Nuremburg then near Munich, where there were 140,000 of us, all half starved. We were liberated by General Patton at the beginning of May. Nobody had told us the war was over. I had been a POW three months, it felt more like thirty years.

Horrax did not know for certain what had happened to his skipper until he returned to Sheffield after being repatriated. Ythier's mother, widowed when her pilot son was training in Canada, had another son in France who wrote to the mayor of Neuhausen. The mayor sent him a photograph of the grave where Gerry Ythier had been buried with T-Tare's wireless operator Ron Lewis and mid-upper gunner Bob Conning.The three bodies had all been found in the wreckage of the Lancaster, which had crashed near Neuhausen. Lewis, on his thirteenth operation, had not been hurt during the attack by the German fighter and Horrax believed he should have escaped.

'We can surmise one of two things,' says Horrax. 'Ron could either have gone to the rear exit but couldn't open the door, or the mid-upper gunner may have been injured in the exchange of fire with the Ju88. Ron may have tried to get him out of the turret, he wouldn't have left him.'

The war had been ended over fifty years when Horrax said: 'There's not a day goes by when I don't think about what happened. I think what the hell have I done with that fifty-odd years that was given to me but not to the others?'

BIBLIOGRAPHY

The Bomber Command War Diaries, an Operational Reference Book 1939-45, Martin Middlebrook and Chris Everitt (Viking, 1985)

Combat Aircraft of World War Two, Elke C. Weal, John A. Weal and Richard F. Barker (Arms and Armour Press, 1977)

Jane's Fighting Aircraft of World War II (Studio Editions Ltd, 1992)

The Bombers, the Illustrated Story of Offensive Strategy and Tactics in the Twentieth Century, Robin Cross (Grub Street, 1987)

Famous Bombers of the Second World War, William Green (Macdonald, 1959)

Lincolnshire Airfields in the Second World War, Patrick Otter (Countryside Books,1996)

So Few (The Immortal Record of the Royal Air Force), David Masters (Corgi Books, 1956)

The Life and Death of Adolf Hitler, Robert Payne (Jonathan Cape, 1973)

INDEX

Aachen, 32, 170
Adams, Flt Sgt Pete, 54, 57
Agner, Albert, 51
Aircrew Receiving Centre,
 Lords, 152
Air Sea Rescue, 10
Aitken, Fg Off Jack, 54, 57, 60
Alconbury, 16, 18
Alexandria, 118
Alsager, 81
Amendola, 107, 108, 112, 116-
 119, 126, 127, 129, 131-133
Ammersee, lake, 145
Ankara, 132
Ardbeg, Ontario, 108
l'Armée Secrète, 176, 177
Arnstein, 156, 157
Alfreton, 180
Allan, Sgt Dudley, 8, 11, 12, 14
Argyll & Sutherland
 Highlanders, 113
Ashanti, destroyer, 13
Astley, 162
Auschwitz, 142
Aylsham, 137

Barnsley, 54
Bavegem, 32
Baxter, Wg Cdr, 82
Beachy Head, 56
Beale, Sgt Don, 101
Beale, Flt Sgt Norman, 170
Beaumont, Sgt Jack, 100, 103-
 105
Beckenham, 35
Becker, Lt Phil, 34, 36, 37, 41
Bedouin, destroyer, 13, 14
Belfast, 72, 171
Belton, Sgt Bill, 16-24
Berlin, 7-10, 56, 71, 73-76, 82-
 87, 117, 126, 167, 168, 179
Biggs, Plt Off Billy, 143-146,
 149
Bihr, Karl, 39
Birmingham, 44, 54, 64, 71
Bishop, Sgt Cyril, 153, 154
Blackallar, Sgt Harry, 170, 172,
 173
Blackpool, 15, 162
Blickling Hall, 134
Boldon Colliery, 19
Bomber squadrons
 7 Squadron, 17
 9 Squadron, 80
 10 Squadron, 174
 31 (SAAF) Squadron, 110
 35 (Madras Presidency)
  Squadron, 17

57 Squadron, 34-36, 161, 169
61 Squadron, 71, 73, 78
76 Squadron, 174
77 Squadron, 8
83 Squadron, 17, 82
90 Squadron, 62, 63
97 (Straits Settlements)
 Squadron, 155
102 (Ceylon) Squadron, 170
106 Squadron, 14, 34, 36, 43,
 54, 61, 80, 88, 153-155, 160
109 Squadron, 17
148 Squadron, 110
150 Squadron, 126, 179
156 Squadron, 16-18
166 Squadron, 89
170 Squadron, 179
178 Squadron, 107, 110, 117,
 119, 133
214 (Federated Malay States),
 98, 99, 135, 136, 138, 142
427 (Lion) Squadron, 143
514 Squadron, 25
582 Squadron, 184
617 Squadron, 15, 80, 88, 153,
 154
627 Squadron, 155
630 Squadron, 34, 35
Central Navigation School,
 Rivers, Manitoba 152, 153
Polish 1586 Flight, 110

Other units
12 OTU Chipping Walden, 98
18 OTU Worksop, 180
21 OTU Moreton-in-Marsh,
 125
26 OTU Wing, 88
29 OTU Bruntingthorpe, 152
10 Air Gunnery School,
 Walney Island, 53
Bonn, 54, 78
Bor-Komorowski, Gen Tadeusz,
 112
Boscombe Down, 170
Boston, Lincs, 72
Bouchot, André & Mariette, 51
Boulogne, 7, 56
Bourges, 66
Boxall, Sqn Ldr 127
Brüx, 136, 138, 139
Bracher, Plt Off Dennis, 162,
 169
Brad, Sgt Harold, 153, 155, 156
Bradwell Bay, 102
Bradford, Sgt Stan, 161-169
Bremen, 9, 10, 17, 99
Brighton, 44, 51, 152

Brindisi, 109
Brisbane, 27, 64, 81
Bristol, 153
British Bombing Survey Unit,
 184
Brocklesby Park, 90
Brunswick, 27
Brussels, 32
Buchanan, Flt Sgt Graham, 63,
 64, 67, 70
Buckley, Sgt Ted, 180, 182, 183,
 186
Bugle, 108
Bulawayo, 108
Bulmer, Flt Sgt Steve, 64, 66,
 67, 69
Burford, Flt Sgt Sam, 26-32
Burns, Sgt Bob, 152-160
Burton, South Wirral, 143
Bury St Edmunds, 100
Burxdorf, 149

Caen, 25
Cabourg, 65
Cagney, James, 108
Calais, 7
Callister, Sgt Jimmy, 100, 101
Cambridge, 64, 65, 106, 153
Camp D'Avord, 66
Captains of the Clouds, 108
Carey, Fg Off Bill, 80
Carlisle, 61
Carter, Sgt Martin, 26-29, 31-33
Carter, Wg Cdr, 155
Cashmore, Sgt Joe, 64, 67, 70
Catford, 90
Chalk, Sgt John, 137, 138, 140,
 141
Chamberlain, Neville, 144
Chappellier, 68
Châteaudun, 155
Chemnitz, 179
Cheshire, Wg Cdr Leonard, 15,
 88, 154
Chester-Master, Flt Sgt Bob, 25-
 33
Chichester, 136
Ching, Flt Sgt Bill, 35, 36, 42
Chipping Walden, 98
Choloy military cemetery, 52
Churchill, Winston, 107, 150
Cirencester, 52
Clarke, Sgt Inis, 180, 182, 184-
 186
Clarke, Sgt Ray, 91, 93, 96, 97
Climie, Sqn Ldr Ken, 99
Coal Aston, 152
Cobham, Sir Alan, 152